A Passionate Pacifist

Essential Writings of Aaron Samuel Tamares

Translated and Edited by
Everett Gendler

With contributions by Ri J. Turner and Tzemah Yoreh

Teaneck, New Jersey

A Passionate Pacifist: Essential Writings of Aaron Samuel Tamares ©2020 Everett Gendler. All rights reserved. No part of this book may be used or reproduced in any manner whatsoever without written permission except in the case of brief quotations embodied in critical articles and reviews.

Published by Ben Yehuda Press
122 Ayers Court #1B
Teaneck, NJ 07666

http://www.BenYehudaPress.com

To subscribe to our monthly book club and support independent Jewish publishing, visit https://www.patreon.com/BenYehudaPress

Ben Yehuda Press books may be purchased at a discount by synagogues, book clubs, and other institutions buying in bulk. For information, please email markets@BenYehudaPress.com

Permissions and Acknowledgements:

Grateful acknowledgement is made to the Yiddish studies journal In Geveb (ingeveb.org) for permission to reprint Ri J. Turner's translation of Aaron Samuel Tamares' Autobiography.

Earlier versions of some of this material appeared in *Judaism* and *Tikkun*

ISBN13 978-1-934730-79-9

23 24 25 / 10 9 8 7 6 5 4 3b   20240102

Contents

General Introduction 1
Acknowledgements 7

Part I: The Autobiography
    Introduction to the Autobiography 11
    Autobiography of "One of the Sensitive Rabbis" (1926) 14
        (Translated by Ri J. Turner)

Part II: Selected Sermons
    Introduction to selected sermons 49
    From *The Ethics of Torah and Judaism* (1912)
        Preface 50
    From *Pure Faith and Popular Religion* (1912)
        "Pure Faith" (Emunah T'horah) (1904) summarized 51
        A Preferred Pathway to God's Presence (1908) 58
        "Love Motivated Turning" (Teshuva me-Ahava) (1908)
            (Parts 1 and 2) 62
    Introduction to "A Sermon on Liberty" and *On Judaism and Liberty* 68
        "A Sermon on Liberty" (1906) 70
        On Judaism and Liberty (1905) 93

Part III: On War
    Introduction to *The Community of Israel and The Wars of Nations* 122
    The Community of Israel and the Wars of the Nations (1918) 127
        Chapter 1: Theories of War 130
        Chapter 2: Dreams of the "Messiah" 132
        Chapter 3: Supernaturalism and Naturalism in the Legends
            of "Gog and Magog" and "The Messiah" 137
        Chapter 4: The Exile of the Presence and the Presence
            of the Exile on page 149
        Chapter 5: The Freedom of Torah and the Arrogance
            of The Sword 162
        Chapter 6: Israel's Global Mission and its Separation from
            the World 171
        Chapter 7: The Land of Israel 201
            (Chapters 6 and 7 translated by Tzemah Yoreh)

Part IV: On Zionism

    Introduction to Tamares on Zionism.. 210
    From *Three Unsuitable Unions* (1930)
        "The Pairing of Zionism with the Revival of
            Hebrew Language and Culture.............................. 213

    Bibliography of Aaron Samuel Tamares.. 230

General Introduction

It is New Year's Day, 2019. Traditionally on such occasions, we look ahead, speculating about what fresh, novel experiences may await us in the calendar year just beginning. Yet here I sit looking back 150 years, musing on two figures whose birth sesquicentennials we mark this year. One of them is so famous that his teachings are known even to billions who lack the basic tools of literacy, the other so obscure that even for scholars of modern Jewish thought, there is barely name recognition. Yet these two, Mohandas Karamchand Gandhi and Aaron Samuel Tamares, share 1869 as their birth year.

More than a birth year, Gandhi and Tamares share a deep characteristic: both were committed pacifists, dedicated to the pursuit and realization of valued ends by strictly nonviolent means. But whereas the philosophical underpinnings of Gandhi's views are well-known, those of Tamares remain largely unexplored. Few of his writings have been translated from their original Hebrew and Yiddish, and even the original-language texts have long been out of print. This volume aims to correct that omission.

Born in 1869 to a Jewish family in Maltsh, a village in the Grodno district of Poland (now Belarus), Tamares was early recognized as an "ilui," a child prodigy whose capacity of mind yielded childhood mastery of Bible, Mishnah, Talmud, and Codes. His further studies at yeshivot (rabbinical seminaries) in Kovno and Volozin saw him ordained as rabbi, and in 1893 he became rabbi of the village of Milejczyce (in the Bialystok region of Poland), succeeding his father-in-law in that position, where he served until his death in 1931.

The brief notices of his life and writings in standard reference works already suggest unusual qualities in this idiosyncratic ilui/prodigy. "[A]n Orthodox rabbi who fought against the fossilized *halakhah* in a completely original style and who attacked nationalism and political Zionism as anti-Jewish phenomena" is how Yehuda Slutsky summarizes Tamares in the *Encyclopedia Judaica* (1972). More specifically, Slutsky points to Tamares' early advocacy of Zionism, his attendance at the Fourth Zionist Congress in London in 1900, his disillusionment with the political aspects of Zionism, followed by his denunciation of nationalism and his advocacy of pacifism in his first book (1905). In *The YIVO Encyclopedia of Jews in Eastern Europe*, Gershon Hundert also emphasizes Tamares' strong endorsement of "nonviolence as a Jewish value."

The YIVO entry also mentions the 1912 invitation to Tamares "to take over the yeshiva and rabbinical seminary that Haim Tchnernowitz had founded in Odessa." Among those urging him to accept the position were such luminaries as Mendele Mocher Seforim and Haim Nahman Bialik. However, "Tamares found the city uncongenial and, reportedly, after only two days there, returned to Milejcycze1." He spent the next 40 years as rabbi to the shtetl/small town of Mielyczyce, Poland, providing this Thoreau-like explanation of his attachment to the life of his small village. Speaking of himself in the third person, he relates:

"His process of self-liberation was greatly assisted by the location of his residence: the little town with its beautiful pinewood forest. It was in the forest (where he spent most of his time during the summers)—in the company of his most intimate friends, the beautiful evergreen trees, and under the open skies— that he perfected his own training in the theory of morality and freedom: he penned most of his work in the forest. And the small town in which he lived left him free to conduct his life according to his principles."

Are these words from Milejczyce or from Walden Pond? Tamares' village is just 25 miles from the heart of the Bialowieza Forest, Europe's last remaining primeval forest. A Google Map reveals that even today, large sections of uncleared forest remain just to the east of Milejczyce. The Bialowieza Forest itself is a World Heritage Site, and the continuing subject of a newsworthy dispute between Polish logging interests and the European Court of Justice. (*The Guardian* and *The New York Times* have given it prominent coverage.) Tamares is both remote and very present, from long ago and yet contemporary. He is not a distraction but, to the contrary, a prescient thinker, a bulwark and beacon for us today. How might this be?

The early twenty-first century has been an age of unprecedented rapid change. Technological developments join with the massive erosion of previously established cultural and ethical guidelines to leave us with a sense of being unmoored, disoriented and adrift. The planet-interlacing effects of the internet are matched by the explosive actualities of "smart" bombs and drones, not to overlook the unpredictable consequences of robots, driverless vehicles and Artificial Intelligence. Combined with radical changes in corporate understanding, reducing the earlier sense of responsibilities toward shareholders, workers, and communities to a single focus on shareholder profits, employment conditions themselves have been radically altered and seem destined for further, unpredictable changes. These represent a startling challenge, especially against the societal reality of the splintering of once commonly shared cultural traditions and behavioral norms.

This universal condition in developed societies is compounded for Jews today by two massive additional events: the devastating destruction of central and eastern European Jewish life, and the establishment of the State of Israel

---

[1] A fascinating, fuller account can be found in the opening autobiographical sketch, crisply translated from the Yiddish by Ri J. Turner.

as a territorial, power-political nation-state. Some of the implications of this latter event are searchingly explored in such volumes as Ehud Luz's *Wrestling with an Angel* (Yale University Press) and Noam Pianko's *Zionism: The Roads Not Taken* (Indiana University Press), to cite but two of ever so many volumes.

With respect to the Nazi-directed murder of 6,000,000 Jews and the consequent erasure of that rich, irreplaceable cultural resource, Abraham Joshua Heschel's unforgettable tribute, *The Earth Is the Lord's*, can be supplemented by Zbrowsky and Herzog's *Life Is With People*, writings of David Roskies and Ruth Wisse, and countless other volumes. These can contribute to preserving, at least in our awareness, some sense of what was so cruelly destroyed and consequently denied us as our rightful cultural inheritance. That loss remains keenly felt, and for many of us, it makes all the more difficult our assessing and trying to control the direction of the current flood of challenging developments with some guidance from our immediate past. Shards of human warmth, communally shared values, personal consideration for others, recognition of neighbors—for all the challenges of living in intimacy with one another, how appealing today are those qualities from the shtetl to our dispersed, displaced, anonymous, isolated "society."

It is against this background that I suggest viewing Tamares as a bulwark, not a distraction from the past. Tamares' writings, five volumes of essays and sermons, plus a sixth of responsa on ritual matters, all published between 1905 and 1931 in Poland and Russia, are tangible, visible, material survivals of that culture whose loss we lament and whose values we affirm. Not imaginative reconstructions of the past, they are vital testimony to that past which is still materially present through the printed page.

Are they typical of that culture? Not necessarily, although they surely represent values of that culture in the quite distinctive expression of a gifted member and leader of that community. They are incontestably authentic, genuine expressions of that culture in one fervent formulation. Addressing timeless issues of ethics, morality, communal morale, and Judaism in relation to the world at large, they can, indeed, serve us as a rampart from which to define clearly and defend vigorously the traditional values that we most cherish.

With respect to Tamares as beacon, illuminating future goals and paths leading to them, his trenchant critiques of political Zionism and of the institution of war are, indeed, forward looking in quite relevant ways. Among those who knew or know of Tamares, there is a tendency to dismiss his specific criticisms as simply naïve. Even Aaron Zeitlin, who had once met Tamares and who commemorated his 30th yahrzeit in the *Yiddish Morgen Zhournal* of September 22, 1961, seems to me too quickly dismissive. While affirming Tamares' "compassion" and characterizing him as "a brilliant and original scholar," Zeitlin goes on to offer the opinion that "the Mielyczycer rov did not understand Herzl, could not make sense of political Zionism." I would argue the contrary: Tamares grasped the realities of Herzl's Zionism with astonishing acuity. Himself an early supporter of the movement and a delegate to the Fourth Zionist Congress in London in 1904, his critique is illuminating even for us today. Tamares' searching critique of the nationalist foundations of the modern ethnic nation-state, together with his sensitivity to the feelings for that land, make him a valuable companion for our challenge to work toward a resolution of the mutually valid, mutually conflicting claims of Jews and Palestinians.

Tamares' pacifism seems to me more of an obstacle to his receiving the thoughtful hearing he deserves. As an example of what I'd call a too complaisant dismissal, look at some of Zeitlin's further comments in the same yahrzeit column: "outdated...an absolutist pacifist...his almost childlike extremism in such matters, which require a sense for facts." Advocates of nonviolent struggle, even those with a firm grasp of the realities of power, obedience, and the chain of authority through which power is exercised, are accustomed to such purportedly "realistic" critiques. These readily accepted opinions surely reflect what the Brandeis sociologist, Professor Gordon Fellman, has dubbed the Rambo culture, the glamorization of military heroics. To the contrary, I would argue that "a sense for facts" demands a searching consideration of the realities of military conflict today, along with a reconsideration of earlier accepted dismissals of the power of nonviolence to effect profound societal change. Combined with increasing evidence that military violence has failed in vital areas affecting our security and our lives today, Tamares' pacifism, strategically applied, may speak to our condition more directly than we realize.

The ability of nonviolent strategies and tactics to affect and transform existing power relations is now well established. Beyond the widely recognized nonviolent campaigns led by Gandhi in India and Martin Luther King, Jr. in the United States, it is important to keep in mind that famed monopolists of military might such as the Shah in Iran, Marcos in the Philippines, and many others were overthrown by unarmed civilians through nonviolent actions. Based on extensive analyses of numerous nonviolent campaigns and movements, organizations such as the Albert Einstein Institution and the International Center for Nonviolent Conflict (ICNC), to name but two, have large bodies of well-researched, sophisticated material readily available. The one-hour video "Bringing Down A Dictator" offers an ideal introduction, at once informative and entertaining. It is a filmed account of how unarmed students in Serbia, by careful planning and organizing, enlisted broad sections of Serbian society to topple "the butcher of the Balkans," Slobodan Milosevec by "people power," without the use of weapons or military tactics.

Thousands of additional examples are well-documented and invite our scrutiny. A powerful overview of this literature can be found in the 20-minute TED talk by Professor Erica Chenoweth. The tale of her 3½-year statistical research on the comparative effectiveness of violence and nonviolence is a carefully documented study of every recorded campaign to overthrow a government or achieve territorial liberation during the past century. In the more than 1,100 such campaigns involving 1,000 or more participants, the results surprised even Professor Chenoweth, a sociologist specializing in this topic: "From 1900 to 2006, nonviolent campaigns worldwide were *twice as likely to succeed* outright than violent insurgencies." This trend has been increasing over the past fifty years, "even in extremely repressive, authoritarian conditions." (Full details can be found in the Columbia University Press volume co-authored with Maria J. Stephan, *Why Civil Resistance Works*, or the 2020 Oxford University Press volume, *Civil Resistance*.) Any would-be realist must take into account these unexpected statistical findings before dismissing nonviolent activism as nothing more than misguided idealism.

As early as 1905, Tamares was advocating active cooperation between Jews and the non-Jews among whom they reside. In his essay on Judaism and Liberty, he proposes both internal projects that will orient and prepare Jews for cooperation with their neighbors, and external projects to activate such cooperation in matters of common concern. He urges vigilance in monitoring false claims by the ruling authorities that would that would distract both Jews and non-Jews from their common exploitation at the hands of the rulers. While far from a fully outlined program, both here and throughout his writings he speaks of attitudes and actions that we would now call acts of civil resistance. Ten years before Gandhi's discovery of "the method," Tamares at times seems to suggest some awareness of such possibilities.

We see echoes of Tamares' insights in the hard-to-believe, successful, non-violent campaign by some 1,500 Aryan German wives of Jewish husbands for the release of their husbands from arrest and, in some cases, from imprisonment in Auschwitz. The demonstrations took place in 1943 on Rosenstrasse, in front of the Gestapo headquarters, and were audacious beyond belief. One of the most deeply held Nazi prohibitions was that of foul Jewish blood defiling pure Aryan blood, especially that of pure German women. Yet here were 1,500 of Germany's blondest Aryans protesting, with growing support from neighbors, friends, and other pure Germans, the application of this law. And the Gestapo yielded! 1,500 German Jewish men lived in Berlin with their non-Jewish wives through the entirety of the Second World War.

How explain this? What dynamics were at work? A meticulously documented, probing presentation of this singular case is Professor Nathan Stolzfuss' *Resistance of the Heart*. It is not a full answer to the case of the extremely ruthless opponent, but it does raise profound questions about power, the exercise of power, and what enables power wielders to succeed or causes them to fail. It is also a most improbable, yet true, adventure tale.

Were there "special circumstances"? Of course, every specific struggle, every individual battle has its own special circumstances; history is a vast panorama of individual events. But this undeniable historical incident should caution us against dismissing Tamares' pacifism as simply utopian, unworldly, without practical application.

There is a strong temptation to write more about the practice and theory of strategic nonviolent struggle, but that is for a different occasion. For now, my hope is simply that these brief clarifying remarks will enable the reader to read, with greater openness, these eloquent essays of "One of the Passionately Concerned Rabbis." I retain the conviction that he, indeed, points us directly toward the future even while anchoring us in the finest values from the past. Like his sesquicentennial birth-mate Gandhi, he seems to me decidedly a resident of the future, not simply a relic of the past.

It is often the attempt of introductions to place the subject more fully within the context of his/her times. In this case, my attempt is to place the subject more compellingly within the context of our times. He, along with the prophet Amos and Henry David Thoreau, has been for me a cherished companion, a veritable bulwark and beacon, for ever so many decades, thanks to the incomprehensible beneficence of a most gracious God.

The selections that follow represent a substantial portion of Tamares' published writings, but they are by no means a complete collection of his works. Neither are they introduced and accompanied by a full scholarly commentary. Rather, they are selections that I think speak directly to us today, as we find ourselves confronting issues painfully similar to some that confronted Tamares in his era. The brief introductions provide sufficient context, I hope, to help the reader situate the essays in their environment, at the same allowing them to offer us some guidance for our own issues.

My hope is that Tamares may contribute as well to your own comprehension and appreciation of the incomprehensible gift of life on this earth, with all its challenges, its trials, and its joys.

Acknowledgements

It was Gerson Cohen, later Chancellor of Jewish Theological Seminary (JTS) but at that time the Librarian, who introduced me to the writings of Rabbi Aaron Samuel Tamares of Milejcycze, Poland, "Ahad Harabanim Hamargishim," "One of the Passionately Concerned Rabbis." Happening across one another in a hallway back in 1956, when I was a student at JTS, Cohen greeted me with a warm, mischievous smile and said: "Gendler, come into my office, I have something to show you." Compliant, I followed him, and saw there on his desk a small, thin, cardboard-covered volume. Lifting it high, he handed it to me with a flourish and said, "Gendler, you're an Iowa Quaker, you'll like this!" His gleeful smile indicated that this brief encounter was now ended, and off I headed to try to decipher the thin, tattered, intriguing volume that was my introduction to the writings of this original Jewish moralist, thinker, and community "rov."

The timing was auspicious. I was approaching my senior year at Seminary, and struggling with the question of whether I could, in good conscience, serve in uniform as a Military Chaplain, or whether I needed to do two years of Alternative Service. At that time of the U. S. involvement in Korea, we who enjoyed a 4-D theological exemption from the draft were expected to make ourselves available for chaplaincy service upon ordination. The volume in hand was *Knesset Yisrael uMilchamot Hagoyim, The Community of Israel and the Wars of the Nations*! As I slowly deciphered the elegant, impassioned Hebrew, I found myself confronting an uncompromising condemnation of World War I and war as such, from exclusively Jewish sources, by the observant rabbi of a small Jewish community in the Grodno district of Poland.

I had certainly read such critiques in my adolescence and later at college, but these were largely from secular philosophical or peace-church theological perspectives. There were also pamphlets from the Jewish Peace Fellowship that emphasized the supreme value of peace within Jewish thinking, and a few principled advocates of such positions among Jews whom I knew. Not before, however, had I seen such a perspective articulated so forcefully by one who could hardly be characterized as a Polish Quaker! No, Tamares was an authentic shtetl yid, Jewish through and through, hence the importance of his writings as testimony to a genuine Jewish ethical outlook on the world. At the time that I was a student at JTS, 1951-1957, numbers of pre-World War II European printed Hebrew volumes were circulating among used book sellers, and I was able to obtain copies of all five volumes of Tamares' published general essays. A sixth volume, his responses (teshuvot) to questions that he had been asked about Jewish law and practice, is currently available as *Yad Aharon*.

Tamares has remained a companion for now some sixty years, Bless God for such longevity! On several earlier occasions, excerpts from his writings that I have translated have been published in *Judaism* magazine (1963, 1968), *Tikkun* (2003, 2010), and *Issues* (2003, 2010). The translation of his major critique of political nationalist Zionism, written in 1929 following the Hebron riots, had been accepted for publication by a journal in 1969, but a sudden change of editors provoked by its acceptance resulted in the manuscript being returned to me unpublished.

As a consequence, until now Tamares has been little known among students of Jewish thought and within the wider Jewish community. At this time of radical challenge to received assumptions within the Jewish world and the world of politics at large, it is my conviction that Tamares' fresh voice can make a major contribution to our clarification of urgent issues such as war and peace, means and ends, particularism and universalism, and other dilemmas. Most recently, 2017, Ri J. Turner has offered in *In Geveb* her translation from the Yiddish of Tamares' autobiographical sketch. Now Larry Yudelson of Ben Yehuda Press has indicated interest in making available significant portions of Tamares' seminal writings. I am grateful for his publishing initiative, and pleased at the prospect that some of Tamares' challenging ideas will now be available to help us critique and clarify various propositions that lay claim to our efforts.

Original encouragement for this project came from Professor Daniel Smith at Loyola Marymount University and Professor Daniel Weiss at Cambridge University. My preparation of this material has been immeasurably helped by Crisse MacFadyen's invaluable organizing abilities, operating with determination but with simultaneous encouragement and good cheer. I appreciate, also, the help of Fruma Mohrer at YIVO, and of Alexander Sikorski, a member of the Yale University Class of 2020. A special word of appreciation to Ri J. Turner and Tzemah Yoreh for their permission to include their translations of Tamares material. Finally, appreciation to Sharon Strassfeld, Mary Gendler, Naomi Camper, and Tamar Gendler for their invaluable help with some challenging editing issues. I am also moved by the realization that the singular outlook of Tamares became available to me through the dedication to scholarly openness that Gerson Cohen exemplified. Living out the finest traditions of Talmudic disputation, John Milton's *Areopagitica*, and John Stuart Mill's *On Liberty*, Cohen entrusted to the arena of free, critical discussion of ideas, an intellectual position that he, personally, likely found alien. It is my fervent hope that we may confront Tamares' outlook in a manner that will yield both clarity and consensus concerning goals, characterized by civility and mutual respect in their pursuit.

Part I

The Autobiography

Introduction to the Autobiography

If we were in possession only of Aaron Samuel Tamares' sermons and essays, without this autobiographical sketch, we would already confront material that challenged some of our perhaps unconsciously held stereotypes of the "shtetl Yid," the Jewish resident of the small town or village in Eastern Europe. Narrow in outlook, limited in awareness of the larger surrounding world, acquainted with and concerned about only fellow Jews; dismissive of "goyim," non-Jews, as lesser human beings; so absorbed in study of sacred texts that there is no awareness of nature: whatever our explanations of these presumed characteristics, such were the character traits that we might have felt compelled to account for.

If every one of these is challenged by the content of Tamares' published but not previously translated writings, his autobiographical memoir, written in Yiddish near the end of his life and here translated in lively, engaging fashion by Ri J. Turner, quite demolishes the stereotype. Here is an *ilui*, a child prodigy, master of sacred texts and extraordinary Hebrew stylist, whose "most intimate friends, the beautiful evergreen trees...perfected his own training in the theory and morality of freedom; he penned most of his work in the forest."

A consultation with Google maps reveals that Milejczyce, the village where he served as rabbi for more than thirty five years, is just 40 kilometers from the very heart of the Bialowieska Forest, the last remaining primeval forest in all of Europe. The importance of this Forest is attested both by the recent European Union Supreme Court of Justice decision (17 April 2018), and by the chapter on Bialowieska Puszcza in Alan Weisman's stunning volume, *The World Without Us*. Much of the forest, although not in the Park preserve proper, even today extends to Milejczyce. It was likely here, in this iconic primeval preserve, that many of Tamares' essays were written—a most intimate interweaving of the two sacred texts of Scripture and of Nature.

Here is a rabbi, a dedicated Jew, whose "awareness of the depravity of war" was first formed by the reaction of a non-Jewish neighbor to news of the death of her son in the Russo-Turkish War (1877): "The fallen soldier's mother wept bitterly at the news—and the little Jewish boy wept with her." This image remained with him throughout his life, and helped him retain his focus on the utter impermissibility of war in the pursuit of human values. It is surely worth remarking that this quintessential Jew finds nothing remarkable in this natural association of Jew and non-Jew in establishing a common human value.

Here is a little kid, often bullied by the non-Jewish ruffians living in his neighborhood as he walked to *cheder*, the village Jewish school, who first experienced "the oppressed" as Jews only. In his early teens, however, he heard about "shoshalists" (socialists) in Saint Petersburg who wanted to overthrow the Czar because he oppressed the people. A few were Jews, but most were non-Jews. Tamares immediately understood that "goyim," also, were sometimes persecuted, exploited, and that the struggle for freedom, for liberation, so central to Jewish tradition, was thus a universal value, applying to all peoples, not just to Jews. As readers well know, this is not a universal reaction following experiences of childhood ethnic-racial bullying.

As Tamares assumed the duties of rabbi in this small community, his self-understanding of his task was "to repair the world...to bring harmony to the world." How? "Insofar as the Jewish people was, in his opinion, called by duty to purify the entire world—then his first task was to purify the Jewish world itself." This clear, persistent, unflinching commitment to the petty particular and the grand universal, their intimate linkage and unrelenting claim, motivated Tamares throughout his life.

Toward this end, in sharp contrast to most of his traditional colleagues, he became an early, ardent supporter of the Zionist movement. Sent as a delegate from Brisk to the Fourth Zionist Congress in London in 1900, he there confronted a reality quite at variance from his understanding of the stated Zionist aims as "a movement devoted to freedom and justice, to the struggle against enslavement and evil." Instead, he found it to be a movement fighting "for the redemption not of people but of territories ...independence, i. e., the opportunity to lord it over others." He also observed, most presciently, that European governments were proposing to "provide reparations for their wrongdoings by handing over foreign property." Stunned by these discoveries, Tamares returned home and spent a year in nearly complete public silence while he digested these discoveries. His searching critique remained a focus to the very end of his life.

There is a temptation to continue underlining distinctive features of Tamares' understanding of Judaism, but he is more than capable of speaking for himself, the purpose of this volume. Let me simply clarify one divergence of translation of Tamares' pen-name, Ahad Harabanim Hamargishim, used for years for self-protection by concealing his identity: "One of the Sensitive Rabbis" or "One of the Passionately Concerned Rabbis." Both are valid and reflect a slight difference of emphasis.

The three letter root, r-g-sh, Biblically designates "be in tumult or commotion; thunder, be in tumult." Turner rightly emphasizes Tamares' special sensitivity revealed in his autobiographical sketch. Translating during the Vietnam War of the 1960s, I felt moved to emphasize both his passion and his concern. "Concern" is a classic term in Friends/Quaker discourse for involved engagement. During those turbulent times of the military draft, association with the Quakers was a sustaining element for those of us resisting the draft. As for Tamares' passion, his self-characterization of some of his writings as "volcanic" is surely warrant for the term "passionate." *E-lu v'e-lu*, "both these and these" are valid renderings.

Added to this consideration for use of "concerned," I recently happened across an additional compelling reason for connecting "margish" with "passion." In his touching tribute to his mentor at Princeton, John Berryman, W. S. Merwin includes this quatrain in "Berryman."

> he said the great presence
> that permitted everything and transmuted it
> in poetry was passion
> passion was genius and he praised movement and intervention

Almost every word of this remarkable passage can be applied to illuminate and augment our understanding of Tamares. "Transmuted" with its alchemical overtones of transformation; "movement and intervention" with their overtones of purposive development; "genius" with its generative overtones from its Latin roots—all of these help us view Tamares as directly in the line of his rabbinic predecessors in the Mekhilta, whose interpretation of the triumphal Song at the Sea truly transmutes it from a celebrative battle hymn of triumph to a celebration of the power of spirit and learning in the world of power relations. Standing similarly in this familiar religious re-interpretive tradition is Tamares' sesquicentennial birth-mate, Gandhi, who performs similarly transformative feats with the Bhavagad Gita in Hindu tradition. Merwin expresses with astonishing insight and brevity this recognizable pattern in religious phenomonology. An initial revelatory insight is refined and given nuance by subsequent generations of religious visionaries. The initial flash of illumination is followed by considered, reflective re-formulation. I submit that it is helpful to view Tamares with this appreciation of poetic passion as a vital force in religious development.

Autobiography of "One of the Sensitive Rabbis" (1926)

(Translated by Ri J. Turner)

INTRODUCTION

Rabbi Aaron Shmuel Tamares was born in 1869 near Maltsh, Grodno Governorate. After distinguishing himself in traditional studies, he inherited his father-in-law's rabbinic post in Milejczyce, a small town which recalled for him the setting of his rural childhood, much to his delight. Tamares joined Netzach Yisrael, a student branch of Hibbat Tzion, while studying at the Volozhin Yeshiva; but a decade later, after attending two Zionist assemblies, Tamares realized that the organizational culture of the Zionist movement clashed profoundly with his own "aesthetic" preferences and his deeply held beliefs about the essential character of the Jewish people (apolitical and pacifist, above all). At that point he left the movement, and after a short period of doubt and exploration, spent the rest of his life writing articles, letters, and books (primarily in Hebrew) expressing his critiques of modern Jewish politics and his visions for an alternative approach.

In 1929, Zalman Reyzen would include an entry about Tamares in his *Leksikon fun der yidisher literatur, prese, un filologye*. As a basis for this entry, Tamares composed an autobiographical essay (probably ca. 1926), in Yiddish, about his life and work, with an emphasis on the formative moments in his political development. Characteristically, the essay is extremely long (seventy-six handwritten pages), trenchant to a fault, and redolent with the prickly false modesty of a man who spent his adult life refusing to join any movement (no small feat in the Jewish Pale of Settlement at the turn of the last century). In contrast, the entry that Reyzen eventually included in the *Leksikon* is only five columns long, and, naturally, devoid of Tamares's sardonic, charismatic voice.

To the best of my knowledge, the essay, which resides in the YIVO Archives in New York, has never before been translated into English. A Hebrew translation by Shlomo Zucker appeared in 1992, along with a facsimile of the original Yiddish text, in Ehud Luz's anthology of Tamares's selected Hebrew writings, *Patsifizm LeOr HaTorah* (Jerusalem: Dinur Center, Hebrew University). The essay, which provides a rare window onto the margins of Eastern

European Jewish political life during the rise of Zionism (and includes cameo appearances by the likes of Mendele Moykher Sforim and Chayyim Nachman Bialik), is intriguing not only for historical reasons, but also from a literary and psychological perspective. Jewish history has no shortage of figures whose acuity, stubbornness, and prophetic tendencies have prevented them from participating cooperatively in the political and cultural projects of their era. In his autobiographical essay, Tamares tells us exactly how he became one such figure—and he expresses a galvanizing, sometimes self-contradictory confluence of political ideas (pacifism and liberationism, humanism and Jewish triumphalism, individual conscience and communal sovereignty) that are all still very much alive today—and still just as difficult to reconcile as they were in 1926.
—R.J.T.

Translator's acknowledgments and copyright information:
Many thanks to Rabbi Everett Gendler, one of Tamares's intellectual and spiritual heirs and his primary translator into English, who pointed me toward this document. I am grateful to Dr. Barry Mesch of Hebrew College in Newton, MA, who advised my master's thesis project out of which this translation sprouted. Thanks also to Fruma Mohrer, Senior Archivist at the YIVO Archives in New York, Dr. Ehud Luz of Haifa University, and The Dinur Center for Research in Jewish History at Hebrew University for their assistance with reproductions and copyright permissions. The Yiddish manuscript is housed at the Archives of the YIVO Institute for Jewish Research in Collection RG 3 (Yiddish Literature and Language), Folder 3222. The manuscript was reproduced in the book *Patzifizm LeOr HaTorah* (Ehud Luz, ed., Jerusalem: Dinur Center, 1992), which also contains Shlomo Zucker's annotated translation of the manuscript into Hebrew, as well as a detailed introduction to Tamares's life and work written by Ehud Luz, both of which I consulted extensively in the process of translating Tamares's autobiographical essay into English.

Chapter I

Rabbi Aaron Shmuel Tamares, well-known for his writings published under the pseudonym "One of the Sensitive Rabbis," was born in 1869 in a village just outside the town of Maltsh,[2] Grodno Governorate, to a poor yet distinguished family. His father, Moshe Ya'akov Tamares, was a grandson of the Maltsher rabbi, Reb Arele, who in his time (the 1840s) was known in the Polesie region as a tzadik[3] and was called the Maltsher Maggid.[4]

He was brought up in the old-fashioned way, with an education in religious studies only. He distinguished himself in the field, that is, in Talmud, and earned a name throughout the region as the "Maltsher illui.[5]"

Alongside his intellectual talents, he was from childhood on also quite sentimental and sensitive to all the subtler realms, whether aesthetics, morality, or religious ardor. Outdoors, he became so enchanted by a beautiful tree or a grassy hillock that he could not tear himself away. And in the beys-medresh,[6] he used to pray with more devotion than any of the other boys.

When he was around six years old, a maggid delivered a eulogy in the beys-medresh for the well-known rabbi Reb Eliyahu Lider,[7] who had passed away around that time. He characterized the loss to the community in the wake of the tzadik's death: "From now on, no one remains who can safeguard the generation." The eulogy made a greater impression on the little boy than on anyone else in the beys-medresh. He wept bitter tears and prayed ma'ariv[8] quite devoutly, immediately taking it upon himself to cultivate torah and mitzvot to make up for the loss of the tzadik who had served as the "safeguard."

However, the pint-sized acolyte didn't prosper, poor thing (in contrast to most of the "pious" among the grown-ups), because a group of smart alecks made a habit of entertaining themselves at his expense. After the eulogy incident, they would approach him saying, "Hey Aaron Shmuel, did you hear? Such-and-such a rabbi from such-and-such a city"—they would devise names of rabbis and of cities—"has passed away." And the boy would run

---

[2] Today Malech, Belarus.
[3] *Tzadik*: an especially righteous man.
[4] *Maggid*: an itinerant preacher.
[5] *Illui*: child prodigy in the realm of traditional Jewish learning.
[6] *Beys-medresh:* house of study, also used as a place for prayer, delivering sermons, etc.
[7] Reb Eliyahu "Elinke" Schick of Lida, also known as the "Ein Eliyahu."
[8] *Ma'ariv*: the evening prayer service.

away in consternation.

He used to get quite upset about any misfortune; his heart would melt with sympathy. And if he saw someone commit an injustice, he could not rest until he had responded in some way.

A few anecdotes would not go amiss here. They are minor in scope, in accordance with the child's tender age; however, in content they are extremely characteristic, and illustrate the claims made above.

1) One of his acquaintances took up the habit of smoking. However, he was poor and did not have the means to purchase tobacco, so he used to stand around in the beys-medresh while someone smoked a cigarette, and wait for him to fling the butt onto the floor. This the poor little smoker would pick up, and from such gleanings, piece together a sort of cigarette for himself. This pathetic sight used to tug at the heartstrings of the future Sensitive Rabbi, and whenever his mother gave him a kopek to buy a treat, he would run to give it to the wretched young man for cigarette money. However, that did not suffice to replenish the smoker's tobacco deficit, because the mother of the future "One of the Sensitive Rabbis" was also quite poor, and could only rarely spare a kopek for him. Thus, he hired himself out to bring drinks of water to the yeshiva students who were learning in the beys-medresh. He would trudge through the autumn evenings, up to the knee in the Maltsh mud, to earn the going rate in the beys-medresh at that time: a cigarette apiece for each drink of water. As soon as he got hold of the cigarette, he ran to relieve the privation of his friend, the hapless smoker.

2) In the kheyder he attended, a couple of wild boys cooked up a scheme targeting a certain quiet boy, and drew the rest of the kheyder-boys into their plans. They badgered and tormented their victim, teasing him every which way. But the future Sensitive Rabbi did not get swept up in the tide. He was the only one to stand up for the persecuted child, and he fought on his behalf against the entire student body.

Chapter II.[9]

The development of his inborn aesthetic and moral sense was enhanced, on one hand, by the beautiful atmosphere of the village setting—the green fields and blooming orchards that provided the backdrop for his upbringing—and on the other hand, by the tragic circumstances of his parents' lives—refined Jews who made their home in a large village full of half-wild

---

[9] Chapter markings don't appear in the Yiddish text until Chapter III; I follow Zucker in marking the first chapter break here (see Shlomo Zucker's Hebrew translation in Ehud Luz, ed., *Patzifizm LeOr HaTorah*, Jerusalem: Dinur Center, Hebrew University, 1992).

goyim. The natural beauty of the rural environment affected his aesthetic sensibilities in a positive manner, by weaving his spirit into the forests and the fields. And the lonely predicament of a refined Jew in an environment full of boorish goyim who interacted in a hard and coarse manner even amongst themselves, and all the more so toward a Jew, a "heathen" (although the snakelike anti-Semitism of our "civilized" era was as of yet unknown to the naive peasants of the boy's early years), affected his sentimental sensibilities in a negative manner, i.e., caused him to hate rudeness and mean-spiritedness. Most of all, he was turned against human malice by the troubles inflicted upon him by the peasant boys and their dogs on his walk through the long village each day in order to reach the kheyder in the nearby town.

In addition, the contrast that the boy perceived between the raw character and rude behavior of the Gentile neighbors, as opposed to the delicate character and refined behavior of his parents, and the fact that the latter was intertwined with a strict observance of the religious laws—had no small impact on his religious feeling; it caused him to become quite pious, and planted within him a deep enthusiasm for yidishkeyt.

His religious disposition was also influenced by the Sabbaths and holidays that he experienced in his parents' home. The indescribable Sabbath-spirit that hovered in the small cottage of a genteel, lonely Jew in the midst of a great village of boorish goyim; the indescribable Sabbath-idyll, which descended upon their little house suddenly as if from Heaven itself every Friday evening, when his mother, after an entire week of tumult with the goyim in the aqua vitae business, of wearing herself out to scrape together a few groschen for Sabbath delicacies, used to sweep out the house and spread the floor with yellow sand, bless the Sabbath candles with a quiet, fervent prayer, and blot out the existence of the accursed tavern for the duration of the Sabbath . . . An hour later, his father would return from the beys-medresh in town and make a devout kiddush. And the Sabbath meal, the way the special Sabbath dishes alternated with apt passages from the Zohar, which he studied by the table with his father, who explained the exalted words in Yiddish—all of this transported the sensitive child straight to paradise.

However, the shy youngster's Eden was occasionally disturbed by the presence of a neighbor, a goy who—out of pure curiosity—would enter in the middle of the meal, sit himself down, and puff on his pipe until the entire house filled with smoke, looking upon the scene with something close to reverence.

Chapter III.

Despite his parents' isolation among the goyim, and his own troubles at the hands of their offspring, the boy harbored no animosity toward the Gentiles of the village, and in fact was on quite intimate terms with a few of them. In the summertime he used to sit in one of the neighbors' courtyards near his barn, reading his Talmud lesson while the neighbor stacked sheaves or threshed in the barn.

During the Russo-Turkish War, this same neighbor received notice that his son had been killed in battle. The fallen soldier's mother wept bitterly at the news—and the little Jewish boy wept with her. From that moment on, the boy's consciousness was consumed by an awareness of the depravity of war. The same woman had a painting from the war hanging in her house, which depicted Russian soldiers attacking the Turks with bayonets. The boy used to stand glued to the image for hours on end, bewildered by the idea that human beings could become accustomed to such acts, and wondering how the soldiers could endure such dreadful circumstances. He was also quite astonished that the bereaved mother could tolerate having such an image in her home, compelling her always to look upon the cursed event which had left so many mothers bereaved.

As mentioned above, the existence of evil in the world tormented him from a young age—man's maltreatment of his fellow man. But at that time, his concept of "the oppressor" was limited to "the goy," considering his daily encounters with the village peasants, their wild progeny, and their ill-tempered hounds. And "the oppressed"—were Jews only, as far as he could conclude from his own and his father's[10] state of isolation in the village.

Later on, when he was about thirteen or fourteen and could learn on his own in the Maltsher beys-medresh, he caught wind of a rumor that a secret society existed in Saint Petersburg, called "the shoshalists,"[11] who "wished to overthrow the Czar because he oppressed the people." Some Jews were counted among the "shoshalists," but most members were Gentile. "Could it be that goyim are sometimes also persecuted?" the boy wondered, astonished. He then quickly came up with an example, remembering the fallen soldier whose death he had mourned for several years alongside his

---

[10] [Sic]—it is not clear why he excludes his mother here, considering that he includes her in the previous chapter; perhaps he is envisioning the archetypes of "oppressor" and "oppressed" here chiefly in terms of males acting in the public and/or political sphere.

[11] ציצילסטן—A corruption of the word "socialist," as spoken by rural people who did not know what the word meant, or with a mildly mocking connotation (see for example the usage in "Nakhes fun Kinder" by Joseph Tunkel). Here Tamares seems to be representing the word as it sounded to him the first time he heard it as a young teenager.

unfortunate neighbor.

The young man came more and more to see war as the epitome of evil and slavery. Even all the constraints that Jews faced (and not only Jews in villages who suffered at the hands of the goyim, but also, as he had learned by then, Jews in the cities who suffered at the hands of the "nachal'stvo"[12]) were, in his mind, as naught in comparison with the gruesome notion of stationing men in an open field and exposing them to a hail of bullets and shrapnel, not to mention the ignominious fact that the soldiers were conscripts who had been dragged there by force, like rams to a slaughterhouse.

When he was about nineteen, he traveled to Kovno to the Kollel HaPerushim,[13] where he studied Talmud diligently. But in his free moments—unlike all the other young scholars, who used to discuss practical matters, such as rabbinic ordination and which cities had vacant rabbinic posts—he (and a few other scatterbrained dreamers he had collected in order to expound before them) spoke only of the slavery and evil afoot in the land, and the need to fight against them. By "slavery and evil," he meant, again, war. And by "fight against them," he did not mean terrorism—he did not advise throwing a bomb under some official's stagecoach: firstly, because that would contradict the spirit of the Talmud, and secondly, because that in and of itself would be an act of war. Rather, the most desirable strategy was to educate the public: to instill in people the ability to differentiate between good and evil.

Once while walking in the city of Kovno, he passed a company of soldiers with switches[14] tucked under their arms, on their way to a bathhouse. "Woe, woe," he mourned their predicament in his heart, "they're on their way to be massacred, yet meanwhile the poor things drag themselves to the bathhouse, just as if they were living men who could expect to have a future . . ."

Another time he encountered a throng of soldiers singing as they marched across a bridge. "Tfui! May their memory be blotted out, the harebrained lot of them," he thought to himself. "Tomorrow they'll be lined up underneath a rain of shrapnel with only their skulls to protect them, and yet they spend today carousing in the streets." They really did seem to have a screw or two loose, which only strengthened his conviction that education was the answer—half the problem was that people had terrible taste . . .

In 1890, he left Kovno for Volozhin, where he spent two years in the

---

[12] начальство, Russian, "authorities."

[13] Established by Rabbi Yisrael Salanter, founder of the musar movement.

[14] For the purpose of gentle flagellation in the bathhouse, in order to open pores and enhance circulation.

yeshiva, advanced further in his studies, and was deeply affected by the passion for Torah that characterized the atmosphere there. He also caught a whiff of haskalah, and acquired some knowledge of the Russian language.

In 1893, without the least bit of effort on his part, he was hired as the rabbi of Milejczyce, succeeding his father-in-law,[15] who had passed away. But the struggle for freedom interested him more than the rabbinate; what interested him was not bringing harmony to his congregation, but rather bringing harmony to the world . . . .

And he did not lack the courage to dream of something as grand as "repairing the world," despite the materially weak position of the Jewish people in the wider society, and his own materially weak position amongst the Jews.

Firstly, by that time his inborn tendency toward beauty and purity had fully ripened, and he was steel-willed in his pursuit of justice and integrity. In addition, he was by then worldly-wise: he had a deep, penetrating insight into the psychology of man, and therefore could orient himself with respect to society's complications.

Secondly, his sense of vocation to "repair the world," to fight for its liberation, rested primarily upon the merits of his ancestral nation, the Jewish people. For if according to his conception the problem must be confronted not by means of bombs but rather with "enlightenment" and moral education—who, then, is more fit for this task than the People of the Prophets and the Tannaim,[16] a people whose history is fraught with martyrology?

Thirdly, vocation or no vocation, what did it matter? Either way, he was burdened, together with his tendency toward spiritual purity, with a fiery temperament that allowed him no rest as long as his most sacred values were being trodden underfoot. Had the world ever asked him what he wanted? Of course not! So why should he start asking the world for permission?

Chapter IV.

Insofar as the Jewish people was, in his opinion, called by duty to purify the entire world—then his first task was to purify the Jewish world itself. He treated every rabbinic sermon as an opportunity to awaken his audience to the necessity of moral improvement. But the town was small, and local propaganda could bear only a negligible amount of fruit—so he also began to write for the newspapers. He became an author because the needs of the hour drove him to pour out his soul before the world, despite the fact

---

[15] It is interesting that Tamares does not choose to mention his wife or his family life as an adult anywhere else in this "biography," aside from this quite oblique reference and one other (see part 2, chapter IX).

[16] *Tannaim*: the rabbis whose debates were recorded in the Mishna (ca. 0-200 CE).

that he had not yet had any training in the profession, and in fact had a poor command of Hebrew and had never even learned any grammar (later on he perfected his Hebrew and also acquired a certain amount of secular education). But the fire that burned within him forged its own language. His internal volcano, with its eruptions of sarcastic reproof against stupidity and evil, drew its lava from his mental warehouse of Torah: Talmudic aphorisms, Mishnaic expressions, Biblical flourishes. Those were the raw materials which he soldered into a unique style, and with which he cleared a pathway for himself into the public eye.

If the force behind his writing was a volcano, then it goes without saying that the articles themselves were made of fire. Those who were of the same mind warmed themselves at the flames and glowed with pleasure. As for the others—they gnashed their teeth.

At that time he encountered one of the spiritual impurities blighting the Jewish community: the habit of "sin-seeking," or "Jesuitism."[17] He began to rail against this despicable phenomenon. Despite his fervent love for Torah and yidishkeyt, which he believed to be the best sources for the uplift of the spirit, he nevertheless considered compulsory piety to be an abomination. To presume to barge into someone else's private space in order to sniff out a "posele tsitse"[18]—this he considered to be an act of utter vulgarity and swinishness—the kind of barbarism that would be most likely to tarnish yidishkeyt in the eyes of the younger generation.

Chapter V.

A little later, in 1897 and thereafter, the Zionist movement appeared on the scene: Herzl, congresses, Max Nordau on the platform lecturing down to his audience; his accusations against the nations and their governments in response to their persecution of Jews; and his demand: that they provide reparations for their wrongdoings by granting the Jews the Land of Israel. (Why they should make recompense for *their* wrongdoings by handing over foreign property, *Ottoman* land—this was a question which it did not occur to anyone to pose at that juncture....)

The aforementioned rabbi threw himself body and soul into this young movement, because he believed that Zionism was a movement devoted to

---

[17] Jesuitism: hypocrisy, holier-than-thou behavior. The use of "Jesuit" to mean "hypocrite, sly manipulator" has been widespread in English as well during certain time periods (see the 1832 edition of Webster's Dictionary, for example).
[18] A fringe on the corner of a garment (in accordance with Jewish law, as based on Numbers 15:38-39) that is invalid for a ritual reason.

freedom and justice, to the struggle against enslavement and evil. It was Nordau's speeches that misled him thus . . . because he had not yet developed the insight necessary to evaluate the calls for "justice" which were ever-present on the lips of the Zionist activists—those activists who fought for the redemption not of *people* but of *territories*—or the copious tears which they shed over "stolen liberties" despite not yet having won independence, i.e., the opportunity to lord it over others. Unfortunately, he was not yet equipped to appraise the value of these antics, particularly since it was too early then to observe what would become of these dainty do-gooders once they got a taste of their preferred kind of "freedom" . . . the way the poor creatures would come to wring their hands and choke on the plague known as "freedom" . . .

At that time, the Sensitive Rabbi also believed that Zionism would provide an avenue for the spiritual uplift of the Jewish people and the revival of Jewish culture. He was misled on this count by the slogan "Merkaz Ruchani,"[19] which had just then emerged on the Jewish political scene, and which, aided by the polished, enthralling style of its author,[20] captured the hearts of all of the Maskilic yeshiva students,[21] for whom such a style—due to their unfamiliarity with European literature—was still a thrilling novelty. They were blinded by the brilliance of the style, and failed to recognize that it disguised an absence of content—it is a choice spirituality, a fine Judaism indeed that is dependent on possession of "our own courtyard."

The moderates among the Orthodox[22] population were similarly misled by the sycophantic kloyznikes,[23] the well-known breed of kloyznik who is enamored of "Europeanism" in general and the title "Doctor" in particular. So as soon as "Herzl the European," "Herzl the Doctor" deigned to descend from his elevated spheres into the "Jewish street,"[24] and expressed his readiness to serve as its mayor—the kloyznikes jumped at the chance

---

[19] "Spiritual center": slogan of religious Zionism and source of the acronym "HaMizrahi" (religious Zionist party founded in 1902).

[20] Ahad HaAm (see footnote to Shlomo Zucker's Hebrew translation in Luz, p. 6 n. 6).

[21] Although Tamares does not explain this explicitly in the essay, we know from other sources that he first became involved in religious Zionism during his time in the Volozhin Yeshiva. This appears to be an allusion to that period.

[22] Religious, as opposed to secular or Reform.

[23] Religious scholars; men whose occupation was to study in the beys-medresh—meant pejoratively, with the connotation "idler, good-for-nothing."

[24] The Yiddish expression "di yidishe gas" (lit. "the Jewish street") refers to the general public political and cultural realm of the Jewish community.

to become his lackeys. They pledged themselves to his service, along with all that was holy to them. Their propaganda was replete with lofty Bible verses and purple Rabbinic prose, which they showered upon the Zionist movement and upon its "great leader" (who, shortly prior to that, had had talks with a cardinal in Vienna about "repainting"[25] the entire Jewish people) ... In this way, the kloyznikes captured many hearts, including the better part of Orthodoxy.

Additionally, the Sensitive Rabbi was also drawn deeper into Zionism by the fact that the old guard of Orthodoxy had taken a stand against Zionism in the name of "sin-seeking," a pursuit toward which this proponent of purification of the religious milieu was already quite ill-disposed from previous experience. And what's more, he thought to himself, how dare these "God's policemen" impose their "sin-inspections" upon the heroes who have set forth to redeem the world?

In short, it was too much. So he came out with fiery articles under the title "Recompense for the Controversy of Zion"[26] (in *HaMelitz*, 1899[27]),

---

[25] This probably refers to Herzl's meeting with Antonio Agliardi, the papal nuncio in Vienna, in 1896, as part of the process of trying to recruit Vatican support for Jewish territorial control in Palestine. Later, in 1904, Herzl went to Rome to meet with Pope Pius X. The Pope's response was notoriously unsympathetic: "... if you come to Palestine and settle your people there, we shall have churches and priests ready to baptize all of you" (see Paul Charles Merkley, *Christian Attitudes Towards the State of Israel*, Montreal: McGill-Queen's University Press, 2001, p. 138). The implication here is that Herzl is willing to "turn the Jews over to the Pope" in return for territorial control in Palestine, an accusation that is not unfounded: Herzl once envisioned mass conversion as a road to full assimilation (see Jacques Kornberg, *Theodor Herzl: From Assimilation to Zionism*, Bloomington: Indiana University Press, 1993, pp. 115-116), and considered suggesting it to the Pope as a bargaining chip for support of the Zionist project (see Merkley, 137). Here Tamares uses the image of "repainting" both to represent the idea of Jews who are willing to betray their "true colors" for the sake of Zionism, and to evoke the aspergillum, an implement similar in form to a paint brush which is used to sprinkle water during the Catholic rite of baptism. See also Tamares's use of the same image below in Chapter VIII (third paragraph).

[26] See Isaiah 34:8.

[27] Vol. 39: Nos. 56-70, excluding No. 61 (19-23, 29-31 March and 4-7, 9-10 April 1899). See also his second series of articles published under the same title, also in *HaMelitz*: Vol. 40: Nos. 14-29 (30-31 January and 1-2, 4-9, 11-16 February 1900).

signed as "One of the Sensitive."[28] In the articles, he aimed a much-deserved tongue-lashing at the "Orthodox Jesuits," and at the same time showered the Zionist "idealists" with the customary praise.

At that time he was still young and inexperienced. As a result he believed that "Jesuitism" was a peculiarity of Orthodoxy;[29] he did not yet know that all ruling parties demonstrates such a tendency, and that the Orthodox exhibited "Jesuitism" only because it was they who ruled over the "Jewish street" at the time.

The reading public seized upon his articles and devoured them with great anticipation. There were readers who did not have the patience to wait for the postman, and ran straight to the post office to pick up the next installment.

After *HaMelitz* ran the aforementioned series of articles, the Sensitive Rabbi received a request from the Kovno Zionists for permission to reprint the articles in pamphlet-form. He gave his permission.

Chapter VI

However, his foray into the Eden of delightful fantasies about Zionism and Zionists did not last long. Soon after the publication of his articles, he was invited to Vilna for a large seven-district Zionist convention, along with quite a few other rabbis who were sympathetic to Zionism. At the conference a board was elected, consisting entirely of young whippersnappers with clean-shaven mugs, twirled mustaches and jaunty, self-satisfied grins. From their perch at the board-table, these "jaunty grins" pelted the audience of delegates, and in particular the rabbis (who were seated right under their noses in the front row), with reports of the "Zionist work"—in Russian—for nearly two days without cease. The rabbis, for their part, sat barely breathing, lest they disturb the "grand intellectuals" with their fancy

---

[28] Author's footnote: "This is how he signed the first of his articles in the series 'Recompense for the Controversy of Zion,' in order to conceal the fact that the author was a rabbi, and also in order to emphasize that the reader should not expect a polished style or scientific proof, but rather the sentiments that gush forth from a pumping heart. However, the editorial board of *HaMelitz* revealed that the author was a rabbi, out of a desire to heighten the effect of the article. Therefore, in the subsequent articles, the author did not feel the need to conceal his profession, and signed the articles 'One of the Sensitive Rabbis,' which remained his standard alias thereafter."

[29] Specifically the organized religious Jewish community as it existed as a political force in his era, rather than orthodoxy as an abstract sociocultural or theological generality.

Russian and their unfamiliar, "elegant" words such as "agitation," "propaganda," "party discipline," etc. The rabbis beheld this whole rigmarole with great respect, like new recruits sitting at attention before their commanding officer as he tutors them in slovesnost,[30] lecturing on topics as engrossing as the birthdates of Grand Dukes Pavel and Kirill . . .[31]

Not a single word of Yiddish slipped out of these upstarts' mouths throughout the entire gathering, let alone any trace of ennobling Jewish thought. Instead, for nearly forty-eight hours without pause, they sat around their little table and doused the rabbis—including some quite elderly ones—with reports (in Russian, a language which most of the rabbis did not understand) of "concerts," "banquets," proselytizing, and fund-raising.

"One of the Sensitive Rabbis" sat and watched the proceedings in amazement. Were these, then, the "idealists" upon whom he had heaped his praise? But he silently justified their torrent of Russian by surmising that the permit for the conference had been granted on the condition that the proceedings be conducted in Russian.

How astonished he was, then, at the comic conclusion on the second day. By chance, a policeman passed through the courtyard, and the entire pack of Russian-blabberers fled hatless out the back door. From that incident he realized that the gathering had in fact been clandestine and illegal, and the Russian that the upstarts had yammered so relentlessly had been gratuitous—that is to say, voluntary. Or, more accurately, willful: They were honing their bureaucratization skills, preparing to lord it over their constituents in the future Zionist state . . .

He left the assembly with a crack in his earlier enthusiasm—and he began to falter in his faith that Zionism would revive the Jewish spirit.

A month later, in the summer of 1900, the Sensitive Rabbi was chosen by the Brisk Zionists as a delegate to the Fourth Zionist Congress in London. He agreed to go. The pure emptiness, bureaucracy, and officiousness which he had encountered at the Vilna conference was present to an even greater degree at the London Congress—and apart from those features, the Congress was utterly devoid of content, with a single exception: The audience of delegates, who had been dragged together from every corner of the world,

---

[30] A Russian word (словесность) that literally means "literature," but encapsulates the idea of the historical and cultural literacy needed to serve the nation (see for example Olga Litvak, *Conscription and the Search for Modern Russian Jewry*, Bloomington: Indiana University Press, 2006, p. 48)—presumably, basic Russian cultural literacy lectures were a rite of passage for new draftees in the Russian army.

[31] Kirill Vladimirovich (1876-1938) and Pavel Aleksandrovich (1860-1919).

were beaten over the head with the "happy news" that Dr. Herzl had been, shortly prior to the Congress, "invited to lunch by the Ottoman Sultan"...

The Sensitive Rabbi's fantasy that Zionism would uplift the Jewish spirit and serve as a vehicle for the fight against bondage, dissolved into nothingness. Without delay, while still in London, he dispatched a message to the Kovno Zionists forbidding them to reprint his articles in a pamphlet. He himself returned home devastated by the disappointment.

Chapter VII

His warmth toward Zionism had disappeared. That is to say, his attitude toward Zionism had not retained a single ounce of anything positive, although on the other hand, at this point nothing negative had yet sprouted. As a result, he felt even more desolate and gloomy than he would have if he had been ready to declare his opposition.

He also had to bear the disagreeable experience of being bombarded from all sides with questions—with demands that he account for his sudden transformation.

But it was difficult for him to explain, because in fact the unpleasant things he had witnessed provoked his withdrawal from Zionism only indirectly. It was as if a single bullet had been fired, which in and of itself would not have caused much damage—but that single bullet flew right into a powder keg, where it set off a catastrophe. Just so, his direct encounter with the empty spectacle of the Zionist functionaries and their entire party apparatus, had torn open a sealed chamber in his heart full of hidden feelings—his innermost "I"—which was not in the least attuned to the Zionist ideal, and which rendered the bond which had bound him to the Zionists for a short while, unnatural.

As time passed, his own worldview would crystallize—in complete opposition to Zionism. But as of yet, all was still murky. He was visited by a sudden presentiment, which muttered to him that relief for the Jews would not be found in Zionism—but he could not articulate this to others, and as a result fell into despair for quite a while after the London Congress. He felt impotent and could not concentrate on anything.

He was also quite downhearted about the fact that he had previously attacked the Orthodox opponents of Zionism, including the most senior big-city rabbis. He had needlessly provoked their rage—the rage of the Orthodox world's greatest authorities. He also began to feel a prick of conscience: Who knows? Perhaps these rabbis were more perspicacious than he, and had immediately recognized the problems which had taken him longer to grasp....

The Sensitive Rabbi traveled to a nearby city, one of the centers of Orthodox opposition to Zionism, in order to find out to what extent his onslaught against the Orthodox had been unfounded: had he attacked the innocent? However, once there, his doubts were laid to rest. These Orthodox hadn't the faintest idea about the truly repulsive aspects of Zionism that he himself had uncovered. When it came to Herzl's dog-and-pony show—his "audiences with royalty"—they too were quite impressed. Even here in B. they were smacking their lips over the lunches he had eaten with the Sultan in Constantinople. As a result, they did not dare speak against Dr. Herzl himself, and primarily cast their fire and brimstone upon the local Zionists for their lack of piety. For these Orthodox, everything boiled down to their obsession with pointing fingers at the "sinful" . . .

This discovery relieved him of his prick of conscience. He returned home much encouraged, and once again capable of constructing his spiritual vision, in which the fight against human evil occupied pride of place.

Chapter VIII

He understood then, however, that he would not be able to throw in his lot with any party—that he would not find his place in any of the movements currently in existence, even though they supposedly shared his goal of repairing the world.

Even when it came to the socialist movement, which at first glance was more in accordance with his views than any of the other parties because of its emphasis on freedom and equality—he nevertheless could not devote himself to it because of its three enormous faults: First, its dedication to the tactical principle that "the ends justify the means"—the movement did not forswear violence. Second, it set aside the sacred—the main quality which renders a person noble and his life sweet—and laid everything at the feet of coarse materialism. Third, it operated in service of "special interests" rather than ideals. The members of the movement testified to this trait with their endless refrain, "We the proletariat," and their ever-present plaint in response to any social ill: "After all, that could cause injury to the working class . . . "

The latter fault, by the way, was endemic to all the parties, which, like the notorious missionaries, went around searching for ways to capture as many souls as possible for their own camp. Whom else could the parties consist of, if not the "interested"? After all, it's not as if a simple man of flesh and blood, who one minute earlier was going around looking for a morsel to put in his mouth and jabbing his elbow into the ribs of any fellow he encountered on the road, could turn into an idealist the minute he was sprinkled with the party paintbrush.

Thus, having recovered somewhat from the disappointment of London, the Sensitive Rabbi withdrew entirely into himself and began to orchestrate a singular "liberation campaign" from the Torah-Jewish perspective—a perspective which knows nothing of "class," of "politics," of "cultivating social organization" (busying oneself endlessly with combing out society's tangled locks)—but knows, rather, of the cultivation of the human heart, the rectification of the human character—*as a natural result* of which society's locks will not become tangled in the first place . . .

The words "as a natural result" are emphasized here because according to the Torah-Jewish perspective on freedom, "society" is a matter of secondary importance: the central matter is the liberation of the individual. And thus the urgency of the rectification of the heart—because the liberation of the individual depends on the refinement of his moral-ethical sense. Having a clear conscience, scorning evil utterly, means—being a free person.

The greatest specialist[32] of Jewish moral literature, of the Jewish perspective on freedom, justifies his prozbul reform in the Mishna[33] not by pointing out that it enables the needy to obtain loans—but rather with the warning that "thine eye be evil against thine needy brother, and thou give him nought."[34]

Chapter IX

From the London disappointment onwards, the Sensitive Rabbi dedicated his full attention to the matter of "liberation via the development of disdain for evil." He sat cloistered in his private corner, secluded from the world, and authored books on the subject. From time to time he also came out with passionate newspaper articles. These were prompted by impure incidents which affronted his moral-aesthetic sensibility and his yearning for the Jewish world to be ethically immaculate.

Through this work, he became the theoretician of the "moral approach"

---

[32] Hillel the Elder.

[33] A legal reform that weakened the Biblical requirement to forgive all debts in the sabbatical year, which increased the willingness of creditors to lend money to the poor in the latter years of the sabbatical cycle (see Mishna Gittin 4:3 and Shevi'it 10:3).

[34] Deuteronomy 15:9, rendered here simply in Yiddish: "People will become cruel, and not wish to do favors." Tamares probably raises this here (and points out Hillel's concern about the effect of generosity, or the lack thereof, on the giver rather than the receiver) in order to emphasize that morality is in the best interest of the moral person himself, and to underscore his emphasis on the well-being of the individual, rather than the benefit for society.

to the fight for freedom.

For the world, i.e., for others, he was no more than a theoretician—but for himself, for the purposes of his own liberation, he gradually became an experimentalist as well. Over time, he carved out for himself thorough autonomy in his conduct. He became a truly free man in all of life's endeavors.

His process of self-liberation was greatly assisted by the location of his residence: the little town with its beautiful pinewood forest. It was in the forest (where he spent most of his time during the summers)—in the company of his most intimate friends, the beautiful evergreen trees, and under the open skies—that he perfected his own training in the theory of morality and freedom: He penned most of his work in the forest. And the small town in which he lived left him free to conduct his life according to his principles.

The gentle stream of life in a small town, with its modest population, negligible wealth, and distance from high society, did not have the power to compel him to conform to local custom—in contrast to the big city, with its rushing river of people who, however negligible they may be as far as "quality" is concerned (and in fact each one is generally worth much less than the average townsperson), are nevertheless quite a hit on the social stage: "aristocrats," "politicians," "dignitaries," and the like. And to break free of their influence is an enterprise unto itself.

At home in the small town, he could live his life like a regular freewheeler. Not only did he fling off the societal customs and fashions that did not accord with his ideals, but he even refused to bother with objectionable matters that supposedly fell under his purview as the local rabbi.

A few telling examples: When a couple of fellows came to him for a din-Torah,[35] he would tell them the ruling straightaway according to the Choshen Mishpat[36]—who was the winner and who the loser. But if the winning party started up with demands that the Sensitive Rabbi use his rabbinic position to compel the losing party to fork over the penalty, he categorically refused further involvement, based on his principle that a rabbi should not act as a policeman, particularly in financial conflicts, in which justice is not necessarily on the side of the party in whose favor the case is decided.

And once, a young, childless man who lived in the town collapsed and

---

[35] Din-torah: a religious court case (here, as a means of resolving a business dispute).

[36] A field in Jewish law (in particular, the eponymous sections of legal tractates Shulchan Aruch and Arba'ah Turim) having to do with business transactions and financial ethics.

lay at death's door. The young man's wife's uncles and aunts, accompanied by a whole gaggle of local do-gooders, rushed to the rabbi to demand that he order the invalid to give his wife a bill of divorce.[37] But he dismissed their suggestion out of hand. He had no intention of pursuing such a "gallant" act—what, he should berate a dying man, saying "Since you're dying anyway, set your wife free so that she can marry someone else"?!

Another time, a group of "god-fearing" householders came to him to suggest that it was time to replace the local ritual slaughterer, considering that he was elderly and there was reason to suspect that his hands trembled.[38] The Sensitive Rabbi answered them saying, "It's better to eat defiled meat than to defile the livelihood of one of our own kosher citizens . . . "

On account of his attachment to the autonomy that he enjoyed in the small-town environment, he refused the frequent invitations that he received to apply for rabbinic posts in big cities. But the main reason he rejected such opportunities was that he was a villager by birth, and he was drawn to his roots, to the wild lap of nature. That wish was fully satisfied for him in the pinewood forests of Milejczyce, which by the way had become almost like a hometown to him, considering that he was married there at the tender age of seventeen and proceeded to live there for the rest of his days. As far as he was concerned, life in the boiling kettle of the metropolis with its stifling air would amount to pure hell.

In the year 5672,[39] when the Rav Tza'ir[40] was on the verge of moving to Berlin from Odessa (on account of the persecution he was suffering there at the hands of the mayor), he sent letter after letter to the Sensitive Rabbi begging him to move to Odessa to assume the leadership of the yeshiva he had founded and operated there for several years. The Sensitive Rabbi was not easily won over. But in the end, he did not dare to snub the Rav Tza'ir, who implored him in his last letter to come to Odessa to take a look, at the very least: "Perhaps you will unexpectedly develop enthusiasm for the prospect."

So he agreed to go. Halfway through the journey, he had to change trains. He boarded the second train, and found himself in the same compartment as a madman who was being transported somewhere by a couple of attendants. The madman sat and sang, drawing the attention of the entire compartment. As soon as he caught sight of the Sensitive Rabbi, he started

---

[37] Probably in order to release her from the obligation of levirate marriage or *halitzah* after his death (see *Shulchan Aruch*, Even HaEzer 145).

[38] During the act of slaughtering animals, which raised suspicions that he was not able to fulfill his role in accordance with the laws of *kashrut*.

[39] 1911 or 1912.

[40] Chaim Tchernowitz, 1871-1949.

shouting, "A rabbi, a rabbi!" and raised a ruckus in an attempt to get the rabbi to sit next to him. In order to placate the madman, which by then all the other passengers were begging him to do, he was compelled to stand up from the seat where he was already settled and reseat himself next to the madman. But the madman's corner was right next to the little furnace which glowed hot and spat fumes, and the "Sensitive Rabbi" suffered greatly from the poor air quality. While he was sitting there, he wondered whether this experience mightn't be symbolic of his visit to Odessa in general . . .

He arrived in Odessa and stopped off at the residence of the Rav Tza'ir, who invited the gabbaim from the yeshiva to come over to get acquainted with the guest-candidate. However, the latter announced immediately upon entering that he was only there for a temporary visit, for the sole purpose of explaining to Rabbi Chaim Tchernowitz and his attendants his reasons for turning down the position.

And that is exactly what he did. For the entire ten days of his visit (the other purpose of his trip was to hurry along the "Moriah" press, which was in the process of publishing one of his works), various parties—the Torah scholars as much as the literati—campaigned for him to move to Odessa and scolded him endlessly, saying, "How is it right for a person to hide himself away in a small town for all of eternity?"

The Sensitive Rabbi paraded various excuses before each of them. He told one person that the condition of his health would not permit such an undertaking; that is, living in the big city and teaching a yeshiva class. To one of the yeshiva-gabbaim who would not leave him alone, he said, "You tell me how to convince myself to accept a change in my circumstances. In Milejczyce, every wall of my house contains a window through which the broad blue heavens peek in at me. Here in the yeshiva, on the other hand, three out of four walls are windowless, and the one and only window in the fourth wall offers a view of nothing but the soot-covered ramparts of the building opposite." But the gabbai, a prominent banker who owned many estates in the city as well as a luxurious summer villa in the country, made a laconic and logical reply (the kind of logic that underpins the Procrustean beds into which such fellows magnanimously invite the poor): "Tsk! So the big city is full of tumult. What do you care? You will dwell within the 'four cubits of halacha.'[41]"

"And in this crowded city, I'll be forced to dwell within four cubits of physical space, too," thought the Sensitive Rabbi to himself.

To "Grandfather Mendele"[42] (who also tried to persuade him to move to

---

[41] See Talmud Bavli, Berakhot 8a.
[42] Mendele Moykher Sforim (Sholem Yankev Abramovich), 1836-1917.

Odessa) he told the story of the encounter with the madman on the train, saying that he was certain that the incident was a kind of mystical omen about the meaning of his visit: "Madmen have latched onto me and want me near them, even though I will suffer a lot here and find it crowded and boring . . . "

"Grandfather Mendele" was quite taken with the fable, even though the joke was on him. But nevertheless, he didn't let up in his pursuit.

Only one person, Bialik, who was also originally among the agitators, eventually decided to leave him alone. On Bialik he tried the tactic of rebuke. "You too?" he asked. "Even you have no sensitivity to the soul of your fellow?" This reproach silenced Bialik on the spot. Had the Sensitive Rabbi chosen the right words to awaken empathy in Bialik's poetic heart for his own aching soul? Or perhaps it was Bialik's internal "natural man" (Bialik was also born in a village) who raised a sudden protest from his secret hiding place: "Listen up, you! Why are you bothering the country bumpkin? Is it not enough that you yourself betrayed the forests and fields, and fled to the big city to stare at the sooty walls and rub shoulders with the rich and famous? Must you also press him to do the same?"

But the rest of his recruiters refused to relent. By the end of his visit, he was nearly ill from the rain of reproof showered upon him for "hiding himself away in a small town" by those who wanted to make him "a man among men.".... He escaped from Odessa with difficulty, and fled home to his beloved friends, the trees of the forest. Good people had tried to tear him away from them, and he cast himself upon them with even more love than before.

Chapter X

As time wore on, The Sensitive Rabbi further developed his principle: instead of repairing the world, it was better to focus on repairing the individual—polishing the faculty of discernment between good and evil. And if the essential goal was to repair the individual—why, that in and of itself was no small task. And the individual whom he had on hand at all times in the forest—that is, his own "I"—was, needless to say, a world unto itself . . .

He dedicated himself primarily to improving his own spiritual well-being—finding his way toward full freedom of conscience, so that he would not be towed under by the vagaries of fashion or unduly influenced by the mainstream.

However, his withdrawal into his internal world was not an indication that he had despaired of tikkun olam, or believed that the world was a lost cause. On the contrary: he believed that the redemption of the world, its rebirth in a better form, was bound to come. But at the same time, he was firmly convinced that the renewal of the world would not come at the hands of sly politicians or a clever rearrangement of society—but rather through the refinement of moral-aesthetic taste, a sense of discernment between good and evil. And because that approach was rooted first and foremost in the individual "I"—in order to be a freedom-fighter it was not at all necessary to live in a central city among the cramped masses, or to carry out demonstrations in the street. Rather, one could dwell in the tiniest village, or even in the forest, and still pursue the liberation of the world.

And indeed, the Sensitive Rabbi dwelt in his small village among his friends, the trees of the forest, and fought in his own way for human freedom. Day by day, he sharpened his commitment to integrity and his revulsion toward depravity. He also strove to cultivate a morally pure atmosphere in his immediate circles. Occasionally he burst out with attempts at "disinfection," sometimes even venturing farther afield: Whenever a rumor about a case of persecution made its way to him from somewhere else in the region—in particular when he heard that one victim had been beset by a whole gang of tormentors—he would whip up batches of fierce letters condemning the hooliganism . . .

But his primary occupation was writing books whose theme and purpose was to arouse integrity and discourage evil conduct. He also frequently published articles in the press. This he did whenever an incident which took place in the world struck a chord in his heart.[43]

In the year 5664[44] he printed a pamphlet entitled "Judaism and Freedom,"[45] in which he laid out a sharply sarcastic critique of a "nationalism" that was empty of any Jewish content, and stemmed merely from a slavish desire to imitate the goyim. The same pamphlet ridiculed the Zionist dog-and-pony show, with its sensationalization of Herzl's success at clawing his way up to "audiences" with "all the king's horses and all the king's men."

In 5672[46] he published *The Ethics of Torah and Judaism*,[47] a collection of sermons which he had delivered on various occasions, elaborating his particular worldview and the ample spiritual and ethical resources which serve as the foundation of Judaism. The sermons depicted the Torah as a

---

[43] Author's footnote: "See in the omitted portion." (See Luz p. 13 n. 16: "It appears that the author intended to add here a footnote containing particulars about his articles, but ultimately did not do so.")

[44] 1903 or 1904.

[45] *HaYahadut vehaHeirut*, Odessa, 1905 (despite the date he indicates above).

[46] 1911 or 1912.

[47] *Musar HaTorah vehaYahadut*, Vilna.

source of illumination, and reprimanded those who sullied and crippled the Commandments of the Torah by exploiting them for their own debased ends.

That same year, he published his book *Correct Piety and the Religion of the Masses*,[48] which treated the same theme as the sermon collection, but in a literary form. The ideas discussed in the book prompted a massive protest against the plans that were underway at the time in certain Orthodox circles to collaborate with the Czarist government and other Russian reactionary forces for the sake of hizuk hadat.[49]

Chapter XI

At first, "One of the Sensitive Rabbis" did not intend his essays, which he wrote in the forest surrounded by trees, to be read by a public audience; nor did he intend to use them to repair the world from which he was so cloistered. Rather, he was driven to write political essays by an inner urge—the same urge that drives the poet to pen odes to the wonders of nature—with the single difference that the poet who becomes inspired by the lovely woods where he has taken a stroll pours out his feelings on paper in order to be able to share his impressions with society; but as for the Sensitive Rabbi, whenever he became upset by an impure event that took place in society, he fled to the forest and poured his heart out before the innocent trees—and, with their help, put pen to paper.

That was generally the first phase. Afterwards, when his seething soul had been somewhat soothed by the process of expressing itself on paper, his inner "freedom fighter" would emerge and demand its share. At that juncture he sought avenues to bring to the public those writings which he had initially jotted down for his own eyes alone.

But even the "freedom fighter," in its quest to publish his words, had *himself* in mind first and foremost—above all, the desire to free his own "I" from the corrupt influence of the reigning mores. And this is the reason he did not restrain himself from speaking quite frequently to the world, even

---

[48] *HaEmunah HaTehorah vehaDat HaHamonit*, Odessa.

[49] Hizuk hadat: "Strengthening of the faith"—in this case, meaning that Orthodox leaders hoped to induce the Czarist regime to back policies that would counter the trend toward secularization in the Jewish community, and in return, the Orthodox leadership promised to support the regime's crackdown on revolutionary activity, among other things. See Vladimir Levin (2009), "Orthodox Jewry and the Russian Government: An Attempt at Rapprochement, 1907–1914," *East European Jewish Affairs*, 39(2), pp. 187-204, especially p. 191, as well as p. 189, where Levin points out that there was even an Orthodox political party called Mahzikei Hadat.

after experience taught him that the world was deaf as a post in the face of honest speech. Indeed, his venture was invulnerable: whether or not society inclined its ear to hear his words, he himself tore free of its dominion by skipping the preliminaries and saying to its face the truth that was in his heart.

The fact that his primary purpose in writing for the public was ensured from the start enabled him to confront injustice without flinching. Reassured by his own steadfastness, he allowed himself a tiny hope that in the end, his words would penetrate the hearts of his audience, and he would realize his dream of spreading freedom and purity throughout his surroundings.

His dream of liberating his milieu, i.e., the Jewish world, did not limit itself to those provincial shores; he also dreamt passionately of liberating the entire world—for although he wrote only in Yiddish50 for a Jewish audience, he knew that the Jewish people as a liberated spiritual force would contribute immeasurably to the liberation of all humankind. If the way to liberation was, as he believed, the correction of the heart and the development of moral-aesthetic discernment—why, who was better suited to toil for the cause of freedom than the Jewish people? Who else ought to serve as the vanguard of human liberation and renewal, other than the People of Exile and Torah, who from long experience of persecution have come to learn so many spiritual lessons?

Chapter XII

Immersed in his dreams of world-liberation, the Sensitive Rabbi was of course sympathetic to the socialist movements, which were dedicated to the same cause. Sympathetic—but no more than that. To join them—as mentioned above—was impossible: their Marxism was too dry a dish for his palate. He appreciated the "socialism of the heart," but not the "socialism of numbers." The literature which depicted, on one hand, the sorrowful life of the impoverished cobbler, the way he sits in his dank basement quarters at midnight, his eyelids drooping, bent over a leather sole by the light of a kerosene lamp, groping dimly for his awl; and on the other hand, the formidable luxury, the wine and song flowing freely, just across the street in the large, brightly lit rooms of the banker's house—this literature, whose aim was to awaken compassion for suffering and disgust for depravity and selfishness, spoke to the sensibilities of the Sensitive Rabbi. This sort of literature was familiar to his soul; it was similar to the Jewish musar tradi-

---

[50] [sic]—despite the fact that by his own account, he published the vast majority of his writing in Hebrew. Here he intends "Jewish languages" (i.e., including Hebrew), rather than Yiddish itself.

tion,[51] from which his soul drew its nourishment.

But the literature that attempted to calculate the true worth of the shoe-sole, awaken the cobbler's awareness of the "others" who live off his labor, and inflate his self-image so that he prances around believing that without him, the world will stop turning—this sort of literature was less to his taste. The compassion-oriented literature was designed to liberate those who were suffering, whereas the shoe-sole-appraising literature was designed to relocate despotism to a new headquarters. The money-magnates would be replaced by the shoemaker-magnates, who would cry, "No one but we deserve anything and no one but we have the right to live in this world!"

Indeed, the Sensitive Rabbi knew quite well that in addition to the vagaries and tragedies of war, there was no shortage of misfortune and exploitation even in peacetime. But nevertheless, the horror of war—the sheer notion of wresting people from their homes in order to line them up opposite cannonfire—dominated his consciousness. In his opinion, war stood at the head of all worldly horrors and required a dedicated counter offensive; therefore, he was bewildered by the socialist press, which failed to dedicate the necessary attention to the subject.

"If you throw a stick into the air, it will come back down," as the Talmudic saying goes.[52] The Sensitive Rabbi could not tear himself from his little town, from the forests and fields he had known since childhood—and so too, the battlefield painting that had hung in his neighbor's house, and the weeping of the neighbor-woman over her slaughtered son, had imprinted themselves on his mind's eye and remained perpetually at the forefront of his consciousness.

His belief that war was the matter that demanded the freedom fighter's most urgent attention, further strengthened his conviction that the Jewish people was called to serve as the vanguard of world liberation, for who else is more averse to war, more attuned to the horror of bloodshed, than the Jew?

The story of himself, the little Jewish boy, mourning with the Gentile woman over her son the war casualty, now served for him as a symbol of the international Jewish mission to awaken in all peoples the fitting sentiment of condemnation toward war. For it is the free, delicate Jewish spirit, woven of exile and Torah, which feels most acutely the horror of bloodshed and the disgrace of coercing a person to serve as a stadium-ox.[53] In con-

---

[51] *Musar*: literally, "chastening" or "discipline." The name of an extensive body of Jewish literature, and later a religious movement, dedicated to ethics, moral discipline, and self-improvement.

[52] See Bereishit Rabbah 53:15.

[53] i.e., an instrument of someone else's will to violence. See Mishna Bava Kamma

trast, the goy, the Esau, is more likely to defend his lentil-bowl, his mess of pottage—that is, to react to an offense against his pay envelope—than to resist being dragged like a sheep onto the battlefield, to shoot at others until he is shot dead . . .

Chapter XIII

In 1914 the European war broke out, and the ignominy of the Gentile world unfurled itself before the eyes of the Sensitive Rabbi. He did not know what astonished him more: the slavish acquiescence of the goyish masses, who allowed themselves to be carted off to the slaughterhouse (the Jewish conscripts were exempt from this critique, considering that they were powerless to change their fate—if they had resisted the draft, they would have been branded "enemies of the fatherland"), or the falsehoods spun by the goyish intelligentsia, who went so far as to glorify the whole debacle. And glorify they did, without exception—even the greatest humanitarians among them, the sentimental writers who used to lament the suffering of the poorer classes and bemoan the tragedy of life, now turned into enthusiasts who spoke of war as a path to global redemption. The Sensitive Rabbi concluded from this that any talk of "compassion" coming from the mouths of goyim was nothing more than a superficial affectation.

But more than anything, he was shocked by the discovery that even the socialists in every country (including the Russian socialists), who had been quarreling so bitterly with their governments a moment before—as soon as the latter cried "War!" and invited them to the party, they were suddenly quite pleased, and started to bray "Patriotism, hurrah, patriotism!" and returned to the national fold in order to play their part in the farce of "going off to liberate the nations . . ."

"European Civilization," already long suspect in his eyes, had now been caught red-handed. He was distraught over the opprobrium of the war, but he was also prone to a sneaky sense of satisfaction: European culture, which had humiliated and spit upon the Jew, now took off its mask and showed its true colors—and the Jew could hold his head high again.

His disgust for depravity and his stormy temperament allowed him no rest; they prodded him to respond to the current debacle in some manner. But how? It was dangerous to unveil the charade in the press, and besides, there was no press to speak of—the press had given itself over to the task of glorifying and sanctifying the whole fiasco. Truly, what was to be done?

4:4, "An ox from the arena is not liable to be put to death [for goring], for [it is not that it decides to gore, but rather] he is made by others to gore."

So he sprayed disinfectant in his vicinity, orally and in writing, as far as he could reach. Anytime he had a conversation, he found a way to point out the current fraudulence and distortion. Anytime he wrote a letter, he slipped in a few jabs at the present-day Golden Calf. He couldn't resist including such barbs even in correspondence with officials, for whom "patriotism" was a matter of self-interest . . .

For example, the local Russian priest appealed to him to collect donations from amongst the Jewish community for the Red Cross. He fulfilled the request the first time, but when the priest approached him a second time, he answered him saying, "In my opinion, the entire population that lives in the war-torn regions is already under great pressure, and it is therefore unfair to ask them to shoulder any of the additional costs of war. There is even an adage: 'It is not the rich man who foots the bill, but rather the guilty party.' And our unfortunate population is not guilty in the slightest with respect to the pandemonium that the high and mighty have inflicted on this land . . . "

In answer to the zemskii nachal'nik[54] who invited him to a conference concerning the welfare of the wives and children of the reservists, he sent his regrets, explaining that his state of health did not permit him to travel. "However," he concluded, "if the conference were to address the topic of how to avoid tearing husbands and fathers away from their families in the first place, I would draw upon my last reserves of strength in order to attend."

Around that time, a group of Jewish leaders in St. Petersburg sent a couple of wagons to the Front, laden with various goods to distribute among the soldiers without regard to national identity, with the inscription, "A gift from the Jewish people to the heroes of the battlefield." One of the main organizers was the well-known Jewish lawyer S-g.[55] In a letter that the Sensitive Rabbi sent to S-g around that time concerning a local community issue, he added as a postscript (despite the fact that at the time, letters were generally inspected by the postmaster) that he would have deeply approved of the mission if the inscription had read, "A gift from the Jewish people for those *suffering*, without regard to national identity." That would have been a true sanctification of God, an expression of Jewish compassion. In contrast, an inscription that conveys adulation for 'good brawlers' cannot serve as a consecration of the Name of Israel . . ."

His alarm only increased when he realized that the epidemic of war-acquiescence had spread even to the Jewish community. He had no way to assuage his own anger, except by keeping a private "blacklist" of Jewish

---

[54] Highest-ranking local Russian official.
[55] Probably Genrikh Sliozberg, 1863-1937.

public figures, especially Jewish writers, who were carriers of the disease. He methodically examined every word that emerged from a writer's pen. One single contaminated phrase was enough to earn a writer a place on the list.

Chapter XIV

The newspaper *HaTzefirah* was one of the first to be infected, as far as the Sensitive Rabbi could tell from the newspaper's appeal to readers, in which it attempted to drum up support by mentioning that "many of our members have gone off to fulfill their duties to the Motherland . . . " Of course, he needed this piece of evidence only at first. Later on, it was quite obvious that *HaTzefirah*, like all of the Russian newspapers, was besmirched with the prevailing putrefaction. When Z. Epstein[56] wrote an editorial in *HaTzefirah* scolding the readership for allowing the only extant Hebrew newspaper to waste away, the Sensitive Rabbi replied with a letter to the effect that in an era in which the press is being debauched by the military Asmodeus, it is preferable for a respectable newspaper to go to its eternal rest, rather than surviving only to fall into disgrace.

As far as the Sensitive Rabbi was concerned, when a writer uttered an expression like "Indeed, we are living in momentous times," it was enough to earn him a designation as a fool at the very least, if not a downright villain. Needless to say, when a writer bemoaned the "Jewish tragedy"—that a "Jewish soldier should have to shoot a brother, a Jewish soldier from another land," or (as the Hebrew poet Y.C.[57] put it) that "a Jewish mother does not know to what end her only son was slaughtered in the war"—the Sensitive Rabbi naturally sensed that the Zionist Fatherland's "pimp" was speaking through his mouth.[58]

But no one disgusted the Sensitive Rabbi more than the Zionist leadership, who not only spoke like war-pimps, but also acted as such. Anyone with a sharp mind and a clear conscience necessarily developed an aversion to the slogan "Fatherland" at the outbreak of the global orgy of destruction, given that it was the banner under which the Destroyers rushed headlong to light the world on fire. In contrast, our Zionist "romantics" scrambled over to warm themselves at the flames. Their beady eyes began flashing with wolfish sparks, in hopes that the time had come to manifest their lofty dream of a "Fatherland." And to that end they began hobnobbing with the

---

[56] Zalman Epstein, 1860-1936.
[57] Ya'akov Cohen (1881-1960), in the poem "Kinat Em" (see Luz p. 18 n. 18).
[58] Because the poet imagines that the mother of the slain soldier would *not* have felt that her son had died in vain if he had died for the Jewish homeland (see Luz p. 18 n. 20).

Chief Arsonists of the World, and danced before them on their hind legs, garlanding them with praise: "Oh ye Liberators of the Peoples . . ."

Even some most unpleasant facts did not deter their hymns of praise, such as the tens of thousands of Jewish victims who were afterward slaughtered in Ukraine, Hungary, and the rest of the little countries who relied on the gang of "Liberators" like sons-in-law of kest[59] and received a bellyful of provisions from them, not to mention armaments—and who served as their vassals, instruments of their will. They were similarly undeterred by the merciless anti-Semitism that flared up beginning after the "War of Liberation" in all the lands under the aegis of the "Liberators," anti-Semitism which oppressed and tortured Jews to death. Like Wilhelm II's "true statesmen," who are ready to sacrifice their entire people for the sake of one clod of earth from the "Fatherland," our Zionist leaders forgave the world powers all the tortures that they had inflicted upon Jews in the lands of exile, in return for one small favor: that they speak up on behalf of the "Jewish National Home"; i.e., that they shout, "Accursed Jews, beat it—make yourself scarce here, onward to Palestine . . . "

His distaste for Zionism was augmented by the interpretation of the World War that was embraced even by the likes of Max Nordau. For even Nordau, the Zionist hero, earned his place on the list of writers whom the Sensitive Rabbi suspected, based on a single impure statement, of war-pimping. That particular "hero" made it onto the blacklist when at the signing of the Treaty of Versailles, he was heard to state the following: "In the name of the seven hundred thousand Jewish soldiers who fought on every front, the Jewish people has the right to appeal to the Nations and make its claim upon the Land of Israel."

This so-called Zionist prophet, who had so enchanted the Sensitive Rabbi and captured his heart for Zionism with his charismatic harangues against the oppressors of the Jews which he had delivered at the early Zionist congresses (because the Sensitive Rabbi was a young man at the time and was not yet acquainted with the lingo of politicians, not yet able to discern between freedom and "freedom," did not know that even the greatest despots take the liberty of ranting about the abstract idea of an "enslaved people" and an "enslaved land," while simultaneously oppressing the real live people under their power)—in short, this "prophet" who had once upon a time helped to draw the Sensitive Rabbi into the Zionist movement, now did his part to ensure that the Sensitive Rabbi would utterly reject that movement, which had revealed itself during the world-Bacchanalia to be a blood relative to

---

[59] *Kest*: The (primarily economic) support received by newly married men living with their wives' families during the early months or years of marriage.

all the world's monstrosities.

Chapter XV

But the Sensitive Rabbi could not quell his dismay about the war by means of such trifles as branding one or another writer as a carrier of the war-lackey pestilence, or throwing a barbed comment into a letter to this or that war-opportunist. No—he could not rest until he had immortalized his reaction in some kind of printed work. In fact, he had already prepared a manuscript of a poem in Hebrew, entitled "The Day of Reckoning is Here,"[60] which he had composed during the summer of 1914 in response to the mobilization proclaimed by the Czar (whose minions came in the middle of the night to drag the reservists out of bed and ship them off to the war). In the poem he assigned each sector of society its portion of guilt for the war-fiasco, and justified the consequences which each had suffered as a result. However, he was unsure whether the poem would be able to pass the inspection of the current censor, so instead he undertook the task of composing his book *The Assembly of Israel and the Wars of the Nations*.[61]

He wrote the book in a serene tone, without turbulence, because it chiefly expressed the secondary feeling that the events of the war had evoked in the author: satisfaction about the bankrupting of European civilization, the chief agent of the persecution of the Jews. In the book he carried out a scientific analysis of the reasons for the war, and came to the conclusion that the war was no coincidence, but rather an unavoidable result of the entire corrupt, crippled, hypocritical lifestyle led by the so-called "civilized peoples." In a serene tone but with sharp humor, he ridiculed both the leaders who herded masses of people to the slaughter, and the masses who allowed themselves to be herded. He also awakened self-appreciation among Jews—awareness of the dignity of yidishkeyt, which stood above the swamps of war, above the bloodbaths into which all peoples were sinking. He did this with full confidence, despite the fact that, to his disappointment, no small number of Jews had already revealed themselves to be war-pimps. He was convinced that these swindlers did not nurse at the breast of Judaism, but rather had been infected by the Gentile neighbors to whom their souls were enslaved.

At first, one thing troubled the security of his pride in the uniquely Jewish attitude toward war, namely, a rumor that not all Gentile socialists had submitted to their governments and lent their energies to the war-Bacchanalia. Rather, a number of socialists (called Bolsheviks) were in fact opposed to the war. By chance, however, a Bolshevik book entitled *Against the Current*

---

[60] "Ba'u yemei hapekudah," see Hosea 9:7.
[61] *Keneset Yisrael uMilhemot HaGoyim*, Warsaw, 1920. *Infra* p. 123.

fell into his hands, and from reading it he discovered that the Bolsheviks were also quite comfortable with mass murder—they merely gnashed their teeth over slaughter carried out for the benefit of the "capitalists." They called upon the "world proletariat" to redirect the bloodbath toward the objective of the Marxist ideal—that is, to fight as long as it takes to establish the Socialist World Order, i.e., to decimate the entire world for the sake of establishing the socialist "paradise" for the next generation . . . The Sensitive Rabbi knew that a movement whose struggle for freedom stems not from any moral-ethical principle, but rather from "special interests" (and whose entire body of "freedom-propaganda" lacked even the smallest shred of heart, but rather was filled with a hard, dry accounting of the percentage of the laborer's profit that ended up in the boss's pocket), was unlikely to reject war as a means to an end, as long as it was advantageous to the state of the worker's wallet—but he was nevertheless shocked to find such sentiments written in black and white by the supposed elites of the freedom movement.

After that, it was clear as day that not a single sector of the goyish world was untouched by Esau's vocation, "and by thy sword thou shalt live,"[62] and that the one and only people capable of true insight into war, and an appropriate feeling of hatred toward it, was the Jewish people.

By then he had given up entirely on the idea that mankind in its sickly state could expect to receive any relief from the socialists. "What a movement you have," he thought to himself about the socialists. "It's so dull-witted as to be entirely insensible to the horror of war; it lacks the insight to assign that horror its unique status as the zenith of human evil; and it confuses the horrific and universally unjustifiable disgrace of despoiling a man of the freedom to carry his head on his shoulders with the convoluted problem of labor and capital. You postpone the cure for the atrocities of war until after the wage for the leather shoe-sole has been regulated, and you even consider making use of the gruesome war-cudgel as a means to effect that regulation . . . May your befuddled minds thrive," he continued to himself, "in corresponding proportion to the likelihood that you'll manage to overthrow your tyrants, considering that you count yourselves among the backers of their very worst deed: warmongering."

At that, he sat down with ironclad confidence to write the book *The Assembly of Israel and the Wars of the Nations*, in which he invested all his hopes for human redemption in the Jewish people, that is, in the techniques of improving the human heart and uplifting the human spirit—techniques which have forever stood at the center of Jewish culture, and which comprise the historic mission of the Jewish people. He published the book in

---

[62] Genesis 27:40.

1920, and thereby immortalized his impressions of the period during which European civilization went bankrupt and showed its true face.

In 1923 he published a book of insights into Torah entitled *The Hand of Aaron*,[63] with a literary introduction about the importance of studying Torah.

In 1926, the Zionist leadership decided to demonstrate yet again that their tendency to cozy up to the great powers of the world was not merely a stratagem motivated by their fetish for a "national home," but rather reflected the deepest inclination of their careerist souls . . . They cooked up a big celebration in honor of the "flag of the Jewish Legion," which they dragged all the way to Jerusalem to stick into the ground of some holy site.[64] Even though the Sensitive Rabbi was already estranged from Zionism, Zionists were still Jews, and it irritated him that they were ruining his holy dream about the Jewish people which he had elaborated in *The Assembly of Israel and the Wars of the Nations*. So he printed a protest article in the *Vilner Tog*, in no. 37[65] and five additional installments.[66]

---

[63] *Yad Aharon*, Piotrkow, 1923. Although this is the last of his books that Tamares lists here (and probably the last book he had composed at the time when he wrote this essay), he did also ultimately publish a sixth book: *Sheloshah Zivvugim Bilti Hagunim* (Three Unsuitable Partnerships), Piotrkow, 1930. See Infra, p. 213.

[64] For more on this incident, see "A Winter in Palestine," Abbi Samuel, *The Jewish Transcript*, Seattle, WA, 19 Feb 1926.

[65] 12 Feb 1926.

[66] No. 41 (17 Feb), No. 43 (19 Feb), No. 44 (21 Feb), No. 47 (24 Feb), and No. 49 (26 Feb).

Part II

Sermons

Introduction to selected sermons

Reading some of Tamares' sermons, my first reaction is a likely violation of the prohibition against coveting: How I wish that he had been my rabbi! His sensitivity to the personal lives of his congregants, his fresh and profound understanding of the ritual and the liturgy, along with an abiding sense of the mission of the Jewish people, combine to yield a discourse that moves me deeply.

Without detaining the reader unduly from Tamares' own words, I do want to note briefly his profound and subtle interpretation of "inui nefesh," a key phrase of the Day of Atonement liturgy that is generally rendered "afflict your souls," "fast," or "practice self-denial." Tamares sharply distinguishes this from "sigufim," "bodily torments," instead inclining it to this spectrum of meaning for "anav:" abstinence, modesty, humility, gentleness. It immediately calls to mind the "anavim piety" of the meek and humble righteous (cf. Psalm 37). It also invites, for Tamares, thoughtful reflections on the purpose of ritual observances generally, along with a sharp distinction between idolatry and true belief and their differing understandings of ritual. For him, the primary purpose of religious observance is the positive enhancement of human life!

His opening prefatory apologetic for the sermonic form is prompted by the fact that his earlier published writings have been more analytical, discursive essays. Anticipating the puzzlement of his readers at his resorting to this "old fashioned" form of discourse, he provides a rather touching defense of the continuing validity of the sermon. As practiced by Tamares, the form has much, indeed, to recommend it!

The collected sermons reflect the custom during that period of twice-yearly sermons: the Sabbath before Passover (Shabbat Hagadol, the Great Sabbath) and the Sabbath between Rosh Hashanah and Yom Kippur (Shabbat Shuvah, the Sabbath of Turning/Repentance).

Following the paraphrase of the Sabbath of Turning sermon, there is a full translation of the Sermon on Liberty with a separate brief introduction.

—E.G.

The Ethics of Torah and Judaism (1912)

Ethics of Torah and Judaism
A Collection of Sermons
by
Aaron Samuel Tamares
From Milejczyce, Poland
"One of the Passionately Concerned Rabbis"
Vilna, 1912

Preface to collected sermons

Those acquainted with my published essays, many written under the name of "One of the Passionately Concerned Rabbis," may be surprised to find here a collection of sermons, a form of discourse often associated with "idlers."

However, different forms of expression are appropriate for different purposes. Sermons are a time-honored form of speaking from the heart to address the hearts of the listeners. Our Sages employed this form of discourse in expounding some of the most sublime of moral teachings, and I grew up in this milieu. So these sermons are quite in character with my more discursive, intellectually oriented writings.

Sermons have understandably earned a bad reputation when they have been misused for purposes of self-display or for special pleading that distorts the meaning of verses being expounded. I hope that the interpretations that follow will be coherent and true to the spirit of the passages that they cite. It is written in the spirit of the "old school" by a protagonist of the prophetic ideals and aspirations there expressed, ideals confirmed by recent crises and societal upheavals. May it satisfy the longings of those who thirst for a reaffirmation of the most exalted teachings of our sacred tradition.

For youth seeking clarification of issues of religion and faith compatible with scientific thinking, I hope that they, also, may find substance here to satisfy that longing, addressing both heart and mind, feeling and thought in a lucid manner true to the intention of traditions cited.

"Pure Faith" (Emunah T'horah) (1904) summarized

In which is explained that the purpose of faith and religion is to improve the human heart; and in which is established the difference between purified/examined faith and confused faith
Delivered the Sabbath of Turning, 5605/September 17, 1904

1.

Repentance/Turning: the traditional term of teshuvah refers to the correction of misguided actions, together with the resolve to follow the correct paths in the future. But not immediately evident is the answer to the question, which are the mistaken ways to be avoided, and which is the correct path to be followed?

A further question is the connection between correcting misguided actions and the term teshuvah itself, with its overtones of turning back to the original correct path. This may be appropriate for one who was, indeed, originally on the right path. But what of one who was on the wrong path? How can a term of "turning back" apply in this case? The answer will emerge from a proper answer to the original question, which are correct paths to be followed and which are perverted paths to be avoided?

2.

We must take care not to be misled by outward popular observances of these Days of Turning: denying oneself favorite foods, gloomy moods, sighs and wails, an anger with the self and with the world. These actions and attitudes make it seem as if our lives during the previous year were somehow sinful as such, as if managing simply to live were itself somehow a misdeed. Perhaps when the Temple stood, and "all sat beneath vine and fig tree, with none to make them afraid," we had reason to regret certain pleasures. But in our persecuted circumstances, with anti-Semitic limitations and desperate conditions of earning the most meager of livelihoods, what excessive pleasures have we to bemoan?

Let us note the fact that during the days when the Temple existed, no dark, dispirited clouds descended during the "Days of Awe," as has been the case in later generations. In stark contrast stands the assertion of Rabbi Simon ben

Gamliel: "Never was there a more joyous festival than the 15th of Av and the Day of Atonement" (Taanit 26).

From the perspective of Torah, also untenable is the current popular association of the pleasures of living with the need for gloomy confessions of sins and misdeeds. Torah is a repository of methods and ways to enhance the enjoyment of life, all within appropriate limits. The Torah is filled with mandates to "choose life!" "Justice, justice shall you pursue that you may fully live!" "Follow My edicts and judgments that, performed, yield life." Yom Kippur, the anniversary of Moses' descent with the second set of life-enhancing commandments, should shed light on all of life, not cast clouds of despair.

3.

Yom Kippur can shed light on two differing explanations for the commandments of Torah to worship God. One is that they fulfill a Divine need, so to speak, providing benefits to the Divine analogous to servants fulfilling the needs of their master. The other is that they fulfill a human need for worship that will improve and sweeten the quality of our lives as human beings. The latter opinion does not deny that God derives pleasure from seeing His creatures behaving in a life-enhancing manner. The most defensible position is reflected in the Midrash: "The commandments were given to improve and purify God's creatures."

This answer helps explain the strength of condemnations of idolatry, for idolatry asserts that the Divine is in need of our offerings for survival. Contrast this with the portrayal of the Divine as "great, mighty, and awesome," without beginning or end, Whose power is directed toward justice and righteousness, the relief of suffering among all creatures, concern for the widow and the orphan. The Biblical portrayal of the Divine is of a Mighty One whose concern is ceaselessly for the weak, the less well off, the disadvantaged.

In the Talmud, Rabbi Jochanan sums it up: "Wherever you find mentioned the greatness of the Blessed Holy One, there you also find mentioned God's gentleness/meekness/modesty/humility" (Megillah 31b). It is the unbounded Greatness of the Divine that explains the simultaneous unbounded concern for humility and justice. Note well the three supporting verses from Torah, Prophets, and Writings.

The first, from Torah: "The Eternal your God is the ultimate Supreme Being and the highest possible Authority, the great, mighty and awesome God, Who does not give special consideration or take bribes; Who brings justice to the orphan and widow, and loves the foreigner, granting him food and clothing. You must also show love toward the foreigner, since you were foreigners in the land of Egypt." (Deuteronomy 10:17-19, Aryeh Kaplan translation).

The second, from the Prophets:

"For thus saith the High and Lofty One
That inhabiteth eternity, Whose name is Holy
I dwell in the high and holy place,
With one also that is of a contrite and humble spirit,
To revive the spirit of the humble,
And to revive the heart of the contrite ones."
—Isaiah 57:15

The third, from the Writings:
"Sing unto God, sing praises to His name;
Extol Him that rideth upon the skies,
whose name is the Eternal;
And exult ye before Him.
A father of the fatherless, and a judge of the widows,
Is God in His holy habitation."
—Psalm 68:5-6

Assuredly not acquitting those cruel leaders who grind the faces of the poor and the helpless, the weak and the oppressed: this is the nature of God, the God of Israel!

4.

When a person connects with and embraces this Absolute Deity, the person is intimately bound up with the Source of justice and ethics, from which emanate rays to illuminate the good, the straight paths of life that are to be followed.

As for the objection that no one can truly cleave to the Divine since the Deity is "a consuming fire," cleave to His attributes (midot): "As God is compassionate, so be you compassionate," etc. By cleaving to these attributes of the Source of holiness and purity, so will you become holy and pure.

This is quite the opposite of those who cling to idols, to incomplete, erroneous misrepresentations of needy deities demanding offerings from exploited human beings, sources of human pain and suffering (cf. Molech worship, for example). This helps explain the intensity of the Biblical condemnation of idolatry: It misleads its followers to paths of human misery, not of compassion and mercy.

Let us now return to the substance of the Day of Atonement.

5.

At first viewing it may appear that Yom Kippur is two-edged in relation to humans. On the one hand, God assures us of Divine forgiveness and mercy for our sins. On the other hand, the afflictions, the deprivations imposed as part of Yom Kippur seem the opposite: God may gain something from them, but for us humans they are pure punishment.

A closer inspection of the specifics of the prescribed afflictions reveals that this is not at all the case. If Torah had commanded, "u-s'gaf-tem," you shall mortify/castigate yourselves, inflict pain on your bodies, one could argue that the commandment is purely punitive. Lacerating the flesh, to walk about naked in sleet and snow: these would suggest that Torah was commanded for the benefit of God and to the detriment of humans. However, the Torah commands "v'i-ni-tem," be humbled, be lowly, be deprived, sounding essentially different overtones. The five mandated deprivations are: eating; drinking; bathing, perfuming, and anointing the body; wearing leather; engaging in sexual pleasure. All of these focus on the body, on corporeality. "With all of created existence, the tragic law of life is that the sustenance of each living creature involves the destruction and consumption of other living creatures."

The physical deprivations of Yom Kippur are not punitive but revelatory. They ask us to recognize the inherent tragedy of our being creatures, to echo within ourselves the words of the piyut: "A day without eating and without drinking, a day without envy or strife." For at least this one singular day, let us distance ourselves from this tragic implication of being the matter-based creatures that we are. This insight also contributes to solving the philosophical question of the nature of the human being.

6.

What is the nature of the human being? Is this creature basically good, with the demands of livelihood and survival at times distorting the innate goodness? Or is s/he basically evil, with survival requirements of social cooperation accounting for generous behavior at times? Philosophers construct arguments for both positions.

The Torah perspective is that "in the human being, two inclinations exist together, simultaneously: the inclination toward good and the inclination toward evil." If we were all good, Torah commandments for goodness would be superfluous; if we were all evil, those commandments would be ineffectual. The discipline of Torah presupposes this duality of inherited inclinations.

The power of Torah to re-enforce the good inclination derives from its putting us in direct contact with the Completeness that is the Divine. This helps us answer accurately the questions: Who am I? What am I? Whence my origins? Torah helps us become aware that we emerge not only from the limitations of the material but also from the completeness that is the heavenly, the spiritual.[67]

Rivalry stems from the anxiety of there not being materially enough. God

---

[67] (N. B. Tamares' full discussion of this is subtle and nuanced beyond the flatness of this summary.)

as Creator assures us that on this earth there is, indeed, sufficient for us along with all our fellow creatures. This is the implication of "I am the Eternal" that concludes the mandate, "You must love your neighbor as [you love] yourself" (Leviticus 19:18). Look toward the Eternal, toward the Source of all existence, the First Cause, and you become aware that you and your neighbor are equal in God's eyes; that insight validates the commandment.

The power of Torah to incline human beings toward the good derives from its putting us directly in touch with the Creator of all, the Source of goodness and generosity, thus rekindling the spark of our Divine awareness.

7.

All of these comments about Torah and the human character are hinted at by the Day of Atonement. The promised pardon and forgiveness assure us of God's love for us, and confirm that the purpose of Torah and the commandments is to enhance our lives. Motivated by this assurance of God's love, our love for our fellow creatures is reawakened. The five bodily abstentions bring us closer to identification with the Perfection, the Completeness which is the Divine, and thus strengthen the Divine magnet hidden in the human heart that draws us closer to our fellow human beings.

Unlike all the other Holy Days that combine the spiritual and the material, Yom Kippur focuses only on our basic nature that is distorted only by our material circumstances. Hence the rabbinic dictum: "The tempter has permission to tempt human beings only 364 days each year; but on Yom Kippur he has no such permission" (Nedarim 32b).

This also accounts for Leviticus 16:30. "For on this day atonement shall be made for you, to cleanse you; from all your sins shall you be clean before the Lord." "On this day you shall have all your sins atoned, so that you will be cleansed. Before God you will be cleansed of all your sins" as you recognize intuitively that your soul is a portion of the Divine.

8.

Confirming the foregoing interpretation is the explicit rejection (Yoma 74b) of "sitting in the sun or the cold to suffer," that is, bodily mortification, as the meaning of inui nefesh, the humbling of the self. It is important that we understand clearly that God seeks our well being, not our suffering; for if God does not seek our benefit, we will not seek our neighbors' benefit. Deuteronomy 30:19, "Choose life!" stands as a perpetual reminder that the Torah was given to enhance human life, to enliven both yourself and your fellow human beings along with you. Hence we must understand "v'i-ni-tem" (Leviticus 23:27) as denoting abstinence, modesty, humility, gentleness; not commanding punishment of the body but rather simple abstinence from food, drink, and other animal needs. Thus we are able, on this Holy Day, to return to our Creator, the Source of Perfection which is simultaneously the Source of humility. "Wherever you find mentioned the greatness of the Blessed Holy One, there you find also mention of Divine humility, concern for the poor and humble." By physical abstention and even inattention to our bodily needs, we can identify with the Perfection of our Creator, and hence focus on matters of justice, not of self-interest.

From this precise understanding of "v'i-ni-tem" we can appreciate that the Jubilee freeing of all slaves is rooted in Yom Kippur. This day is a day of forgiveness and pardon from God, and of purity and abstinence by human beings. How appropriate to give this expression by loosening the bonds of the captives, in removing all traces of one person dominating another. The human soul is pure and aspires to human love and unity; it is our bodily needs that distort this relationship and divide us into dominators and dominated. With release from material needs on Yom Kippur, no one is subdued and domination is ended. We return to being brothers and sisters to one another.

The shofar, the ram's horn, is surely the appropriate instrument for proclaiming the advent of the Jubilee Year on the Day of Atonement, for it is associated with the most exalted of Biblical events. At the Giving of the Torah at Mount Sinai, "There was the sound of a ram's horn growing louder and louder" (Exodus 19:19). On the New Year, the Festival of Enthronement of the Blessed Holy One, we sound the ram's horn. And on the Jubilee Year, when slaves are emancipated, we again sound the shofar, the ram's horn, the instrument whose very sound simultaneously summons humility and justice. It is an instrument designed to purify the human being, whose very sounds plant within the human heart a passion for truth and for Divine justice, a passion even unto death, as exemplified by Isaac.

However, as a safeguard against misconstruing Isaac's baring his neck to mean that God desires human sacrifice, the shofar reminds us immediately of "a ram caught by its horns in a thicket," and the episode concludes with the explicit command: "Do not harm the boy. Do not do anything to him" (Genesis 22:12). The beneficent God, the Source of Perfection, created humans for life, not for death, and the vision of the Binding of Isaac is intended to fan the spirit of determination in us to resist, even unto death, whatever defiles the soul within us. Thus the ram's horn sounded thrice, at Revelation, the Enthronement of God, and the Jubilee, proclaims the triumph of true freedom in freeing the slaves from the physical shackles of their slavery and their masters from the moral chains of their evil dominance.

This profound correction of human society, returning it to its intended original state of goodness, explains the appropriateness of the term "t'shuvah/(re)turning," for designating this deep correcting of our inner selves on the Day of Atonement.

This life-affirming explanation of the true intention of the Day of Atonement is especially important today, in that all too many identify the holiday with chest-pounding confessionals and loudly-voiced pleas. Too often these are uttered in a spirit of irritation and anger, thereby negating the life-enhancing intention of the Holy Day. Again we must reiterate that the Blessed Holy One does not delight in human pain or self-inflicted mortifications, but rather in the genuine cleansing and purifying power of the House of Study to correct our mistreatments of one another if we engage in study in a positive spirit.

9.

The concluding testimony in support of this as the correct interpretation of Yom Kippur is the prophetic portion from Isaiah 57:14-58:14. "Cry out, spare not, raise your voice like a trumpet, and show My people their transgression... 'Why have we fasted,' they say, 'and You do not see it? Why have we afflicted ourselves, and You take no notice?' Behold, on your fast day you seek your own pleasure and afflict your workers. Behold, you fast to quarrel and fight, and to hit with the wicked fist." To fast while holding onto petty interests and the desire to dominate others is to nullify the purpose of fasting.

"Is not this the fast that I have chosen? To loose the bonds of wickedness, to undo the bonds of oppression, to let the crushed go free, and to break every yoke?...Then your light will break forth like the dawn, and your healing will come soon."

Soon, in our own days, Amen Amen!

A Preferred Pathway to God's Presence (1908)

In "The Melancholy of Exile and the Jewish Soul," a sermon delivered on The Sabbath of Turning, 5669/October 3, 1908, Tamares is disdainful of speculative, philosophical attempts to establish a felt, living relationship with the Divine.

Citing "Diogenes' Lamp" (literally chavit, vessel), Seneca, and the reflection of exhausting mental effort in the musculature of Rodin's sculpture, presumably "The Thinker," Tamares has a different recommendation. (Inviting scholarly research are the sources of Tamares' citations of both philosophers and of a recently unveiled (1906) Parisian sculpture. Pretty en courant in that shtetl!)

Below is a translation of this excerpt from the sermon.

The true path where the Divine Presence resides, along with light by which to reach the Divinity, is the path of feelings of the heart that are stirred by the revelation of God that becomes visible to the human eye when a person goes for a stroll upon the broad face of the earth, to contemplate the abundant outflow of Divine blessing and goodness. There one observes the Godly harmonies that reign in the midst of the marshaled legions of the earth in all their variety.

This is the highway from which David the King, may he rest in peace, saw so clearly, with his spirit greatly rejoicing, the vision proclaimed in Psalm 104:

> Bless the Lord, O my soul.
> O Lord my God, you are very great.
> You are clothed with honor and majesty,
> wrapped in light as with a garment.
> You stretch out the heavens like a tent,
> you set the beams of your chambers on the waters,
> you make the clouds your chariot,
> you ride on the wings of the wind,
> you make the winds your messengers,
> fire and flame your ministers…
> You cover [the earth] with the deep as with a garment;

the waters stood above the mountains...
You make springs gush forth in the valleys;
they flow between the hills,
giving drink to every wild animal;
the wild asses quench their thirst.
By the streams the birds of the air have their habitation;
they sing among the branches.
From your lofty abode you water the mountains;
the earth is satisfied with the fruit of your work.
You cause the grass to grow for the cattle,
and plants for people to use,
to bring forth food from the earth,
and wine to gladden the human heart,
oil to make the face shine,
and bread to strengthen the human heart.
The trees of the Lord are watered abundantly,
the cedars of Lebanon that he planted.
In them the birds build their nests,
the stork has its home in the fir trees...
You have made the moon to mark the seasons,
the sun knows its time for setting.
You make darkness, and it is night,
when all the animals of the forest come creeping out...
Yonder is the sea, great and wide...
There go the ships,
and Leviathan that you formed to sport in it.[68]

When David had contemplated at length the broad, harmonious pageantry of the glories of the natural world, waves of song lifted him to the heights of the Creator himself, culminating in a flame of sacred song and praise to the Creator:

"May the glory of the Lord endure forever;
may the Lord rejoice in his works....
I will sing to the Lord as long as I live...." (vv. 31, 33)

Additionally, future benefits accrue from the moral state of human beings whose spirits are lifted through this awe, this reverence before the Divine. For behold, when humans approach the purity and beauty of the natural

---

[68] (Quotations from Psalm 104 exactly as cited by Tamares, NRSV version.)

world of the Creator, then according to the vision of the divine Psalm-singer,

> "Sinners will cease from the earth,
> and the wicked be no more." (v. 35)

For the beauty of nature and its purity will bring them to a state of moral purity, the beauty surpassing all beauty.

The contemplation of the beauteous harmonies of this earth and life upon it, is the gateway to the Divine open to every human being, fashioned of matter, to recognize and to reach God. And not only to know God intellectually but to feel God, to become intimate (y'did) with God, to touch and embrace God in the fellowship of Torah and good actions (mitzvot) that flow from the human heart. That is to say, feeling testifies to the benefits of these good actions, even as spirit rejoices in them.

In the words of Deuteronomy 30:11-14, "This Torah mandate that I am prescribing to you today is not too mysterious or remote from you. It is not in heaven, so that you should say, 'Who shall go up to heaven and bring it to us?'… It is something that is very close to you. It is in your mouth and in your heart, so that you can keep it."[69]

The meaning is this. The Blessed Holy One stands and exhorts Israel as follows: Know well that this Torah that I have given you is to spare you the ordeal of seeking a sense of God with no prior connection to the Creator, like a devastated, deserted wife. Such a ladder of ascent to reach the Deity does not exist in this world. But I have given you a path to reach me, the chapter of "Bless the Lord, O my soul." Awareness of this path gives you the ability to achieve intimacy with the Creator…

This "Bless the Lord, O my soul" approach to God gathers from resources both heavenly and earthly. The bountiful blessing that God has implanted upon this earth broadens and inflames the human heart. It attracts it, enfolds it within a loving embrace, to fuse with the Godhead ("ha-elohut") that peers forth from the breadth of creation, becoming one sound within the universal harmony of creation. In this way human life is enriched with a sublime, exalted content, love from heaven. This joy of life is so clearly comprehended, so keenly felt that it is not diminished even by the specter of perishing and non-existence. It is bonded to the universal, eternal Creator.

This is the reason that at the end of the psalm, when the seeker of God's presence is so aflame from contemplating the harmony of nature, he exclaims,

---

[69] Aryeh Kaplan translation.

"May the glory of the Lord endure forever;
may the Lord rejoice in his works," etc.

These words seem directed against the angel of melancholy, which stands ready to weaken the enthusiastic rejoicing by saying: Of what profit is any of this to you, since all of these phenomena that so expand your vision of the moment are fickle, fleeting, ephemeral? And you the observer, are you not also fleeting and destined to perish? Against these words, the inner feelings of one who longs for God reply: Look, the Creator of all this is everlasting, "his glory endures forever," "he will rejoice in his works unto eternity." Even if their forms be changed, even if they now wear different garments, "I will sing to the Lord as long as I live." This is to say, the specter of destruction leaves me unmoved at this moment, for notwithstanding all this, I am now alive, I rejoice at these present semblances of the Divine, and my destiny is to unite fully with the Eternal Completeness (shalem).

Love-Motivated Turning (Teshuva me-Ahava) (1908)

In which will be explained that the most excellent Turning cannot be achieved without clarifying the concept in Torah. Then one will understand and recognize that the substance of Turning is to approach the "God of Purity," to love that Purifying Deity and to cling to God's ways without clarifying the concept, trying to "bribe" a "Wrathful Deity" with fasting and loud confessionals is likely to be mistaken for Turning; not only does this not help human beings, it diminishes us.

1.

The prophet Isaiah proclaimed,
"Seek the Lord while He may be found,
call upon him while He is near." (55:8)

To which the rabbis ask (Talmud Rosh Hashanah 18), "And when is He near and most easily found?" And they reply, "These are the ten days between the New Year and the Day of Atonement.

We must now explain why these particular days are designated especially suitable for awakening the sense of Turning.

The majority of our people understand this quite simply. During this period, winds of sadness hover over our community from the portrayals of calamity that the tradition presents as dominant in "heaven." There abound Seats of Judgment before which people and their deeds are arraigned; there abound Books of Life and Death in which are inscribed their fates to come in the year ahead, whether they shall remain in their places here in this world, or Heaven forbid, whether they shall be severed from it.

And paired with this sobering portrayal of the heavens above, nature here on earth below answers like an echo of that above, as Autumn ushers in the feeling of "after the wedding." Charming, beloved Summer, that for nearly half a year has delighted the earth, brightening her, warming her, fructifying her, covering her surface with grasses, plants, blossoms: Suddenly all this slips away into the abyss. Chill winds begin to blow from all directions. The sun, sire to all the abundant plant life, suddenly seems aged, strength diminished and weakened. One day he energetically rises from his bed to shine forth, then two days lies listlessly in bed while clouds surround and displace him. And when he does appear, how hard it all seems: With toil and trouble he manages to rise from his bed, but with dripping eyes and impaired strength, fewer hours each day, yawning, burping, bones tense, sight dimmed. Before he can properly rouse himself, already he begins to sink back onto his couch. Now all the plants and the leaves on the trees, with aching hearts observing the exhaustion of their beloved father, the sun, cast themselves downward and return to dust.

In a word, the entire environment of humans at this time of year is absence and destruction, reminding us of our own frailty and transience.

It is with this depressing mood that most of our people, it would appear, have associated Turning, thus expressing Teshuvah exclusively in sadness and wailing, the multiplication of confessionals, breast-beating, deprivation of sleep and of food, all of this in funereal mood. There is every appearance that Turning is a despair of life, a strong, singular focus on the end of life, with lamenting over the end of life and our descent to the netherworld.

Let us now consider if this path of Turning is the desired path.

After a bit of reflection, it is clear that this path is recommended neither by reason (chochma) nor by Torah. From the point of view of reason, what value does a person derive from focusing his/her thoughts upon depressing images? What reason can there be to depress the head in order to stare at the crater of Sheol and Eternal Nothingness that lies beneath our feet, until we are dizzy and apoplectic? Can this prevent or slow the tragedy? Since it is an absolute decree, would we not be far better off to seek to derive from it wisdom and strategies for dealing with it, rather than reawakening images of calamity, thereby making the few days of life granted us harder and more bitter than death itself?

All the more is this not the path desired by Torah. Deuteronomy 30:15,19 declares: "See, I have set before you life and prosperity, death and adversity; choose life." Notice: the "Creator," in creating human beings, desired that we live out the days of our lives on this earth with joy and desire, not that we embitter our lives with despair because they are bound to end at the determination of the Merciful One. Humans should not carp at or complain about this, but rather let their hearts accept in simplicity, "The Divine will do that which is good in His/Her eyes." When the time comes, by Divine will, one will be gathered to the Divine, likely to ascend from this lowly world to the higher realm of souls. For now, however, whatever time the Divine will strengthens us to live life on this earth, we should be engaged in life enhancing activities and improving the world, not focused on death and desolation. "God created this world not for desolation but for habitation" (Isaiah 45:18).

Concerning Turning itself, the prophet Ezekiel declares: "Say to them, As I live, says the Lord, I have no pleasure in the death of the wicked, but that the wicked turn from their ways and live; turn back, turn back from your evil ways; for why will you die, O house of Israel?" (33:11) Notice, again the matter of Turning is a matter of life, not of death.

There is also a substantial promissory note due Turning as popularly practiced by the masses, if we calculate the quantity of forgiveness that it should have earned. For the Talmud states (Yoma 76b): "Great is Turning for it brings redemption near," as is said, "And a redeemer will come to Zion, and unto them that turn from transgression in Jacob" (Isaiah 59:20). Yet our eyes see that even as we engage in our current methods of Turning, with repeated Confessionals and visits to the graveyards, redemption appears to recede ever further.

It is fitting, therefore, to consider if we have targeted correctly the way of Turning. Perhaps the actions we have seized upon so eagerly, repeated recitations of our misdeeds so that we are totally mired in them, is not the true way of Turning. Worth considering is that our misdeeds are like a thick, confusing forest. One who loses the way and runs from path to path while confused, will likely end up only further lost and confused.

In reconsidering the true path of Turning, it is worth noting that in "the Eighteen Blessings," the blessing for Turning comes after the blessing for Knowing. Without Knowing there can be no Turning, no true separating from evil. Without Knowledge, one can call evil good and good evil, and beat one's breast for not having sinned the more! An example of this was the reported lament of the wife of a notorious Jew-hating official at the time he was dying. "O Master of the World, why do You cause us such suffering? Did we not oppress and afflict the accursed Jews, Your deniers? Be gracious to us, Compassionate One, for the sake of their blood that our hands shed like water!"

It is evident that the path of Turning must be accurately identified and clearly marked.

2.

Understanding the concept of Turning is not isolated from understanding basic general concepts of Torah. Along with the petition for Turning in general, there is "Turn us, our Father, to Your Torah;" similarly, "Turn us with a complete turning before Thee." This is because Torah itself is dependent upon the blessing of understanding (da-at). Without knowledge there is no Torah, as implied by the Rabbinic adage, "For one worthy/pure, it is a life-giving drug; for one unworthy/impure, it is a death-dealing drug."

This saying, although evident as it stands and in no need of further explanation, nonetheless will not be harmed by a bit of additional scrutiny relating to the difference between "the pure" and "the impure," life-giving for one, death-dealing for the other.

The difference depends upon one simple, yet basic and fundamental distinction that we repeatedly emphasize in our writings: namely, the basic purpose of Torah commandments. Are they intended to enhance the well-being and success of the human being, or are they tax and tribute for the benefit of the Creator, who desires that human beings behave as servants before their master? Each of these two basic concepts moves the human being along a distinctive path, and the entirety of Torah ethics, relations among human beings and between the individual and his/her own self, differ depending upon which concept is understood as basic.

It is well known that the commandments of Torah fall into two categories. One is "between oneself and fellow human beings," how to comport with others, to avoid injuring them and doing all possible to help them. The other is "between oneself and the Divine (Makom)," to perform and fulfill those commandments. According to the first point of view, God's purpose in giving the Torah was for the success of the human being. Hence the rules for behavior "among human beings" that are intended to sweeten the common life, are to be understood as simple, basic; whereas "between oneself and the Divine" must be understood as preparation for the primary goal of enhanced life among fellow humans. For cleaving to the Divine purifies the self and firmly plants virtuous ways of living (midot tovot).

By contrast, from the second perspective, in which God brings forth the human (God forbid!) primarily for Divine advantage, the reverse is the case. Here "between oneself and the Divine" is primary, simple and basic: to serve God like soldiers who serve the king. On the other hand, the societal injunction, not to oppress one another, now becomes a prerequisite for serving the Divine: it is forbidden to injure one's fellow because s/he is Divine property, needed to serve the Divine. It is parallel to earthly authorities severely punishing those who injure police officers or soldiers, even in countries where the human being is not valued, and where the humiliation of the simple citizen is not protected by law or authority.

This is not simply a theoretical distinction; from it flow numerous practical consequences, affecting both social relations and the solitary individual. From the first perspective, the duties toward our fellow humans derive from the duty of loving one's neighbor. This is unconditional, without exception, irrespective of whether that neighbor is devoted or slack in serving the ruler. If at times there flares up within us anger at those who are slack in their worship of the Divine, an impulse to punish them out of our felt devotion to the Divine, we must recognize this as the counsel of the evil impulse. This is not zealousness for the Divine but for ourselves, anger at those who dare choose a different path for worshipping the Divine. We must exercise self-control over this impulse, as supported by the Talmudic passage[70] (Baba Metzia 32a-b): "Unload the donkey of the friend or help load the donkey of the enemy? Assisting the enemy takes priority in order to curb his negative impulse (yitzro)."

But notice, please: Wherever in Talmud we find the word "so-neh, foe/enemy," it refers to a transgressor, an evil-doer, not simply a person you dislike. Notwithstanding, the Talmud cautions you to restrain the negative impulse, not to inflict harm but rather to respond positively, to respond with goodness "in order that the transgressor may curb his negative inclination (yitzro)." This is to say, with cords of kindness, by good examples, you shall draw the heart of the transgressor to the way of Torah far more effectively than by outright punishment. Even the Holy One of Blessing loves transgressors of his commandments so long as they do not harm their fellow human beings. "Either way, foolish or wise, transgressors or faithful, they are called Children of God" (Talmud Kiddushin 36a). Commandments between the Omnipresent and the human were given by the Creator in order to broaden the human heart, so that the human is a lover of all fellow creatures, not conditional to judgments about to whom or not compassion shall be shown.

(Following are paraphrases of portions of the remainder of the sermon.)

How shall a person regard him/herself so that there be preserved within the way of Torah and ethics? From the perspective of God creating humans that we might thrive and be happy, there is a strong basis for the ethical laws of love of our fellows: the devotion (kul-tus) to love and heavenly aristocracy. The love implanted within Creation is the strongest guarantor for the love of one another. The firm knowledge that we are of aristocratic descent, from the Sovereign of Creation, is our guardian against descent into baseness. This is the warrant for our living in freedom, enjoying the material pleasures of the world in accordance with natural desires, and worshipping the Creator in joy and contentment. Hence there is no need for flagellations and self-mortifications, nor fear of death or eternal punishment.

---

[70] Cf. Exodus 23:5

......

The established surety for rules of ethics and love of fellows is the positing of Torah for the purpose of enhancing human life, bearing within it the love of the Creator for human beings. Hence spiritual fulfillment does not require mourning, mortification, or fear of death. To the contrary: From the natural joy of life and the self; from the nature of love and compassion planted within our hearts by the Creator; and from the heavenly aristocratic inheritance of every human through Divine instruction (Torah); from this our souls are purified and our spirits uplifted to the highest ethical plane.

In a word: by esteeming human beings and according them this elevated status, their spirits are lifted, their hearts are content, and they are filled with love and compassion for all created in the Divine image.

Introduction to "A Sermon on Liberty" and "On Judaism and Liberty"

The twentieth century revealed, with unprecedented clarity, the pragmatic, practical potential of nonviolence in effecting serious societal change. Gandhi in India and King in the United States did not perfect their societies, but they did contribute to major societal change by means of strategic nonviolent struggle. For both of them, along with later advocates of nonviolence such as the Dalai Lama, the basis of their nonviolent struggles was religious.

In other major world religious traditions, one can point to other prominent figures who advocated nonviolence as the permissible and preferred means for effecting societal change: in Islam, Khan Abdul Ghaffar Khan (1920s); in Theravada Buddhism, Thich Nhat Hanh (1950s). Notably absent from such a list is any prominent representative of Jewish religious thought. This is all the more remarkable in that a highly disproportionate number of those most active in nonviolent peace and social justice movements in the United States were Jews.

In addition, throughout the world during the twentieth century, there were numerous other conflicts that were waged nonviolently, not for religious reasons but from purely pragmatic considerations. There is now an impressive body of meticulous research on the function of such terms as truth, justice, and love in a power political context, not simply as religious ideals.[71] Gandhi's

---

[71] For a succinct, comprehensive view of strategic nonviolent struggle together with brief case studies, see *Waging Nonviolent Struggle* by Gene Sharp (Porter Sargent, Boston, 2005). For a brief, authoritative analysis and summary of some of the principles of power and how nonviolent intervention can function effectively, see the first four chapters of *On Strategic Nonviolent Conflict: Thinking About the Fundamentals*, by Col. (Ret.) Robert Helvey (Albert Einstein Institution, Boston, 2004). For some surprising, solid research statistics on the comparative effectiveness of violent and nonviolent methods in over 1,100 conflicts between 1900 and 2006, see the 2013 TED Talk by Erika Chenoweth.

To read Tamares against this strategic background is quite a different experience from our usual way of listening to sermons or discourses. Issues of social intervention, self-defense, means and ends all come to the fore, and one sees Tamares as an early Jewish explorer of the expansion of religious principles to actual power-political application.

Satyagraha, for example, at root meaning "clinging to truth," comes to denote civil or nonviolent disobedience or resistance. The term thus comes to refer to numerous non-violent techniques and tactics, and truth becomes also a non-violent weapon. King credits Gandhi with having made him aware that love and justice could be terms that applied to social struggle, not simply to individual religious quest.

In our reading of Tamares' Sermon on Liberty (1906) and his Note on Judaism and Liberty (1905), it will be helpful to keep this broader background—the application of "purely religious terms" to actual power issues—as a reference point. Repeatedly and explicitly, Tamares insists that the Exodus is not simply a past historical event or a sermonic opportunity, but rather a continuing paradigm for nonviolent self-defense.

Tamares, speaking and writing in 1905, displays glimmerings of recognition that religious terms such as "justice" and "truth" can have these societal effects. His pragmatism is clearly reflected in the opening of his Note on Judaism and Liberty. It is during this time period that Tolstoy (early 1900s) in Russia is advocating Christian pacifism, and that Gandhi (1895-1915) in South Africa is discovering elements of the method of non-violence.

This is not to suggest that Tamares' commitments to pacifism were not primarily from Jewish sources. At one point he specifically rejects aspects of Tolstoy's pacifism, and it was not until the 1920s that Gandhi published "My Experiments with Truth." It would appear that at this time period, revelations of the pragmatic power potential of religious ideals were being transmitted through such individuals as Gandhi, Tolstoy and Tamares.

One further background note on Judaism and Liberty may be helpful. Apart from Tamares' prescient (1905) anticipation of the great European bloodbath of World War I, starting in 1914, his sketch of developments in Europe in the preceding decades is quite specific. He contrasts sharply "Nationalist" and "Liberal" currents, condemns Bismarck and Junker Nationalism by name, and clearly affirms the proclamations of individual human dignity and rights as reflecting the true meaning of Genesis.[72]

It feels auspicious that this first English volume of some of Tamares' Essential Collective Writings is being prepared on the 150th Anniversary of his birth year, 1869. One notes, incidentally, that 1869 is also the birth year of Gandhi.
—E.G.

---

[72] C.F. Norman Davies: *Europe A History*, Oxford University Press, 1996,(pp. 802-805, 812 ff., 841-848).

A Sermon on Liberty
(1906)

A Sermon on Liberty
In which will be explained:
The substance of freedom and its great excellence;
The substance of tyranny and its great abomination;
That the single means for breaking the yoke of tyrants
is to root out the essence of tyranny found in the heart
and to put absolute and complete trust in the power of
justice.
Preached on the Sabbath before Passover, 5666 / April 7, 1906
by
Ahad Harabbanim Hamargishim
("one of the passionately concerned rabbis")
(Aaron Samuel Tamares, rabbi of the community in Milejczyce, Poland)

1

The wheel of time has turned full circle on its axis and we stand once again on the threshold of that great festival, the festival of Passover. As we well know, the biblical holidays provide the Jew with double nourishment, offering him not one but two kinds of fare: physical provender—meat, wine, fresh garb, and all that is included in the commandment, "and you shall rejoice in your festivals;" and spiritual fare—that ideal upon which each holiday is founded and the ethical notion which follows from it. To this latter the passage in Leviticus 23 refers: "thus Moses declared the appointed feasts of the Lord"—those occasions which bear within themselves the exalted divine message "to the people of Israel"—to humans. which is to say that the festivals have both their divine and their material features.

And as befits this double provision, the material and the spiritual, we find each holiday in the Bible described in dual fashion. First of all, each of the holidays is related to the succession of produce from the fields. "Three times in the year you shall keep a feast unto me. You shall keep the feast of unleavened bread…at the appointed time in the month of Abib…" Thus the Torah characterizes Passover as the spring festival. In like manner Shavuot and Sukkot are related to the seasons and the soil: "…and the feast of harvest, the first fruits of your labors, of what you sow in the field; and the feast of in-gathering, at the end of the year, when you gather in from the field the fruit of your labor" (Exodus 23:14-17). These earth-tied traits of the holidays provide the basis for the material pleasures and joys associated with the festivals, for at those times when the bounty of the Lord is revealed to man through nature—when the fields have produced the first fine shoots for the spring festival, and these have ripened to maturity at the time of the first harvest festival, and the granaries at the final feast of in-gathering are filled to overflowing with their assurance of life and bounty for the year ahead—then men's hearts naturally incline toward rejoicing and celebration.

There is, however, a second characteristic of the Jewish holidays, and that is their connection with the manifestations of the divine in the miracles and wonders performed by the Lord on behalf of Israel in those early times when He was first establishing them as a people unto Him: Passover commemorating the Exodus from Egypt, Shavuot, the giving of the Torah, and Sukkot, "that your generations may know that I made the people of Israel dwell in booths when I brought them out of the land of Egypt" (Leviticus 23:43). It is these divine traits of the holidays which provide the basis for the spiritual sustenance, the ethical message, to be derived from each of them.

And if, when the Jewish people lived on its land in Israel, the nature aspect of the festivals took precedence—their tie with the soil and the seasons being plainly contemporaneous, while their ties with signs and wonders, the spiritual aspect of the holidays, were merely memories of past events—for us in the diaspora, possessing neither fields nor vineyards, neither light nor air (even our air for breathing is but strictly granted), for us the matter is reversed. The nature aspect of the holidays is a thing past, living only in our memories, and so the material celebration of the holidays is weakened accordingly. But in its stead the spiritual significance of the holidays has grown, and the memories of early miraculous events which befell the Jewish people become for us the living present, instructing us how to live our daily lives. For our life in the diaspora depends entirely upon the ethical teachings of the holidays, and without them we should not be able to exist even one hour.

Hence we shall turn immediately to the consideration of the ethical message of Passover.

2

The festival of Passover is designated by the name "the season of our liberation," and this name itself is most interesting, especially in these times when "liberation movements" find men everywhere of conflicting opinions, some praising freedom as very good indeed, others decrying and condemning it. How urgent, then, that we give ear to the declaration of the Torah, that higher wisdom, on this matter.

And for us the children of Israel, subject to bitter exile and great suffering, the redemption from that former exile in Egypt long ago is of special interest; for perhaps from it we can derive some guidance for liberating ourselves from our present state of exile, achieving thereby at least some small respite for our afflicted souls.

And in fact the first incident which the Torah relates concerning the redemption from Egypt, God's appearing to Moses in the burning bush, itself suggests that this redemption is not merely an historical, once-for-all redemption from Egypt, but is rather a paradigm for all future exiles and woeful states which may befall the children of Israel. This is implied in the very wording of Exodus 3:13-14: "and Moses said unto God: 'Behold, when I come unto the children of Israel, and shall say unto them: The God of your fathers hath sent me unto you; and they shall say to me: What is His name? What shall I say unto them?' And God said unto Moses: 'I will become what I will become.'"

The midrash understands this to mean: Just as I am with them in this suffering so will I be with them in future sufferings. But if so, we may well ask, where today are the wonders which the Blessed Holy One previously performed when he made us a nation? Why do our enemies so abuse us from generation to generation, striking us, slaying us, burning us, shaming us, while the Blessed Holy One seems to stand aside, coldly watching our sufferings? Why all this? Where is the promise of the Blessed Holy One to Moses in the bush, "I will become what I will become!"? Certainly this question is not a new one, for Gideon was already asking it in the period of the Judges: "Pray, sir, if the Lord is with us, why then has all this befallen us? And where are all His wondrous works which our fathers told us of, saying: did not the Lord bring us up from Egypt?" (Judges 6:13) We must, then, understand the meaning of that promise as follows. The Blessed Holy One did not assert that He would personally involve Himself perpetually in the performance of miracles on behalf of the children of Israel. As I explained in my book, *Purified Wisdom*, signs and wonders involving the devastation of nature are a very base manifestation of the divine glory, indicating a generation so obtuse that none are stirred on behalf of justice, and righteousness lacks all influence in the world. At such a time the Blessed Holy One is compelled to appear in naked might, shattering and destroying the tyrants. But these signs appear only on condition that the persecuted—until now totally subjugated to the brute power of their oppressors—learn from them the ways of the Lord, the ways of justice and righteousness. If, however, even after such events the creatures still remain foolish and impenetrable, and their hearts fail to perceive the ideal of justice enclosed within the miraculous appearance of the Holy One, blessed be He—if they admire only the external might and power of the miracle—then there is no point in His appearing again through miracles. For the Blessed Holy One is not an athlete performing feats of prowess before spectators in a stadium! It is easy to see, consequently, that the promise of the Blessed Holy One "I will become what I will become," is not to be understood as implying that He Himself will appear on each occasion with a new miracle. Instead, it means that His appearance at that time established a paradigm for all future generations, and that from it the children of Israel might learn how to defend themselves in all future times of trouble.

What manner of self-defense is this to be? We shall explain this shortly, and together with it the significance of the change from the first to the last part of Exodus 3:14. The entire verse reads as follows: "And God said unto Moses: 'I will become what I will become;' say this to the people of Israel, 'I will be' has sent me to you.'" The midrash already asks why 'I will become' is repeated twice to Moses but only once to the children of Israel. Its answer, however, is not satisfactory. For if the reason were simply that Moses objected to making the children of Israel suffer in anticipation of future misfortunes and God acquiesced, why did not God equally spare Moses the sorrow of future sufferings? In the course of our words all will be explained with the help of God.

But first of all, let us return for the moment to the issue of freedom, an issue over which all the inhabitants of the earth today weary themselves, both its supporters and its opponents; and let us pay close heed to the message of the Torah, the message of that higher wisdom.

Now from the holiday before us, we see plainly that with the essential idea of freedom the Torah is in agreement. The Torah abhors exceedingly that despotic trampling upon others, and the proof is that it has established a great holiday to honor and commemorate freedom. However, we must still inquire into the ways in which freedom is to be acquired according to the Torah.

Here it would appear at first glance that in theory the Torah's formulation corresponds to the slogans current among those striving for freedom today. For we established above that the vision of the redemption from Egypt was to serve as a divine paradigm for the children of Israel throughout the generations, instructing them in the proper art of self-defense against their oppressors. Among the seekers after freedom today there is also one basic cry: "We shall gain freedom for ourselves; it is not to be received as a gift." So much for theory.

In actual practice, however, we discern certain differences in the means advocated by the European nationalist parties for "gaining freedom" from those by which we gained our freedom. They seized their freedom at the time of the French Revolution, for example, by means of barricades and bombs aimed at one despot or another. We, on the other hand, strive to achieve our freedom through the enactment of the Seder: by eating matzah, reciting the hallel, etc., each Jew participating in the ceremony in his own home, within his family circle. Which is to say that by recalling and re-enacting the liberation from Egypt we fan within our souls the divine flame of remembrance of His merciful deeds. Let us now consider which of these two means of waging war on behalf of freedom is likely to yield the better results.

At the outset, let us state clearly that we have no right to cast aspersions on those who rose in revolt against their despotic masters during the period of revolutions. We need only recall the murders, devastations, and terrible indignities which the tyrants in those lands inflicted upon the weaker of their own citizens to realize that these wanton cruelties themselves laid the foundation for the revolutions which occurred, as Isaiah said (3:11): "Woe unto the wicked! It shall be ill with him; for the work of his hands shall be done to him." The same prophet devotes his entire fourteenth chapter to describing with piercing irony the fall of Nebuchadnezzar. Also well-known is Hillel's proverb in Abot (2:7): "He saw a skull which floated on the face of the water, and he said, 'Because you drowned others you were drowned; and in the end they who drowned you shall themselves be drowned.'" However, the strategy of these revolutions, the answering of evil with evil, is questionable. It may succeed, but on the other hand, it is just as likely to aggravate the original evil. And even when it does succeed, it is only a short-lived palliative. This we have seen clearly in every land where freedom was seized forcibly by nationalist revolutions: In no time at all the plague of despotism erupted in the flesh of the body politic—just as before. The only true cure for this despotism, the only remedy which removes the evil at its very roots, is the truly revolutionary activity of the Jewish people, the enactment of the Seder—rightly understood, of course, and not merely performed by rote.

To achieve this deeper understanding, it is necessary only to analyze adequately the characterization of this holiday as "the season of our liberation," for from this deceptively simple term, "liberation" or "freedom," we can actually discern both the meaning and the inestimable value of that to which it refers.

What, then, does it mean to be liberated, to be rescued from the crucible of servitude? Does it mean to be relieved of the hunger experienced while a slave? If so, the proper description for such a liberation would have been: saved from the misery of hunger. Or if freedom were meant to refer to liberation from cold, then more appropriate would have been the designation: rescued from cold and provided with shelter and clothing. Or if the complaint were lack of rest and sleep, the liberation would better have been described as: being rescued from nights of toil; etc., etc.

If, finally, you say that freedom refers to the stirring of the feeling of dignity in man, that deep inner refusal to submit to another man and offer complete obedience, even though the master supplies all physical comforts—this at least we have seen illustrated in recent events, when fighters for freedom have chosen to suffer the deprivations of hunger and cold if only they might have the freedom of their souls, rather than sit at the fleshpots of comfort subject to the dictates of their rulers. This refusal to submit to tyrannical rule is deeply felt and deeply rooted in the soul of man, and is a powerful sentiment. But precisely because of this it is not convincing to associate that pervading concern of the Torah for freedom with this natural sentiment. For numerous elements of the tradition center about this liberation from Egypt: the thunderous descent of the Lord upon Sinai to proclaim, "I am the Lord your God who brought you out of the land of Egypt, out of the house of bondage;" the tumultuous verses in the musaf service of Rosh Hashanah: "You revealed Yourself in a cloud of glory to Your holy people. From the heavens You caused Your voice to be heard… amid thunders and lightnings You revealed Yourself to them, and with the sound of the shofar You appeared before them…"—and many others. But is it reasonable, does it make sense that all this glory and grandeur is concerned only with the natural rebelliousness of men against their masters? Is it needed for that? Despite ourselves we must concede that hidden within this notion of freedom is a yet bolder and more universal meaning, one applicable to all the circumstances in which men may find themselves. It is this which we shall now explore.

3

It is well known that the goal of the Torah is the purification of men so that they remain far removed from the contamination of unworthy acts. Men's unworthy acts flow from two sources. Some come from the material aspect of man—-his body; and some from that other aspect of man—his mind. Those deriving from the body we classify as "good" or "evil;" those deriving from the wayward intelligence we classify as "true" or "false." The violences due to the body are those natural acts of murder which are plainly performed, with no rationalizations or justifications. In such cases anger may overcome a man because another has grabbed some desired object, or he may so strongly covet his neighbor's possessions that he at last assaults him bodily. The prototype of such murders is the episode involving natural primordial man, Cain and Abel, where "it came to pass, when they were in the field, that Cain rose up against Abel his brother, and slew him" (Genesis 4:8). Such occurrences still take place occasionally, as when bandits ambush travelers in the forests, kill them, and take their possessions. All such murders are simple ones and do not claim any justification. But those acts of violence flowing from the perverted intellect do claim justification and are accompanied by excuses. Examples of such are centuries-old persecutions of Jews by non-Jews because they refused to accept the cross, or the persecutions within the Jewish community by fanatics claiming to act in the name of true piety. These two kinds of evil are not to be confused, for they differ basically. The plain acts of violence stemming from the body alone, without intellectual justifications, are deeply planted in the nature of man; for man does, after all, covet that which is not his, and he does become angry with those who refuse to perform his will. But those acts of violence abetted by the intelligence, that is, by deception and deceit, do not have their roots in the nature of man. For by nature the spirit of man aspires toward truth and honesty, and falsehood and deception are artificial and unnatural creations. In the words of Ecclesiastes (7:29): "Behold, this only have I found, that God made man upright; but they have sought out many contrivances."

But the difference is greater still in other respects. The violence wrought by the lying mind is both more constant, more widespread, and more destructive than that due to the natural instincts of man. For the instincts of the body, precisely because they are natural, do not attempt to deny the good and the just, which are also part of the natural man; and this holds not only for bystanders but for the murderer as well. Even when overcome by passion the murderer still recognizes that he perpetrates evil, and during the act itself he must fight against the insistent voice of justice which clamors within. And after the deed is done, that same inner voice gives the murderer no rest, as all acquainted with matters of the soul will agree. Natural acts of violence, then, result from a person's having failed to develop his powers of restraint to the same degree that he has nurtured his passions; consequently, at the bitter moment when the beast rages within he is unable to control it. But despite such momentary triumphs the natural passions cannot vanquish or silence the voice of conscience even in the murderer himself, and still less are they able to silence the strictures of others. The murderer may have been overcome by a momentary, uncontrollable agitation, but nothing about such acts persuades others to abandon their own proper values. Hence natural murderers seek forests and the darkness of night for the perpetration of their acts, for in cities and in public view such acts would naturally be restrained by others. Such is not the case, however, with that unnatural evil which is justified by the intellect and which is supported by the deceptions of the mind, for falsehood is insubstantial, perishing, and cannot stand before the face of truth. Falsehood and truth cannot reign beside one another, for truth is not false. Therefore, if you see falsehood making its appearance on the public podium, you may be sure that truth has been set on its head, if not utterly crushed. When falsehood bursts forth from its hiding place to perform its devilish work, it walks upright in the streets of the city and struts about without meeting any opposition from the men around. Unlike the natural killer, who met resistance from his surroundings and from the good within himself, this fraudulent killer meets no opposition from others. In fact, by virtue of his swindling deceptions he actually enjoys the support of the less discriminating; for though he may himself be aware of the nature of his deeds, others are taken in by his falsifications. In a word, this fraudulent evil, this evil justified by the mind—political evil—has become the greatest destroyer on the face of the earth. It is the source of the worst catastrophes which have befallen men since the beginning of the "improvement" of the intellect. For what have we seen? A steady diminution in private, natural crimes of individual violence, but an enormous increase in fraudulent murders: for hypocrisy has united whole nations and entire societies in the pursuit of weaker ones.

This is the secret of all the wars, conscriptions, and organized slaughters which have occurred in the world at large and against the Jews in particular, and this it is which permits entire nations to band together publicly in organized assaults upon the weaker nations. That whole populations are summoned to perform vile deeds openly and without shame requires the help of lying opinions which provide all manner of permissions and justifications for the murders: "The Jews are thus and such, and so they should be killed!" At that hour when deceit runs riot and takes as its task wanton destruction, the victims far exceed those of any natural violence, whose effects, after all, are by its very nature limited. But this fraud, masquerading in the name and with the seal of the Blessed Holy One Creator of the Universe, is utterly appalling in its destructiveness: one convulsion and immediately the earth is covered with corpses.

4

It was in order to clear away these two corruptions—the natural material, and the unnatural ones resulting from misrepresentations of the intellect—

that the Blessed Holy One manifested himself in the world through the giving of the Torah, preceded by the exile to and redemption from Egypt. The Torah itself is valuable medicine for natural wrongs resulting from the body: its love of the holy brings about man's cleaving to the Lord, while its specific prescriptions (separating man from improper relations and forbidden foods) serve to purify and refine man's emotions, thereby strengthening his worthy impulses which check the beast within him. Thus the rabbinic dictum: "I have created the evil impulse"—that is, the material evil—"and I have created Torah as its condiment"—as that which will sweeten and refine natural rebelliousness.

However, despite the therapeutic value of the Torah for natural transgressions, we still have no assurance that the unnatural evil of man's falsifying intellect will not snatch the Torah first, toss it into its valise, and make of it another weapon for destruction and murder. For this is the standard method of the minded murderer: to take the fruits of enlightenment and intelligence, intended to enhance life on this earth, and turn them into their opposites, tools for the angel of death. Consider, for example, the railroad, invented for the purpose of transporting the bounty of the earth from one section to another, distributing the blessings of nature to all the inhabitants of the earth, and in years of famine rescuing from death those in any particular district threatened by starvation. But now look! The impudent diplomat-destroyers from the school of Bismarck boldly commandeer the locomotives, and without shame and without the least regard for the sanctity of science, proceed to fill the freight cars with soldiers, shipping them off like cattle to front lines where they are to kill and be killed. Without a twinge of conscience, they turn the blessing, "Who has graciously bestowed knowledge upon man" into a frightful curse. Or consider the invention of the electric light, intended to illuminate night's darkness that men might not stumble into pits or snares. And now in times of war men turn searchlights upon enemy camps so that they can aim more accurately the muzzles of their cannons! How, then, could there be any certainty that this same fate would not befall the light of Torah? What assurance that imposters, wolfish eyes ablaze upon hearing that the Torah has been given to Israel, would not immediately pounce upon it—not in order that they themselves might understand and fulfill its teachings, but rather that they might persecute others, invoking His name to justify their fiery denunciations of anyone they might catch with an improper fringe on the corner of his prayer shawl!

To prevent such abuses, the Blessed Holy One gave the Torah only after the exile and the redemption from the servitude to pharaoh in Egypt. For servitude, the condition of one having dominion over the person of another, falls under the second category of evil, that evil which pretends some justification. Unlike the man in the forest who ambushes another out of anger or lust, acting from natural passion and invoking no sophistries, the "master" always makes claims: that the slave together with his possessions was legally acquired just like any other object; that the land upon which the slave walks is the master's property and likewise the feet with which the slave walks; that the air the slave breathes is the master's and similarly his nostrils; that his sitting, his standing, his lying down, his going about, in short, his every activity, are not really his but his master's. Such claims can be maintained only by deceit, dishonesty and intellectual fraud, all invented by the masters to legitimate their claims to sovereignty over the bodies of their slaves. Perhaps the slaves are of a different faith, then the masters have permission from their own God to trample the former; or first making sure that their slaves are kept in darkness and ignorance, the masters afterwards pointing to this lowly state as their excuse for bridling and treating the slaves like beasts.

This intellectually abetted evil, its slippery justification at its side, had its inception in Egypt. Consequently, when the Blessed Holy One wanted some "introduction" to the giving of Torah which would make plain its purpose—the removal of evil from the face of the earth—He chose the judgment upon Egypt rather than one of his earlier acts of judgment, for the earlier punishments of Sodom and the generation of the flood were for natural, corporeal evils only. Not until Egypt, the most advanced of ancient civilizations, do we have a clear instance of intellectual cunning operating to justify wickedness. The priceless phrase, "Come, let us deal wisely with them," is the clue. Here, at the very beginning of the exile, the Egyptians started their clever dealings with a variety of lies—pretending that they were threatened by the Israelites and feared lest the Israelites join forces with their foes to banish them from their own land in time of war—and this they continued until the end of the exile, blackening the reputations of the Israelites even as they bent their bodies to the ground, and all the while with their "reasons"—Pharaoh became God and so had absolute justification to trample men mercilessly; for who, after all, can challenge God? Therefore, when the Blessed Holy One wanted to guard the Torah against imposters greedily seizing it to justify and excuse their persecuting, injuring, and inflicting indignities upon other men, He chose to introduce it with his own severe retributions upon Egypt; for the vision of the plagues visited upon those fraudulent evildoers is the most powerful expression of the absolute rejection by the Lord of that most vile falsehood, the domination of one man by another. The plagues of blood, fire, and columns of smoke proclaimed to all the inhabitants of the earth that the Torah was to be personally hearkened to, heeded, and obeyed, not misused for vile purposes of domination. All this is alluded to in the first of the ten sayings uttered by the Blessed Holy One at Mount Sinai: "I am the Lord your God who brought you out of the land of Egypt, out of the house of bondage"—not out of the Egypt of simple, natural killers, but rather out of the Egypt of lying imposters who convinced themselves that they had the right to enslave the children of Israel (hinted at by the phrase, "house of bondage," implying a "right" established by three year's consecutive duration, as in the case of a house or other immovable property), as if to say: You see, Israel, how I despise fraudulent evil, that evil which falsely tries to justify itself; know then, Israel, and take upon yourselves the striving after truth all your days. For this reason, I warn you: "do not make for yourselves any graven image or likeness…"—do not change your religion for that religion of the cross whose Spanish priests forcibly burned innocent souls at their hellish pyres. "Do not take the name of the Lord your God in vain"—never perjure the name of the Lord your God by behaving within your own ranks as did the inquisitors in Spain, forcing your fellow by blood and fire to be responsible for commandments against His will; but instead let each man personally accept upon himself the Torah, observing it in truth, simplicity, and with a willing heart, and this of itself will awaken in others the desire to adopt its pleasing ways. "Remember the Sabbath day to keep it holy," "honor your father and your mother," etc. In all cases, study the Torah in order to understand and fulfill it personally, not in order to twist, distort, and make of it a permit to carry a rifle! This is also the reason for the sublime prescription in the laws of prayer (Orah Hayim, sec. 66), that one should join the word "truth," which opens one paragraph, to the last sentence of the preceding paragraph, which concludes: "I am the Lord your God who brought you out of the land of Egypt to be your God; I am the Lord your God." How appropriate that we attach to this sentence the word "truth," yielding "the Lord, your God, is truth." It is as if to say: By this vision of the Exodus from Egypt it was made known and proclaimed to the whole world that "the seal of the Lord is truth" and that He hates with absolute hatred the schemings of fraudulent wickedness.

5

With this we have completed our analysis of that basic liberty about which the Blessed Holy One so concerned Himself, and have discovered both its glory and its greatness as well as the offensiveness of one man's dominating another. This situation of domination is offensive precisely because it is a complete falsehood, and as such is despised by the Blessed Holy One whose sign is truth.

We shall now explain the ways in which, using the means provided by the promise of "I will become what I will become" from Egypt, the Jews today can achieve freedom from their oppressors.

The prescription is a simple one. The children of Israel must fulfill the commandment "that ye remember the day of your departure from Egypt all the days of your life." That is, the Jews must remember always that their God is the God of truth and justice Who shattered the yokes of their oppressors. They must plant deep in their hearts absolute faith in the power of truth and justice to triumph finally; and they must completely reject falsehood and evil as insubstantial and perishing. This idea, when firmly rooted in their hearts, will itself serve to defend them from all violent and lying persecutors; for if the children of Israel will not esteem falsehood within themselves, falsehood can have no power over them.

When the Blessed Holy One stated at the time of creation, "Let us make man in our image, after our likeness," He thereby placed in man's hands the power to create worlds as He had done. And if it be true, as our sages affirm, that man affects even the higher spheres, then how much more must he affect this very earth itself. Certainly his own situation is shaped by his own hand. The effect of society upon him is but the harvest of those deeds previously sown by him in this world. Good actions set good waves moving in the air, and a man performing good acts soon purifies the air which surrounds him. Evil actions poison the atmosphere, and a man's evil acts pollute the air until finally he himself breathes the poisonous vapors; and such poisons flow from all the actions of a man, whether physical or mental. Were the eye able to perceive it, we should see that when a man raises his fist against another man, the air surrounding him is filled with waving fists; that when a man raises a foot to kick another man, the air registers feet raised high and aimed at him; that when a man casts a designing eye upon another man, the atmosphere reveals designing eyes aimed at him; and that when a man stands inert as clay while another's blood is shed, the air surrounding him is filled with congealed lumps awaiting the hour when his own blood will be shed. The same holds in cases where one man dominates another to the latter's hurt. Such fraudulent domination could not persist for any length of time unless the subjugated themselves respected the lies of their masters. By what power does Hetman the Tartar control his Cossacks, even though he treats them as abominably as his horses, housing them together in stables? Because they themselves behave like beasts, and when given the chance prance upon people as do their horses. By what power was Germany able to send thousands of her sons to the slaughter? Because of the clod-like insensitivity of the rest of the nation, which coldly stood by and in fact even sang and cheered the plague of war with patriotic hymns and prayers; and also because the sacrificed themselves felt only the pain, and not the fraud and injustice inflicted upon them. Please notice, also, that the Torah itself, holy and priceless in its wisdom, suggests that the Egyptians could never have succeeded in dominating and oppressing the Jews had not the Jews themselves deteriorated morally. Constantly seeing the violence and cruelty of their Egyptian masters, however, they themselves began to esteem the power of the fist and to grant it the right and privilege of persecuting and crushing their own oppressed.

The actions of Abraham, our father, described by the Torah as just and righteous, provide a marked contrast. He was notably hospitable: "And seeing them, he ran from the entrance of his tent to greet them." He lived peacefully with his neighbors and was careful not to violate their borders: "And Abram said to Lot: 'Let there be no strife between you and me, and between your herdsmen and my herdsmen; for we are kinsmen. Is not the whole land before you? Separate yourself from me. If you take the left hand, then I will go to the right; or if you take the right hand, then I will go to the left'" (Genesis 13:8-9). He was deeply concerned when his relatives were abducted, and he risked his life to rescue them: "And when Abram heard that his brother was taken captive, he led forth his trained men, born in his house, three hundred and eighteen, and pursued..." (Genesis 14:14ff.). Not only the capture of his relatives but the fate of persecuted strangers also touched his heart, for the same chapter reports his efforts on behalf of the fleeing king of Sodom.

And what was the consequence of actions such as these which he disseminated in the air around him? He was the most deeply honored of all his neighbors and was crowned with the title, "you are the prince of God among us."

What, then, accounts for the later reversal in which the Egyptians freely trample the descendants of the prince of God?

Alas, as the Torah hints, his progeny were corrupted in the course of time and stupidly came to venerate the crude fist of their rulers: "And when Moses grew up he went out to his brethren, and saw their burdens; and he saw an Egyptian smiting a Hebrew, one of his brethren" (Exodus 2:11). Not a single Israelite was stirred to protest this maltreatment of one of their brothers before their very eyes; not even a verbal protest was heard, because their feelings had already been blunted by the internal admission that the Egyptian, sword strapped to the broad red band about his waist, had the absolute right to strike any Jew, even for no reason.

At that moment Moses our teacher was inspired to undertake the work of restoring the crown to its former state. By encouraging the people to recapture those keen sympathies of their ancestor, Abraham, they too might come to feel the pain of their brother, and so Egypt's hold upon them would be weakened. The first example of risking one's own life on behalf of the afflicted he showed them on the spot: "And he smote the Egyptian…" (Exodus 2:12). But very soon after, the next day, in fact, he had to admit that he had erred in his hopes: "And he went out the next day, and behold, two men of the Hebrews were quarrelling." To his sorrow, Moses saw once again how terribly closed the heart of the people had become, and how their common sufferings had failed completely in impressing upon them the need to band together: here they were, unable to leave off even their pettiest personal quarrels! If a bowl of grits were sighted which might somehow be grabbed and gulped down, a man would charge into the crowd and elbow his brothers right and left, quite unconscious of the Egyptian sword hovering over the necks of all of them together. To make matters worse, when Moses tried to save them from destruction by speaking a word of caution to them, they cruelly turned upon him, their compassionate defender who only the day before had risked his life for them, and defiantly took the part of the Egyptians, their brutal oppressors: "Who made you a ruler and a judge over us? Do you intend to kill me as you killed the Egyptian?" (Exodus 2:14). In the face of this abysmal ignorance and insensitivity, Moses was thoroughly discouraged. It was clear that the natural appeal to reason, which had worked so effectively for Abraham in propagating the knowledge of God, had not the slightest chance of succeeding with this demoralized generation, so stupefied by the vile yoke of the Egyptians. And so "Moses fled," despondent and despairing at Israel's bitter fate invited by their own abject moral condition: imminent destruction at the hands of hostile persecutors.

"And it came to pass, in the course of those many days, that the king of Egypt died; and the children of Israel sighed because of their bondage, and they cried…" (Exodus 2:23). And so another line is added to the portrait of that morally obtuse generation. For at a time of unbounded oppression and moral perversion—when, according to the midrash, the king of Egypt himself became leprous and thereby exposed in pus and boils his foul inner state and the rot within his soul ("leprosy comes because of slander and arrogance," says the midrash); when he attempted to end people's shunning him by ordering the slaughter of some male children (believing that he could be cured by bathing in the blood of those whose sense of smell was keenest and not yet impaired by long subjection to the stinking atmosphere of slavery); and when he chose as his victims the most defenseless of all, the children of the Israelites—there is no record of the children of Israel having cried out to the Lord, the God of justice. They failed to sense the injustice and falsehood in the whole situation and could only complain of the pain. "But their cry came up to God." Although Moses could no longer hope for the Jews' rescue by natural means—i.e., by their reaching such spiritual heights that their oppressors would be unnerved and chastened—it did not exceed the Lord's capacity to manifest Himself personally as the mighty and wondrous saviour and redeemer. And there were several reasons to expect such intervention. First of all, whether the Jewish people was itself worthy of rescue or not, the Blessed Holy One could not, while the wicked raged, indefinitely restrain Himself and permit them to inflict upon a poor and defenseless people their cruel schemes passing all bounds. As for the question of their being "worthy," the view of the Lord is not like the view of man. For the view of a man, even one so exalted as Moses, is but a view of the moment, the character of the Jewish people at this instant. But the Blessed Holy One surveys time in its fullness, seeing past, present, and future together. He penetrates to the ancient root of the people, to its origin in the sublime and glorious patriarchs, from which even now there must glow in its innermost heart a spark of feeling and decency, however dimmed this inheritance by the dust heaped upon it. He also foresaw the future, their accepting the Torah so that once again they would be pure like their fathers, if only He would appear this once to rescue them personally from the mire of Egypt. And so, continues scripture, "while Moses was keeping the flock of his father-in-law, Jethro… and the Lord appeared to him in a flame of fire out of the midst of a bush; and he looked, and lo, the bush was burning, yet it was not consumed" (Exodus 3:1-3)—a suggestion that even though at this moment the children of Israel were as desiccated as the bramble in lacking the sap of justice, despite this they would not perish from the world. And Moses, our teacher, on the one hand sustained by the hope of this hint, on the other hand bewildered by the impossibility: for how could a people so abject as this be rescued from the hands of its oppressors? But the Blessed Holy One answered him, saying: "I am the God of your fathers, the God of Abraham, the God of Isaac, and the God of Jacob…"—which is to say, I have looked to their glorious past, to their descent from the loins of the holy patriarchs; and similarly do I foresee their splendorous future, their accepting of the Torah.… "When you have brought forth the people out of Egypt, you shall serve God upon this mountain" (Exodus 3:6, 12). Even though they do not recognize Me as the God of justice and righteousness to Whom they should cry out, despite this "…I have heard the cry of My people because of their taskmasters!" That is, at all events, I can no longer restrain Myself before the cruel wickedness of the Egyptians and the sufferings of the Israelites, and I am compelled to intervene directly by means of manifest miracles, recompensing the wicked and rescuing the persecuted. And this act shall be a lesson for future generations, that they may learn from it how completely they are to loath tyranny and falsehood. And as a result there will be no more need for My miraculous meddling in human affairs, My interfering from outside the natural order of events, for there shall nest within them the presence of God, the God of Righteousness and Justice, and it will defend them against the domination of the wicked. It is in this sense that the midrash understands Exodus 3:14. "I am becoming what I will be; I will be with them in other tribulations just as I am with them now." That is, their power to defend themselves and achieve victory in future exiles should grow from this, My present manifesting of Myself to them.

Obviously, of course, this idea of self-defense which lies as a treasure hidden within that combination of strong faith in truth and justice and the absolute and total rejection of falsehood, was grasped at that time by Moses alone, for he alone felt not only the pain of the persecution but also its injustice and falsehood.

As for the rest of the people, so given to Egyptian ways were they and so respectful of the might of the fist, that from their masters' lashes they felt only the pain of the blows and none of the indignity. Hence they could not grasp this idea of self-defense contained in the belief in the God of Justice, the secret of all future redemptions, without first seeing plainly revealed the mighty hand of the Lord. It was for this reason that the Blessed Holy One instructed Moses: "Say this to the people of Israel, 'I am has sent me to you'" (Exodus 3:14). For the simple people there is no point mentioning the second 'I will be,' the idea of the future redemption, for at the present it is beyond their understanding.

6

The redemption from Egypt, with all the majesty and awe of the plagues which the Lord inflicted upon the tyrants, is a clear revelation to everyone of how completely the Blessed Holy One loathed the deeds of the tyrants and falsifiers. And with this divine paradigm everlastingly established before the children of Israel, this example to which they might look and direct their ways accordingly, they would have at hand the means to defend themselves against persecutions in the lands of their exile, means which would also, in the course of time, succeed in removing entirely from the face of the earth the life of "one man's dominating another to the latter's hurt."

For actually that power, majesty and awe which the Blessed Holy One displayed at that time while intervening on behalf of the persecuted, derived from the higher power of truth and justice. But since at that time the oppressed had been corrupted morally and were dominated by the values of their Egyptian oppressors, the higher power of truth and justice could only burst forth in blood and flame. However, the divine power itself could and had to be appropriated and treasured by the children of Israel deep within themselves, for by its means other fraudulent tyrants could be terrified, toppled, and prevented from dominating them.

What is the nature of this treasure? Its nature is a strong faith in God, in the God of Truth and Justice. But how shall one discern this faith which lies within the heart? Through deeds and actions which are appropriate to such a faith. This means that both individuals and entire peoples must order their lives on the basis of the saying recorded in the Tosefot to Baba Kama 23: "A man should concern himself more that he not injure others than that he not be injured." For when a man tries to keep watch that his fist not injure others, by that very act he enthrones in the world the God of Truth and Righteousness and adds power to the kingdom of justice; and it is precisely this power which will defend him against injury by others. This does not happen, however, if a man is preoccupied with watching out only for himself and keeps his fist always poised to prevent others attacking him; for by such a pose he in fact weakens the power of justice and stirs up evil. When a man constantly portrays in his imagination scenes of terror, when he asserts that everyone wants to obliterate him and that he can rely only on the power of his own fist, by this he denies the kingdom of truth and justice and enthrones the power of the fist. And since the fist is by nature poor at making decisions, in the end defense and attack become reversed: instead of defending himself by means of the fist, such a man becomes himself the assailant and destroyer of others. Hence, like begetting like, others repay him in kind, and so the earth is filled with violence and oppression.

This message was conveyed by the Holy One, blessed be He. In connection with the last of the plagues upon Egypt, when He Himself executed the judgement of death directly by His own power: "For I will go through the land of Egypt in that night, I and not an intermediary." Now obviously the Blessed Holy One could have given the children of Israel the power to avenge themselves upon the Egyptians, but He did not want to sanction the use of their fists for self-defense even at that time; for while at that moment they might merely have defended themselves against the evildoers, by such means the way of the fist spreads through the world, and in the end defenders become aggressors. Therefore, the Blessed Holy One took great pains to remove Israel completely from any participation in the vengeance upon the evildoers, to such an extent that they were not permitted even to see the events. For that reason, midnight, the darkest hour, was designated as the time for the deeds of vengeance, and the children of Israel were warned not to step outside their houses at that hour—all this in order to remove them totally and completely from even the slightest participation in the deeds of destruction, extending even to the watching of them.

With this we can now explain the words of the Braita (Baba Kama 60a): "...And none of you shall go out of the door of his house until the morning" (Exodus 12:22)—Rabbi Joseph explained—"Once He has permitted the destroyer to act, distinctions fall by the way." Now at first glance this appears to contradict the assertion of the midrash, "I and not an intermediary." Then how can the Braita say, "since He has given permission to the destroyer"? But by our explanation there is no contradiction in the words of the Braita, for their purpose is to explain why the Blessed Holy One saw fit to execute vengeance by His glory and might rather than with the participation of the children of Israel. And the answer: in order not to give permission to the destroyer within them, for once having permission there will be no distinguishing between righteous and wicked, and from "defender" one becomes in the end "aggressor."

"...and none of you shall go out of the door of his house until the morning... that there not be in your midst the plague of the destroyer." Which means: your abstention from any participation in the vengeance upon Egypt will prevent the plague of vengeance from stirring the power of the destroyer which is in you yourselves.

Many other verses in the same spirit circulate concerning the exodus from Egypt. For example: these verses preceding the crossing of the Red Sea. "And Moses said unto the people: 'Fear not, stand still, and see the salvation of the Lord, which He will work for you today; for whereas you have seen the Egyptians today, you shall never again see them. The Lord will fight for you, and you shall hold your peace'" (Exodus 14:13-14). Here the word "see" is to be understood in the sense of "esteem." (Cf. the Talmudic expression, "I see the words of Admon," i.e., esteem and agree with.) And the verse consequently means: since this day the Egyptian power has been nullified in your case, and their horses and chariots which met you by the sea have perished. Since this day you have seen the mighty shattering of material might—of the strength of horses and the sound of spears, "you shall never again respect and esteem them." And when this rejection of material might will be well planted in your heart, then indeed "the Lord will fight for you, and you shall hold your peace," which would not have been the case had you participated in the acts of vengeance by the might of your arms, for by such acts you would yourselves have conceded the power of the fist.

We might also refer here to the words of the Torah in Deuteronomy 17:16: "...If you set a king over you...he shall not multiply horses to himself, nor cause the people to return to Egypt, to the end that he should multiply horses; forasmuch as the Lord has said unto you: 'You shall henceforth return no more that way.'" Nowhere has the Lord previously forbidden the "returning that way?" If derived from Exodus 13:13-14, the argument is weak, for there we only have a description of the great salvation promised them but hardly a warning. Furthermore, that whole passage is inappropriate as a basis for prohibiting the multiplication of horses. Finally, what has "not returning that way ever more," the essence of the verse, to do with horses?

The true explanation is this. The entire section of Deuteronomy 17:14-20 comes to present an exalted conception of the Israelite monarchy, forbidding trust in the accumulation of silver, gold and prancing steeds "lest the people be turned again to the paths of the Egyptians," to the ways of the Egyptian tyrants. For "did not the Lord say"—by His personal execution of vengeance upon Egypt and His prohibition against the children of Israel participating in it, "you shall hence forth return no more that way"—the way of the Egyptians who trust in the power of the fist—"ever again."

By this explanation the idea of these verses in Deuteronomy is in fact the same idea as in Exodus 13:13-14.

The children of Israel, then, must derive this lesson from the events of Passover Eve: not to put their trust in wealth and not to put their trust in might, but rather in the God of Truth and Justice, for this will serve to defend them everywhere against those who would dominate by the power of the fist.

7

But beyond this primary lesson to be learned from Passover Eve—that the guardian of Israel is the God of righteousness and justice, not the power of their fists—there is an additional lesson relating to an even more debased idea than self-defense by the power of the fist: that the human being, by the power of his fist, is the guardian of his deity. This rationale, used by persecutors of Jews throughout the generations, has inflicted greater injury than have savage fists alone. This rationale is the very opposite of the Liberation from Egypt, which recognizes the power and strength of the God of truth and justice to defend the human being. It has been the justification for all the hyena-like Jesuits, filled with deceit and idolatry, zealously robbing and persecuting on behalf of their deity. This accursed excuse devoured Jews in the days of Torquemada and the Crusades, and when local priests became inflamed with the idea, rivers of Jewish blood flowed and great communities became a heap of ruins overnight. After all, it is no light matter to defend one's pathetic, oppressed deity!

In its role as a treasured people among the nations, Israel must defend itself against the slanders of its persecutors by purifying itself of any traces of such erroneous beliefs. Jews must purify their conception of God, and hold ever before their eyes the memory of Passover Night. On that night, it was the Blessed Holy One alone who battled on behalf of the Israelites against their oppressors, so that they might understand the true meaning of "God" as the source of justice and truth. Is not truth the foundation of strength? From which it follows that God must be understood as majestic in might, defender of human beings, not human beings as defenders of the deity by insulting the exploited.

In short, Israel must take special care not to make of God, as it were, a weak, despised idol to display as ensign on our backpacks as we set forth to gore, on its behalf, our fellow creatures. This is comparable to groups of beggars who cultivate a particular defect or injury to use as they move from city to city begging for alms. The lesson Israel must learn from Passover Night is that the God of Israel is the God of truth and might Who defends His human worshipers, not they who defend Him. God is presented as strong, mighty, lacking naught, defending those creatures in need of help. Then life on earth is defended by the power of truth, and human lives are secure. This is not the case when humans presume to defend their deity as one weak and in need of creaturely assistance; then all the world is in peril. For if God is weak, human life is not secure. If the Dweller in the Heavens is inadequate, then governance is given to Cossacks below, who trample their fellow creatures to the sound of their horses' hooves.

It is not accidental that in the history of the Inquisition in Spain, it was on Passover Night especially that the demonic inquisitors, filled head to toe with falsehoods and blood lust, made their greatest efforts to ambush and apprehend the pure, delicate souls of Jewish families for the great sin of secretly, in cellars and hiding places, attempting to perform the Passover Seder to the God of Israel. Today we have precious paintings portraying the terror on the faces of these innocents as they realize that the wolves had found them in their underground hiding places. It is again worth noting that the timing of these most ferocious assaults was not an accident. Passover Night, the Night of Watchfulness, teaches that God is the God of truth and might Who defends the human being. This is the total opposite of the Inquisition, which asserts the power of a false deity, a nullity, whose followers support and uphold him at fever pitch. Therefore do these zealots (whose souls give them no rest on this night) seek out those innocent souls who perform the Seder and nestle in the bosom of the God Who is the sovereign of righteousness and Who despises evildoers. The inquisitors want especially to eradicate the continuing testimony in the sacred assembly of the Seder to the falsehood of the inquisitorial thirst for blood.

Precisely because the focus of our persecutors' zeal was our Seder on this Night of Watchfulness, therefore our most vigorous effort must be to understand its essential idea: to enthrone the God of truth and justice as the defender of humankind. By this shall we be saved from the wicked plots of all those who would waylay human beings in the name of their deceptive, ineffectual deity.

8

Solid support for our analysis above is provided by the language of the Midrash. In Midrash Exodus Rabbah, 16:2, this is the explanation of the reason for the Paschal Sacrifice: Because the Egyptians worshiped a lamb as a deity, therefore the Blessed Holy One commanded to slaughter a lamb and so nullify that fear. I now adduce a few expressions from the language of the Midrash.

"Said the Blessed Holy One: 'Because the object of this idol worship is like a senseless stone of no substance, and others must guard it to prevent it being stolen, how can it give life to the sick?'" "Thus you find that when the Israelites were in Egypt, they worshiped idols. Hence the Blessed Holy One said to Moses, 'While they are in Egypt the Israelites worship idols and thus will not be redeemed. Go speak to them and urge them to abandon their evil practices,' as it says 'Pull' and 'take', that is, pull your hands away from the idolatry, take a lamb and slay their Egyptian deity. By this Paschal sacrifice God will pass over you. This is implied in 'By turning and tranquility (shuvah v'nachat) shall you be saved'" (Isaiah 30:15).

The words of this midrash hint at the interpretation we have offered. At the very first hour of the redemption from Egypt, the Blessed Holy One commands that the Israelites deny explicitly the divinity of the Egyptians' "feeble lamb." Such worshipers present their deity as a feeble deity in need of protection and defense by the "Cossacks." From this came all the evil inflicted on the Israelites, and you must slay this idea to begin your liberation, that is, uproot from your hearts the nasty, depraved idea that the human can defend the deity. Proclaim before all that the end has come for swarming charlatans who ruled Egypt with such notions, and who thrashed and winnowed our people without mercy. Now the rule has been transferred to the God of truth and justice. The night of watchfulness has arrived, the night for protection from the destructive forces, from which it is fitting that you now place your trust completely in the God of truth. Henceforth no destroyer or villain will raise such an ensign anywhere in the kingdom of purified faith.

This is the import of "Through turning and tranquility shall you be saved"—That through your quiet confidence in the God of justice when you set Him forth as your defense, without anger or violence, without the oppressive, aggressive actions of Egypt, shall you find strength.[73]

One additional observation is in order about the Passover sacrifice, with its command to "place the blood of the lamb upon the doorposts of the house." Unlike the dependent lamb of Egyptian idolatry, whose devotees stand outside guarding it, the Blessed Holy One stands outside the dwellings of His devotees guarding them. In the words of Onkelos the convert-translator: "A king of flesh and blood sits within while his subjects stand guard outside. In the case of the The Blessed Holy One, his worshipers sit within while He guards them outside" (Talmud Avodah Zarah 11).

What follows from our words is that when the children of Israel make the effort to comprehend fully the reason for the particulars of this liberation from Egypt, they will inherit the true freedom. For the singular expression of Might—the display of Divine miracles of judgment upon Egypt—was compelled to come from outside because of the lowly spiritual state of the Israelites at that time, to become treasured within them, later to impose fearful respect upon the nations for their wisdom, understanding, and honorable behavior.

This also illuminates the meaning of the proclamation that the Blessed Holy One sent through Moses to the Israelites before the Giving of the Torah: "You saw what I did in Egypt, carrying you on eagles' wings and bringing you to Me. Now if you obey Me and keep My covenant, you shall be My special treasure among all the nations that are on the face of the earth" (Exodus 19:4-6).

The explanation of these words is the following: Behold, at the time that you were reduced to the lowest depths, thus giving the Egyptians the ability to rule over you, I Myself was compelled to inflict judgments upon the Egyptians and lift you from the depths on eagles' wings, that is, by sudden elevation to bring you to Me. Now, however, come and I will teach you the counsel that, from this day forward, will give you the power (to defend yourselves) at all times: "If you hearken to My voice and fulfill My covenant." This is to say: If you observe My Torah in the spirit of the liberation from Egypt, a spirit of compassion for the persecuted and hostility toward the persecutors, then "you shall be a treasure to Me from all the peoples." That means, all the peoples will, of themselves, recognize your special qualities and will respect and honor you. This is suggested by the Midrash (Deuteronomy 3), "Blessed are you by all the peoples, for all the

---

[73] Once again Tamares struggles toward asserting "truth-power," very much in the spirit of Gandhi's *satyagraha*, simultaneously a moral term and a strategic, power-political term. It is noteworthy that Gandhi, Tamares, and Tolstoy are all stirred by this idea at this time. This is again re-stated at the end of this sermon.

earth is Mine." To Me, the God of righteousness and justice, belongs the ultimate power and victory, to which all will finally submit.

To give best expression to the idea of Pesach that we have propounded throughout our interpretation, that Israel's victory in the world must come not by might nor by power but by spirit, the prophetic portion (haftarah) for the conclusion of Passover, summarizing the essence of the holiday, Chapter 11 of Isaiah, should now be cited:

> A shoot shall come out from the stump of Jesse,
> and a branch shall grow out of his roots.
> The spirit of the Lord shall rest on him,
> the spirit of wisdom and understanding,
> the spirit of counsel and might,
> the spirit of knowledge and reverence for the Lord.
> He shall sense the truth by his reverence for the Lord:
> He shall not judge by what his eyes see,
> or decide by what his ears hear;
> but with righteousness he shall judge the poor,
> and decide with equity for the meek of the earth;
> he shall strike the earth with the rod of his mouth,
> and with the breath of his lips he shall slay the wicked.
> Righteousness shall be the belt around his waist,
> and faithfulness (in the power of justice, ko-ach ha-tzedek)[74]
> the belt around his loins.
> The wolf shall live with the lamb,
> the leopard shall lie down with the kid,
> the calf and the leopard and the fatling together,
> and a little child shall lead them.
> The cow and the bear shall graze,
> their young shall lie down together,
> and the lion shall eat straw like the ox.
> The nursing child shall play over the hole of the asp,
> and the weaned child shall put its hand on the adder's den.
> They will not hurt or destroy on all My holy mountain,
> for the earth will be full of the knowledge of the Lord
> as the waters cover the sea.

This is the depiction of the redemption that awaits us, soon and in our days, Amen.

---

[74] (Tamares addition)

On Judaism and Liberty[75] (1905)

In my opinion, one of the most important projects for the improvement of our life here is this: the appointing of watchmen to track diligently the relations between the Jews and the people among whom they reside. These relations should be constantly maintained in a state of purity, and such a project should be undertaken both internally and externally.

Internally, there should be widely diffused among our people, both orally and in print, the teaching of our sacred Talmud that Jews should live in peace and amity with all people, whether or not they be of our religion. Likewise, the teaching of our exile not to be angry or resentful over the disadvantages of our status. Above all, not to express this dissatisfaction by deceptions and deceit in dealing with the simple common folk. They are certainly not responsible for the laws that oppress us. Neither are they, the honest workers who contribute much to the world and receive but little from it, the ones who benefit from the damage done to us by the restrictive legislation. On the contrary, it is incumbent upon the Jew to be gracious

---

[75] In 1905 Tamares published his first bound volume, the pamphlet *Judaism and Liberty*, under the pen name, One of the Passionately Concerned Rabbis. It had a dual intent. On the one hand, it was meant to be "a sharply sarcastic critique of a 'nationalism' that was empty of any Jewish content, and stemmed merely from a slavish desire to imitate the goyim." The same pamphlet ridiculed "the Zionist dog and pony show, with its sensationalization of Herzl's success at clawing his way up to 'audiences' with 'all the king's horses and all the king's men'." (See end of Part 2 of the Autobiography.) This fills most of the volume, both the Introduction and the central essay, "Where Are You Headed?"

Attached to the central essay are five footnotes that are, in fact, essays. The longest and most substantial is Footnote 4, "Jewish, Non-Jewish Relations," here translated in full. It is this section that fulfills the first stated intention of the publication itself: "Perspectives on Judaism and Its Aspirations for Freedom and Justice, and an Analysis of Nationalist Zionism from these Perspectives."

Noteworthy are the call to cooperation between Jews and non-Jews based on their common human interests; the allocation of more attention and funds to needs of the local community rather than to a Zionist superstructure; and the unqualified affirmation of the inviolability of the individual human being as the most basic principle of Creation portrayed in the Hebrew Bible.

and forgiving in any dispute that may arise between us and our neighbors, for if we have with us the hearts of the simple people and true peace exists between us, then of necessity the power of politics to harm us will itself be weakened, depending as it always does on its claims to be working for the good of the common people. These are the internal projects.

External projects include the following: Always, whenever plans are afoot to stir up hatred among the common people by intrigues and agitators, to turn to the masses of the common people and, in their language, invite them with soft gentle words to peace and brotherly understanding (think of the prophetic saying, "Have we not all one father? Has not one God created us? Why do we do deal treacherously against one another?"). At the same time we must show them clearly the falseness of the accusations leveled against us by our enemies. We must consider both negative proofs, in order to remove from us the falsehoods of the agitators, and combine with these positive revelations before the masses, the sources of these accusations and the destructive interests of their creators. Their only intention is to distract the eyes of the people from their own interests, which people could investigate if they were not distracted by religious hatred. The proportions of these approaches we must consider carefully, but to permit the plague to spread without any response from our side is not to be considered.

If we devoted to such a project but one small part of the precious funds that Zionism yearly collects for its Herzlism, our people would receive from the project seven-fold the blessing that it receives FROM Zionism. But why do say seven-fold? Zionism is the complete opposite of this project. Anyone who looks into the Zionism literature with a penetrating eye can see that Zionism strives constantly to pour the spirit of depression and despair into the heart of our persecuted people, and attempts to deny its hope, its eternal hope based on the promise of its holy scriptures, that worldwide justice will in the end reign supreme. Zionism never reviews any incident in the world, be it great or small, without proving from it, at the top of its voice, that anti-Semitism is growing ever stronger—all this in order to prove that only from Dr. Herzl can salvation arise for Israel. Our Herzlistic journals have released throughout the world a flock of black ravens, harbingers of evil tidings, ready to pounce upon any foul deed at the furthest ends of the earth, and immediately publicize it to prove thereby that anti-Semitism has cropped up in places heretofore unsuspected, discouraging by this any hope for the cure of the disease in places already afflicted. We read continuously in the world events sections of Hebrew newspapers, reports providing balm for our already aching hearts, from London or New York or Cape Town or other places where Jews are scattered. The reporter, certain that we have not yet received all the blows we deserve, invariably begins the report with these words: "Anyone who says that here in the lands of freedom Jews can live in security, kindly let him note such and such an incident that should hit him where it hurts." Or, "Let him please read newspaper such and such and he will see signs of hatred, and the indications of a pogrom against the Jews are unmistakable; it will surely come, it will not tarry." With pleasant tidings such as these we are honored by our newspapers, spread about the world, to pluck constantly such thorns. It would be impossible to understand why they come to cheer our aching hearts with such encouraging news were it not that reporters themselves never forget to conclude without words such as these: "Therefore we must support with full strength 'our great leader' and only in the shadow his wings shall we find refuge. Selah." Let us at least count this to their credit, that they were not able to restrain themselves and conceal in their hearts the source from which flow the ideas, and the hangouts where their faces are regularly seen.

In one word, all the Zionistic literature is fed exclusively by this plague. It spends all the day long pointing to the evidence of sickness and disease in the relations between Jews and their neighbors. It is easy to imagine how the air is cleared of all impurity and dross by their perpetual effort to prove that the faithful fail among human beings, to cast doubt and slander upon righteous spirits, and to give absolute assurance that deeds of corruption and violence are everlasting visions, ordinances of the world which shall not be transgressed.

How terribly tragic that the Holy Spirit, the spirit of honesty that invested the pages of Hebrew literature in its beginning, has vanished in these later times, these days of shrill slogans of nationalistic moments. In those earlier times, the task of the Hebrew authors was to inspire in the hearts of the people the most basic and healthy life aspirations, both individual and collective. For example, the striving for wisdom and knowledge, for graciousness and consideration, for justice and love: a love for all humans, a love for the larger world, and inclusive brotherly love—these aspirations they tried daily to plant in the midst of our people. Even though this effort resembled the call of the times for the Jew to leave his narrow, separate circle and to join the greater world (for such were the winds blowing at the time), even so, how welcome were these calls to the Jewish spirit, and in fact especially to the Jewish spirit which abides always in the shadow of the divine Torah. For this inspired Torah asks of the Jew to strive for sublime ends, to embrace the whole earth. This is also the case with these aspirations for life and betterment, the improvement of the whole world and all its inhabitants. The Jew saw in this no contradiction or threat to his own world, but just the contrary: the enlargement of his own world over the whole face of the earth, the conquest of all human beings by these strivings. How sweet were the dreams of universal righteousness and justice dreamt by the enlightened human beings of all people and tongues! How did the heart of the Jew throb and expand when he heard the voice of the living God walking about in the land, when he saw shoots of righteousness and compassion for all created in the Divine image sprouting and growing in all the surroundings. How reassuring this honoring of Torah by the realization of the sublime vision of all human life, the end of the exile of the Shechinah, and together with it the end of the physical suffering which was sure to come. How pleasing to the Biblical and Talmudic Jew to stroll among the rows of this literary vineyard, and how very much did he feel himself a rooted, flourishing citizen among them. Their splendid fragrance, the fragrance of Torah and the natural enlightment taught by Torah, were to him as fine oil, and his bruised soul and body breathed afresh with new life once again.

But alas, that splendid period did not last long. A shudder passed through the gross body of the masses, a shudder due to the brilliant, heavenly light which shone upon them suddenly and to which they were unaccustomed; and so they turned back startled. To be more exact we should say this: the shudder and convulsion seized the various leaders of the flocks, the cronies of Bismarck, they who had ascended to power and authority during a period of thoughtlessness and might. They then took counsel to turn aside the hearts of the people from the illuminating sun of righteousness and understanding which destroyed their authority without mercy.

But what scheme would have the possibility of stopping the sun of righteousness in its course, and where could it be found? How could it be enlisted? Notice, we are living in the age of "the science of bacteriology," which has searched and found that one must cure light with light. To defend the body against the infectious bacteria of an illness, one must inject the body with a serum from the same infection itself. Likewise in the case of righteousness, world justice and betterment, which are like a disease in the eyes of those leaders who grow fat from corrupting justice and making crooked the paths of life, these leaders could find no other way to defend themselves than by a similar scheme. They announced that they were not only concerned with the anxieties and problems of the leaders themselves, as leaders formerly were, but they were also concerned with the general needs and welfare of the whole community. However, rather than worrying about the improvement of all humanity, as proposed by certain rash liberals, something too taxing for the intelligence—after all it is no small burden to bear the whole world on one's back—in order to lighten the burden on the mind, the leaders proposed that one must be satisfied, at least for the time being, with each one worrying only about the needs of his own nation or people.

And so by this ruse—and a "Mazel Tov! Treason!" is in order—there was born to us that beautiful daughter, "Miss Nationalism." Soon thereafter the leaders married this charmer, finding her precisely that which their souls did love. This lovely couple was in turn blessed with many fine offspring—may the righteous be blessed!—who came to be known in the world as national patriots, "patriotic volunteers." Their mission was that each gather about him a flock of human sheep, establish the camp by his standard, in order that these "patriots" could purify the masses and set them to work in "public service," each operating strictly within his own flock. Thus the former leaders reappeared as "national patriots."

It is not this in itself that we condemn. Had it been determined that the community projects should be divided into separate sections in order to lighten the burden on the workers, we would not regard with hostility the success which these men are having in their efforts with the public. It is well known that the whole is not greater than its parts, and if the individual parts of humanity be improved, then it automatically follows that humanity as a whole is better off. Why then quibble over an issue where one is better off and the other one is not harmed? The work of the volunteers is easier and the whole community is better off when its parts are combined.

If this were the case, however, how has it happened that in dividing the common work into regions, whose end is only to make the work easier for the workers, how has it happened that, together with this division, the actual content of the work has suffered a fundamental change? "They that turn the many to righteousness" have begun to feed the masses of their communities very strange fare, and to worry on their behalf about very strange and unusual problems. In place of the true material and spiritual needs which are bread, air, light, justice, morality, grace and understanding—all would agree that these are genuine community improvements—our "national patriots" have created for themselves a whole new set of anxieties on behalf of the people. They drum into the people the threefold chant of "descent, language, and ancestral ways." Bread: whether the people eat bread or starve, this is a minor worry. Morality: whether the human be in the image of God, or the beast be in the image of man, this also is easily solved in the opinion of the "national patriots" if only descent, language, and traditional customs be frequent on the lips of the people.

How has it happened that "nationalism," sought by the leaders as a concession to their inability to undertake improving the whole at one time, surely a permissible undertaking, how has it been converted by these leaders to an exclusive working only on behalf of the single part? It is now as if the various patriots had sworn that each would be very careful that from the improvement of his part no advantage should accrue to any other part. To assure this, they established fixed boundaries and divisions. Not only that, but all the community projects themselves came to be of one category only, "official national," and within the domain of the "official," one was not to make the least mention of improving the tree of life itself. Not a single word was to be breathed in the space allotted to that category. The government was busy all the day long setting "the flaming sword which turned every way" on the path to the tree of life, to guard it that no alien might touch it. Beneath the cloak of nationalism, work was given to the Krupp armament factory to prepare weapons to murder men, work in such quantity that the factories are humming day and night. The master of this factory, the provider of all needed instruments, the "Still Angel," has earned the crown of a good name among all the national patriots far greater than all the developers and inventors of constructive devices for living. So great is this adulation that a special "national patriot" personally went to bestow the highest national honor upon the owner of the armaments factory, something that never in history has happened to the owner of the largest factory producing plowshares and pruning hooks to bring forth bread "to stay the human heart." How is this, that the noble matron, "Miss Nationalism," has converted all of Europe into an armed camp? Fortifications and barricades to ambush the blood of men fill the face of the earth in greater numbers than silos, and the voice of drunken songs recounting the wonders of the fist and deeds of destruction burst out from all the barracks windows, filling the whole earth with praise and admiration for might and all the beastly inclinations of humans, silencing by their roar the song of the simple farmer recounting the generous contribution of this worker of the soil. In one word, the barracks, the glorified esteemed barracks, dominate by their scent and spirit all the pleasures and all the purity of thought. The air is filled with the smell of the barracks and our concepts filled with the spirit of the barracks. Why and for what have the forts and barracks multiplied so greatly? To block the path of the tree of life from aliens and strangers, the "national patriot" will reply. But the costs of the fortifications and the barracks themselves have already drained the sap of life, so against whom and what do they defend?

How is this, that the improvement of the parts—divided from the whole with the understanding that the whole will thereby be improved, the basic meaning of nationalism—has been converted into the uprising of part against part, so that air is filled with a fine mist of venom and envy, of nation against nation and people against people? How is it that to the beat of nationalism there have arisen from the earth, like ghosts, all the lies and vicious slanders of earlier ages which were used by scheming murderers to catch their prey, such as blood libels and similar accusations? How is it that these have returned with the growth of the nationalist idea, and along with them the tears of the oppressed and tortured victims?

How is it that from the time that nationalism triumphed even the great luminaries of the enlightenment have been dimmed? That the air of the academies and universities is filled with the plague? That at the head of every warring faction and mass demonstration, one regularly encounters university students with their glittering banners, marching at the head of the parade and shouting "Hit! Strike!," as if they had come to take the place of the young priests with crosses in their hands who marched at the head of the Crusaders in earlier times? Not only this, but frequently one meets these brilliant scholars attacking one another: German scholars opposing Czech scholars like two flocks of kids, each grabbing and bucking his neighbor over the issue of in which language, German or Bohemian, shall one say, " May the darkness engulf you!"

In one word, how is it that the whole earth is filled with biting, kicking, wrestling, and fisticuffs ever since the horn of nationalism was raised on high? What is this? What is this?

It may well be that these events seem wondrous to the simple, who failed to notice the plot against the progress of humanity which was achieved through the birth of racial-political nationalism. The drivers holding the reigns of humanity took advantage of that moment when all were celebrating the birth of that fine beauty, "Miss Nationalism," to reverse the direction of the chariot of humanity from progress to regress. The naïve, who failed to sense anything of this in its hour of accomplishment, and who imagined that the chariot was still proceeding in its forward direction, are of course amazed and startled when they suddenly meet again the barbaric occurrences of the dark ages. The more perceptive, however, are not at all surprised by this turn events, knowing full well that the barbaric phenomena now manifesting themselves are the expected fruits of "nationalism." Already at the moment of birth, this hellion could be recognized as the messenger of the evil power of might, sent to destroy the counsel of goodness and to prevent the further spread in the world of ideas of justice and humanity, even to turn them to the advantage of Mars. To use generosity for cruel ends, the power of love and brotherhood for enmity and hatred, social impulses for divisive ends, joining humans together by compacts and covenants in order to attack those not of their group; fanning to flaming heat the spark of nationalism, not in order to provide heat and light for brotherliness within the camp, but in order to burn and pillage those outside the camp, and then to establish the same predatory order within the camp: the swallowing of the weaker by the stronger, the stronger by one still stronger than he, and so forth within the camp itself.

In short, the birth of this latest version of nationalism was the beginning of cancerous growth in the cells of the body of humanity. It resembles exactly this disease in the body of the individual. At first sight it seems as if the cells have become more cohesive, more "brotherly," for the cells do begin to join more strongly and congregate with one and another. In truth, however, the exaggerated clinging stems from lack, and soon weakens the body, striking at the vital fluids and natural warmth which sustain all the cells of the body equally, and maintain among them harmony and equilibrium. Thus in a state of health, each cell receives and transmits nourishment in equal measure, and each individual cell is recognized as the established resident of its place, the rightful occupant of the base. The basis of life and existence is reserved for each cell for its own sake, that it may itself live and exist. The increment, on the other hand, belongs to the body as a whole. That is, from the very existence of each cell, benefits accrue for other cells as well. But now that disease has struck the body, reducing the flow of natural warmth and nourishment, the brotherliness betweens the cells ceases. They no longer sustain themselves from the increment of the base, each thereby deriving benefit from the existence of its fellows, but rather from the destruction of the brother, from consuming the base itself, the flesh of its neighbor. It is for this end that coalescing and congealing suddenly appear. The stronger cells begin to grab the weaker cells surrounding them, so that they can suck them dry. Corresponding to the manner in which these stronger cells trap, seize, and consume the weaker surrounding cells, in other parts of the body other stronger cells set traps to ensnare and encircle the weaker cells surrounding them, and suck them dry. Thus throughout the entire body lumps appear, traps and snares; in the center of each sit the "volunteer patriots," engaging with great satisfaction in the work of sucking and destroying the other cells, thus preparing the imminent death and decay of the unfortunate body.

Like cancer in the individual body, so is the "new nationalism" in the collective body of humanity. This collective body, of which each individual on the face of the earth constitutes one cell of its tissue, also cannot live and be sustained unless the flow of life follows its normal and natural course within it. The test of healthy circulation is this: equal treatment is accorded every cell, and there are neither oppressors nor oppressed, exploited, but every single cell has its own place, and the right to exist for its own sake. That is, it lives in its own right, for its own sake, and its life belongs to it and not to another. Such equal treatment can exist only where the body-sustaining warmth and vital powers flow as they should. What is this natural warmth that sustains the larger body, the body of humanity? Righteousness, justice, honesty, and human rights. When these principles reign in the world, then "oppression is no more and marauders have vanished."[76] No cell attempts to

---

[76] Cf. Isaiah 16:4

swallow its neighbor, for they will no longer live by a dog-eat-dog predatory system, nor by exploitive economic systems in which the stronger tramples upon and consumes the weaker. Ended also will be the deceptive schemes by which a select few, designating themselves "the whole," cunningly and falsely require the rest of the their fellow humans to sacrifice themselves as bloody prey for the benefit of their leaders, this process being called "for the general good." Such devious tricks will be at an end, and in every heart will be firmly established the clear recognition that the request for this kind of sacrifice is not in any way to be heeded! Absolutely no one has the right or the authority to ask or demand from his fellow that he be his ransom, not the whole from the individual and not the individual from the whole. Every single human being on the face of this earth was created and endowed by the Lord with the capacity to look after his own life (Cf. Rashi on Genesis 9:6) and to worry about death and perishing; each was created for his own sake. The breath which the Lord breathed into the nostrils of Reuben is for the sake of Reuben; it is for him to live and exist by, not to be a bloody sacrifice for the sake of someone else. From his very living and existing, profit and pleasure of themselves accrue to other creatures as well, in as much as he is their brother, helper, and fellow worker in tilling the soil and producing its bounty, benefits which in no way diminish the base. The ground still remains his and for him, the man existing for his own sake, so that he may live from the land, while the fruits, his services and the works of his hands, are of value to the whole society.

In a word: when righteousness and honesty, the natural warmth and vital powers in the body of humanity, are in a state of health, then there is peace for all the cells, for every individual human being. Each and every person sits in his rightful place, and receives from the collective sap of life that which he needs to maintain his own existence, and his friend does likewise. Then the chapter of "sacrifice" and carrion is ended, where one claws and drags away his neighbor and swallows him, whether by the tiger claws of the plain marauder, or the eagle claws of the ideologues, who entice their prey with forgeries in verse and song, seducing them to enter willingly their dance, being consumed while convinced that this is for the betterment of their souls!

Nullified and ended the chapter of "sacrifices," each man swallowing his fellow man. Instead, all will live by the chapter of "manna," each going forth to gather "every man according to his eating, the bread from Heaven," that is from the fields of the earth given to all humans equally—not man eating the flesh of his neighbor!

This is the culture of the Bible, the culture of Creation in the Book of Genesis, which neither knows nor recognizes "nations, peoples, classes, sects," all of the latter created ex nihilo by imaginings of humans. It knows only the individual person formed ex nihilo by the Creator of all in the divine image and likeness, created to live and sustain himself through dominion over nature, not over his brother. This also was the culture of the first nineteen centuries. Liberals, students of the prophets, for whom the Bible was "a lamp unto their feet," and who carried aloft the ensign of the Bible at the beginning of that splendid, glowing period. Then did the rights of men grow and blossom. Then it was recognized that the only compass point which could faithfully guarantee ideas safe passage through the shoals of the darkness was one absolutely fixed point: the foundation of life on this earth in the individual person.

When this point was faithfully followed, the direction of all aspirations and goals was thereby clearly established: toward life and secure existence. For of what value was all the wealth of the individual without basic security, without secure life and existence, the maintenance of life within the body, so that he might go about securely here on this earth all the days that the Lord would keep him in life?

If that fixed point, the recognition of the rights of the individual, disappear, and in its place there be substituted any other term; "community," "society," "nation," as the basic foundation of life on this earth, as that for whose sake was man created, then alas! Already then we find ourselves involved in dark theological concepts, and between these beliefs and the idolatrous beliefs which declare that man was created for the sake of this idol or that idol, there is really no difference at all. Neither is there any assurance that the holders of such opinions and beliefs will not turn out to be stewards of "the Still Angel," nor that their casuistries will not yield death and destruction for the individual human being, offering him on the altar of fine abstractions, sacrificing the actual life, the life of the blood and the spirit, for the rhetorical life of fine sounding phrases fluent on the lips of this or that idolatrous priest.

Life, tangible life, the life of the blood and the spirit, this is the need which must first be sought. The life and secure existence of the individual: these are the basis of life on this earth; from them all comes, and in them all is included! When all is well in the blood and spirit of the individual human, then there is peace for the whole society, and the organism of humanity will grow and blossom, full of sap and richness, like gardens beside a stream.

This goal of liberalism is strengthened whenever justice and honesty—the vital powers of the organism of humanity—are in a state of health. Then social relations between the individual cells are healthy and correct, and the cells approach one another in a spirit of brotherhood. Each derives from the other a benefit in no way harmful to the first, conforming to the true test of mutual benefit: that "brothers should sit together," both living securely, each benefiting from the continued flourishing of the other, not from the demise of the other, neither benefiting from his neighbor's misfortune.

One small ray from this splendid goal did appear in the world for a very brief time, at the beginning of the nineteenth century. But this blessed period, to the world's great misfortune, lasted only a brief time. Shortly after, there appeared a sore within the organism of humanity. Evil and foolish men, together with secretive schemers, conspired to inject disease into the body of the world. This foul injection affected the vital sap of justice and uprightness, the vital fluid within the body of humanity began to decline and dry up. Immediately a terror arose among the cells, the terror that occurs at times of siege and scarcity. Hearts turned to ambush, seizing their neighbors to assuage their hunger by their neighbors' flesh; thus began to spread the cancerous illness of "nationalism," while respect for human rights declined to the lowest rank, replaced by the abstractions of "nation" and "collective." Then did the mightier cells conspire to busy themselves with the task of catching and grabbing weaker cells, each one gathering heaps of weaker cells from which to extract blood. The brotherly intimacy in which one happily rejoices over the existence of one's friend, and derives value from his existence, the natural state of cells when the body is healthy, grew continuously stronger and more powerful, joining one to another ever more securely within each national unit. But suddenly from intimacy of friendship it became the intimacy of devouring, the intimacy of the lamb with the lion. Now every thought of the stronger is simply how to take advantage of the moment and ingest the weaker, making him truly "flesh of his flesh." Thus "the chapter of manna" turned away and departed, the gathering of the heavenly bread, the gaining of substance from the fields of the earth, appointed equally for all humans and valuing fairly the life of each and every person. In its place there began to be heard, with great noise and clamor, the sound of "the chapter of sacrifices." To cover the naked work of devouring, cloaks of song and chant were prepared. The voices of priests from their temples of prayer, the voices of poets from their palaces of verse, all extolled and praised with a single voice the idol of "nationalism," with their sermons and their songs enticing and inciting the people to offer themselves as living sacrifices upon the altar of "nationalism." Despite the wealth of richly covered tapestries which the cloak makers may weave, they cannot prevent the perceptive eye from seeing the content within. It is the appetite to devour which speaks from the throats of all these priests and poets, the desire for prey that moves them to create their exalted masterpieces.

Thus did the cancerous disease of nationalism run its course, burying the rights of the individual and causing tumors to erupt everywhere on the body of humanity, each lump a trap and snare in the disguise of peoples, kingdoms, and countries. Every such protrusion was reinforced and surrounded by a network of barbed wire and bayonets, capped by bullets and grenades, so that anyone coming near might be shocked or swallowed alive in a mound of flame. Upon the face of everyone was spread a mantle of hostility and terror, at the very sight of which a man's heart would melt and he would feel bereft of all trust in life. From every threatening rapacious mound, there burst forth in unison the cry: come hither, son of man! The right to live securely is not the individual's! Long live the nation! Long live the state! To hell with the individual!

After all this, should one be surprised by the spirit of enmity and hostility that has filled the earth since "nationalism" ascended the throne and was duly sanctified as an idea? Shall we be surprised by the greedy dogs pouncing upon every bitter scrap reported in the newspapers, all of them tended by Mrs. Nationalism in order to slander and vilify other nations, especially the weak, and to embarrass them with sharp words? Should this surprise us, when the whole enterprise of nationalism is the enterprise of internal devouring as well, this devouring within the camp, hidden from the eye? Is this not the necessary outcome of the process, and a great factor in the successful concealment of this "clean" work internally, the appointing of public agitators and thugs to incite an open attack on some nation outside as compensation and distraction from needs within? By this means, those who have been plundered within the nation can become plunderers on the outside. Shall we be surprised at evil, destructive, random acts such as the breaking of windows, the burning of homes, the destruction of property, which break out from time to time where a weak nation borders a stronger one, and where the inspiration of nationalism has opened a path? Should we be surprised by the random acts of destruction which occur among the residents from Madame Nationalism's desire to amuse herself a little, inciting the stronger nation by these acts to plot against the weaker neighbor? Should any of this surprise us, when all the serious work of nationalism, carried out openly and publicized, is mobilization, digging trenches and foxholes, launching shells, and making all the other necessary preparations for nation attacking nation? This work totally consumes the vital sap of the present and foretells a great and terrible slaughter for the future.

Our charming matron, Madame Nationalism, has been preparing for some fifty years now a great family sacrificial feast and frightful blood wedding, to which all peoples and tongues shall be invited. The invitees, whom she earlier divided and split from one another, will meet at this wedding from near and far, face to face, to join in that compact where each buries his spear in the chest of his fellow before himself departing this earth for the eternal world. This dividing of individuals into nations has greatly simplified the task of sending invitations to this terrible wedding. It is no longer necessary to invite each resident of the earth individually—an overwhelming task, with no guarantee that simple people would want to rush to this exalted wedding quite beyond their simple understanding. What would guarantee the full attendance of simpler folk, who spent their days beside plow and sickle? They might also fail to be excited by the desire to attend when they consider the personal cost involved: their very lives! Therefore, Madame Nationalism wisely decided first to trap and group men in small constellations, heaping them up, so that all inhabitants of the earth might be grouped as a limited number of "national patriots." These, limited in number, could be educated in the proper spirit of nationalism, inclining their reason to accept this counsel of destruction. Then at the opportune moment, when all preparations were completed for the hellish wedding, she need only whistle to two or three of her circle, "those of advanced intelligence," to join her in the demonic dance. These already regarded their participation in these fresh tales of heroism and wars as the height of good fortune. Their fantasy was always of achieving fame and fortune in roaming the fields of slaughter, like the poets' fantasy in fields of grains and fruits, climbing higher on the platform of life, always from a valley filled with blood and dead bodies. This whole arrangement was also effective because, by virtue of their positions as leaders, the "Black Wedding" presented no threat of loss or danger to them personally. They, these officials, her longtime attendants, would not fault her—why should they fault her?—as they hastened to provide her with sufficient invitees from the flocks entrusted to them: flocks of human sheep, sheep for the slaughter, numerous as the sands of the sea. Now then: if for these fifty years our fine Madame Nationalism has been busy preparing this great provision and terrible feast for the whole family of humanity, a devastation the like of which has never before been seen, not even in the days of the Black Plague, a day of calamity, a "world war" slowly but steadily approaching; if this be so, why marvel at the few small crumbs of this feast that fall from the table into the mouths of the weaker peoples, such as our own? Of what account the shattering of some windows in Jewish homes, the ripping of our clothing, or even the few torn bellies at the time when the tattered and barefoot stride forth? Of what account these small incidents beside the great official slaughter being prepared for all humans, without distinction? Citizen and stranger, buyer and seller, lender and borrower, assaulted Jews and assaulting riffraff: all alike will be offered whole at the great feast which the Grand Dame Nationalism will provide for the entire family of humankind.

 I am, therefore, not at all surprised that a few crumbs of the great general slaughter, rapidly approaching, already fall from the kitchen table into the mouths of "a people dragged about and plucked" (cf. Isaiah 18:2,7).[77] What must be noted, however, as one of the seven wonders of the world, is the short-sightedness and lack of vision of many members of this "driven and plucked people," most especially the Zionists, who have pounced upon "nationalism"—the primary source of the tears of the oppressed in general and of Jews in particular—as a wonderful find, a "kosher metzia," and have hauled it into our boundaries to the accompaniment of timbrel and dance, setting before it a great mob to sing and shout its praises day and night, heralding it as the single salvation and success of our people, beneath whose dark, hellish wings we shall find protection against every sorrow and misfortune. Assisting them is quite a coterie of vacuous writers, most of them educated in the universities of that capital of nationalism, Germany, and consequently not like those religious ne'er do wells who have no idea of what is "customary among the nations." No indeed, they have looked long and hard, these bright students, observing that every Teutonic nation is busy emphasizing its nationalism, with more forts, barricades, and steel helmets appearing fresh each morning. It is only their people, the Jewish people, that sits with its hands folded. The sight is most disagreeable to them, this disgraceful state of their people, and so they have arisen and gone forth to save their people with mighty acts, and have established in its midst a literary foundation for nationalistic nonsense, thereby "rendering for bullocks the offerings of their lips!" Behind them follow a whole stream of small-minded liberals, educated in the swampy borderland of the "Hebrew bibliotheca," envious of their big brothers with glittering banners. So they, too, have gone forth to imitate their hymns. All of these together have combined in a plot to banish utterly the Holy Spirit from Hebrew literature—the healthy spirit of justice and morality which filled our literature in its beginnings—and to make of it the lowly consort of the filthy idol, "nationalism."

These young sparrows have already inundated our world with their floods of nationalistic chirpings. Open any book today and you will meet only one theme: "nationalism," "nationalism," with perhaps an additional two or three words of like manner, such as "might," "Maccabees," "the last drop of blood," etc. These esteemed words are milled and kneaded unceasingly, with no lessening of fervor even the hundred and first time, and each time they are mouthed by their composers (better said, their fabricators) with ever greater arrogance and disrespect for all the sages and men of the

---

[77] Hebrew meaning uncertain. Support for this rendering of "m'mu-shach u-morat" may be found in Brown Driver Briggs *Hebrew and English Lexicon to the Old Testament*, as well as in William Braude's *Midrash on Psalms*, Psalms 87 and 120.

spirit who had earlier arisen in Israel. For in the eyes of these nationalistic chirpers, every previous generation stumbled blindly and never found the path to Israel's redemption until…until they, themselves, appeared and stole the hidden light from the Academy of Bismarck and Schtecker, so that new light now illuminates all the dwelling places of the Children of Israel. This new vision—members of the plucked and driven people beginning to chant the hymn of nationalism, the hymn of the mighty; children of a poor and downtrodden people beginning to make use of the scepter of the mighty—this, my lords, is a very strange sight indeed, a caricature without equal. For while a rich and powerful person, asserting himself strongly about boundaries and limits and bellowing loudly, "What is mine is mine," may not win many friends, at least he is not laughable. But how shall we regard a pauper who, holding tightly his tattered bundle, screams like a crow, "What is mine is mine"? A mighty giant who terrorizes his fellow men may not win many hearts, but at least he is not ridiculed. But how shall we regard a thin and wasted individual, known to be in ill health, who stands shaking his shriveled fist to frighten people while shouting in a pathetic voice, "Watch out or I'll let you have it!"?

It is precisely in this guise that I see the crowd of vacuous Zionists with their incessant chanting of "nationalism, nationalism." Experience has shown that their selecting this lovely word, "nationalism"—whose common meaning is, the strengthening of gross egotism and the private concern for filling one's own belly, politely designated by the word "nation"—is not to be explained away as merely a case of "a worthy doctrine in an ugly, unworthy vessel." Such an excuse argues that the term "nationalism" was borrowed in order to awaken and stir within the Jewish camp a love for the Divine morality and justice, hence serving to contain a different and much more valuable content. Further, it argues, that of the two kinds of separating which may take place under the term "nationalism," these authors refer to the spiritual withdrawal from the surrounding impurities and corruption in order to refine and purify one's own deeds and concepts, not to the dividing of stock against stock and blood from blood for the sake of ethnic exploitation, having as its goal once again the private maw. But experience shows very clearly that our authors of nationalistic poetry have adopted the term "nationalism" with all of its ugly and corrupt connotations, exactly as it is current among others, without a single change. In fact, it is a wonder to behold the duplicity which reigns within the nationalism of our nationalists. Here our ears are deafened by their mighty sounding of the refrain, "nationalism, nationalism," ostensibly a voice crying to Israel to concentrate inwardly and come to appreciate its treasure. But our eyes behold a draining away of that spirit, and a terrible ignorance of Torah wherever the feet of the nationalists have trod. The more they proclaim "nationalism, nationalism," the more do they barbarize our tradition, and the more strongly do they establish the spirit of Edom within Jewish life.

After that speculative criticism, one simple, compelling fact. Were their nationalistic awakening really spontaneous and genuine, caused by the stirring within of their dormant Jewish feeling, then they would not have found it necessary to choose new terms for conveying the Jewish spirit, least of all such a foul and corrupt slogan as "nationalism." Israel already has an ancient and glorious expression, the Holy Bible, which adequately conveys to all the inhabitants of the earth the aspirations of the Jewish heart as well as the aspirations of all the oppressed everywhere. Not only do they not need the term "nationalism," when they already have such a mighty and exalted term as "The Bible," but it is completely incongruous and misleading to use the slogan "nationalism," in as much as it is the complete opposite of "The Bible." For "The Bible" desires only to distinguish between righteousness and wickedness, and loathes every other division among humans; whereas "nationalism" is constantly making divisions among men in order to deliver them into the domain of might and wickedness. But since the awakening of our nationalists did not, in truth, proceed from within, from the stirrings of their Jewish hearts, but from without, from imitating the ranks of Ham and Edom, all the filth, all the violence, and the utter lack of purity and holiness which characterize the general refrains of "nationalism" have been brought within our camp as well.

Of course, as we mentioned above, one must still note the considerable difference between "them" and ourselves, between the heavy giant waving his large fist and the crippled dwarf waving his puny fist; for the latter is nothing but a laughable caricature. Alas, how bitterly laughable to see the wild shouting and dancing by our society of conspirators, presented today on the platform of our literature as the great new find of "nationalism," along with the wild derision that they heap upon the earlier strivings for justice, equality, and the rights of humans here in the world. How strange, how terrible it is to hear the great shout of scorn roared by these scions of a "people driven and plucked" over the demise of the striving for world justice, cut off prematurely by the great spread of nationalism. How dreadful to see them scornfully cast stones from their Zionist literature upon the coffins of those who dreamed dreams of justice and equality. Nor are they willing to forgive their even having entertained such strange notions as the desire for justice or compassion, since they thereby failed to recognize the boundaries of violence and the order which makes it something forever fixed and established in this world. So great and strong is the appetite of our new collection of prophets for this latest invention of Edom, "nationalism," which has murdered the striving for justice, that they outdo Edom himself in their enthusiasm. It is as if our poor, erring assemblage of souls declared the following to the mightier nations that invented nationalism: "Congratulations, fools. It was hard work to murder every attempt to attain the equality and dignity of all humans, but you've succeeded, and you've even managed to gain our acquiescence as well. But now that you've begun to busy yourselves with treaties and pacts, we, too, are released from all obligations of friendship toward you, and we, too, shall begin to fortify our borders so that you shall come to know our displeasure as well."

That such threatening words are laughable from a poor and helpless people hardly requires mentioning. But I must add that these words are also terrible, and dangerous for the world culture in general and for the Jewish people in particular. For even if it were true that the ideas of "nationalism" and might have already captured the hearts of the nations, so that they want to besiege our every step, we being weaker than they, still it is neither worthwhile nor right that we adopt their faith and seize the poisonous term "nationalism" as a defense against the plague of their nationalism. By so doing, we ourselves manifest the same poisonous behavior and intentions, thereby lending sanction to the sway of nationalism and the dominion of violence.

For our people, "the people of the book," "a people driven and plucked," to assent to the rule of might is no small matter, my lords. For since it is recorded in the annals of history that never has there been an honorable or worthy movement which did not include a number of Jews among its leaders, then how logical it is that in resolving issues of justice versus violence or mercy versus might, none should be more qualified than the Jews to solve them, none better equipped to influence the outcome greatly in the direction of either might or mercy. For our people are disciples of the exalted "Book of books" which first proclaimed morality and justice to the world, which first elevated humans from the slime of the pit to the inspiration of heaven, and which has already influenced the inhabitants of the entire world, near and far, to bow respectfully before it. On whom, therefore, does it rest as much as upon us, nurtured by that Book, to bring the final strides of morality and justice to the world?

This is the theoretical qualification that we have for solving the question of justice. But besides this, we have a very great practical qualification as well, the wonderful, sublime designation that we inherited from our exalted prophet: "a people driven and plucked, a nation oppressed and downtrodden." Who is able to know the soul of the oppressed so well as we, who is able to feel all the evil which concepts of might bring to the world as we, sheared and plucked, strangled and stoned these two thousand years?

Let our spirits not be depressed by the words of that famous but confused philosopher who scorns the morality of justice in this manner: "It is the morality of slaves and weaklings."[78] In so far as he attributes the ethic of justice to slaves, we must, with all due respect to his strange philosophy, point out that this is proven utterly false by the clear and well known fact to the contrary. It is precisely the nature of slaves, long sunk in their servitude, to regard the thorns and briars with which their masters thresh them as constituting their lords' rightful power to dominate them. As for those beneath them, they assume their own right to dominate them in turn. From that which the mighty mete out to them, they take their example for their treatment of others. The maltreatment that they receive from the mighty thus sets the example for their own maltreatment of others.

However, in relating the ethic of justice to "the weak," i.e., those spiritually free even if weak materially, our philosopher indeed speaks the truth. Had the ethic of justice not been revealed to us directly through the Torah; had the Creator Himself, Who searches unto the utter ends of His creation, not engraved therein the seal of justice for humanity and declared plainly and definitely that only through justice can the world be established; had the Torah itself not stated this with absolute definiteness; had the notion of justice required a gradual intellectual development through time, like all practical scientific discoveries and inventions; then there is no doubt that the weaker men, those who had experienced the pain and suffering which comes from violent might, would have been the first to present the notion of justice. Even this in no way reduces the intrinsic value of justice, for it is the nature of things, and cannot be otherwise, that all the discoveries and inventions in the world have been initiated by the happenstance of actual needs and experiences. Had it not chanced that early on, humans happened to see sparks flying from two stones meeting, the power of fire might still be unknown today, and the world would be without this useful resource. If some persons had not once suffered a slight burn from coming too near this glittering discovery, thereby learning that it is good to be a friend from afar with fire, we might have been destined at some future time to stumble into a great blaze from which there would have been no rescue.

Like every other discovery and invention in life, so that of justice and the awareness of another person's suffering of necessity had to begin with the actual experience of affliction by an individual who had himself felt and tasted stripes and wounds in his own flesh. Had such a one personally not known affliction and paid attention to the principle of compassion, that person would have regarded as equal the beheading of a fellow human

---

[78] Clearly a paraphrase of Nietzche.

being and the felling of a tree. This was the answer given by the Divinely inspired teacher to the heathen when asked to "teach the whole Torah while standing on one foot," i.e., to give him one fundamental principle, itself natural and reasonable, by which he could understand and remember all the prescriptions of the Torah. As is well known, Hillel the Elder presented the command to love one's neighbor as the basis of the entire Torah. But rather than stating in the words of the Torah itself, "Thou shalt love thy neighbor as thyself," an injunction which itself requires support (for who can prove that it is fitting or worthwhile to love one's neighbor?), Hillel presented the injunction according to its content rather than form: "That which is hateful to you, do not unto your fellow." By this formulation he intended to awaken the man's heart to the recognition within himself of the essential touchstone of justice: that from his own personal experience of suffering he could know the soul of any other unfortunate not himself.

Therefore, if the scornful philosopher would find fault with the ethic of justice because it is the morality of the weak, i.e., the discovery of those who have some experience of the matter, then let him, by the same token, reject all the inventions and improvements in the world. For were not all of them born of trials and experiences? Let him especially reject all those improvements that have come from interested persons who first suffered want and privation before producing their inventions. By this logic, one ought not travel by steamship since it is the invention of mariners whose lives were constantly endangered by previous methods of crossing the ocean. One should not use charcoal since it has been developed by lumbermen, interested parties to the matter. Would that our philosopher himself, so scornful of the ethic of justice since it is the invention of those directly affected, had taken care not to use any discovery or invention of an interested or affected party. In that case, since Gutenberg's invention was undoubtedly intended for his own use and benefit, our author could hardly have put it to use in spewing forth his own putrid thoughts. Thus we would have been spared entirely the necessity of listening to his confused philosophizing! Not only that, but in all probability, this whole deep philosophy of the "superman" would not have developed in his mind in the first place, had it not been first invented for their own benefit and profit by the leaders of that land where militarism was born, Germany, by whose general atmosphere our philosopher was influenced. For it is clear that the leaders of his land are really the ones who caused the birth of such great wisdom as this within him.

But let us return to the matter at hand. The scorn of this confused philosopher should in no way intimidate us, the weak, from raising on high the banner of justice, especially since our turning away from it will, even according to our philosopher, do the idea of justice incalculable harm. For if the weak acknowledge that might makes right, if the smitten kiss the rod of their smiter, what more can the violent and mighty themselves do?

Behold, it finally it falls upon us alone—upon us, at once masters and slaves: masters of the inspiration of Torah in the theory of righteousness and the practice of justice, and slaves in chastisements and affliction—to proclaim and proclaim again, never tiring and never ceasing, the urgent need and aspiration for universal justice. Even if the ideas of "nationalism" and "terror" had already conquered the hearts of all the nations, even so it would be incumbent upon "the people of the book, a nation driven and plucked," that nation most expert in matters of justice and compassion, to withhold its assent. So long as that people dissents, the power of evil cannot be fixed and permanent. Moreover, as is well known, neither have all the righteous perished from among the nations; there are still many many precious human beings everywhere who have not gone astray after other gods, and who will have nothing whatsoever to do with that abstract and deceitful name, "nation," but only with the individual human being having the breath of life in his nostrils, living and experiencing and knowing suffering and indignity. These spit with disdain of soul upon these new concepts which the latter day terrorists have invented to destroy the rights of the individual human being!

Especially in our land, Russia, where due to the peaceful and quiet nature of the Russian people in general[79] and the nature of the government of the land in particular, there is one power maintained above all parties and factions, a power which maintains all the residents of the land in a state of equality beneath its wing. National jealousies cannot very easily develop here, nor can nationalist parties engage in the kinds of struggles and ugly maneuverings that have plagued Western Europe recently. If there be any hope for the restoration of the honor and glory of humanity in Europe, it will proceed from the saintly ones among the Russian people, for only from among this people will there blossom forth the opposition to the reaction that has gripped the nations of Western Europe. This nation that is, at present, last in the progress of its civilization, and which is advancing but very slowly, will in the end establish a civilization upon a proper foundation, so that what is achieved may be maintained and preserved. It will be this rearward of the nations which will, in the end, restore to the other nations of Europe those things that they lost in their all too rapid strides. It is an urgent and sacred duty, therefore, upon every Jew in our land—a duty whose fruits will be enjoyed immediately by us and whose lasting benefits will accrue to all the inhabitants of the world in days to come—to join with

---

[79] Cf. similar sentiments in Nicholas Berdyaev's writings.

all our Russian neighbors who are well-intentioned, and to be at one with them in striving to spread justice and peace among all the inhabitants of our land. Our influence in this endeavor, as will be explained below, is no small matter.

But to our great sorrow, what actually are our successful young people doing, our congregation of mocking youth? All the day long they sit "making cakes for the queen of divisiveness and enmity" with their flood of stanzas about "nationalism, nationalism." These they inflict upon the world, and when they further open their mouths, they declare the vile great, and cast dust upon every aspiration for justice and equality. Toward this end they have even formed an actual society for the advancement of false prophecy, and have removed themselves from all other activities, so that they are actively concerned with only one end: to plant within every heart the pure faith in the permanence of national hatred, and the conviction that the abomination of "nationalism," the rivalries of different tongues, and all the other afflictions of humankind, are lasting, permanent, here to stay, never to be overcome. Therefore the only solution for the Jews is to seek shelter beneath the wings of the newest idol, called "Jewish nationalism," and so set idol against idol, defending themselves against the strange abominations of others by their own insane abomination.

We have already explained at length how tragic it is that refrains such as these, which corrupt and befoul the air of the world, should come from members of "a people driven and plucked." How painfully one must sigh at the bitter irony of this present confusion and upset. One finds the good and decent people among the stronger nations trying to reassure the weak and oppressed, and dry their tears with kindness and consolations in words such as these: "It will be only a short while until such hatreds pass, and wickedness shall disappear as smoke." In reply, our weak and plucked and crushed spread dung upon the faces of their counselors, saying, "You can save your vain consolations; we know better. Wickedness will live forever and ever, and therefore we present you with idol against idol, fist against fist, and so you shall know and see our displeasure!"

The doctors of the West, who were originally assimilationist, but who now dedicate their efforts to building their own private political platform, and who have become leaders in the Zionist movement, indeed tell us at length, as experienced eyewitnesses, that assimilation cannot succeed for Jews. They have tried it and have found that "Karl" or "Friedrich" refused it, and that apparently the latter are not so keen on the idea. Therefore, they tell us, "as true lovers of the Jewish people we have found it advisable to establish for it a nationalist platform of its own Jewish politics. We come to you with a double warning. Be very careful to avoid any further movement in the direction of mingling or assimilation. For you will certainly get no praise or respect from von Hammersteins. Therefore, abide here with us in our "nationalist" shelter which we have founded for you, and you and we shall know goodness all our days." This dire threat has become current on the lips of every man and woman within the pale of settlement, thanks to the "shekel" agitators and "National Fund" workers, who have found its sound most helpful in collecting funds. So when "Itzik Vozilischki," the poor peddler, returns to town from the villages—where he has been mingling with the non-Jews in completely assimilated fashion, trading with them, exchanging matches for old clothing, and at times even eating baked potatoes with them, which they especially prepare for him in a properly heated and cleansed oven—and goes to the House of Study, there he hears the preacher describing the shameful things that have happened to his big brothers there in Paris and Berlin. When he hears that one of them wanted to become a regimental officer in the cavalry, and the head staff refused permission; that another, when he visited the "club" and asked the daughter of a lieutenant-general to attend a dance with him, she simply shoved him aside; immediately Itzik's sympathies are aroused for them. Knowing that the wheel turns in this world, and that there is no guarantee that this same thing might not happen to him tomorrow at the hands of the lieutenant-general, he immediately fishes in his purse (made of a small scrap of linen), draws out his few prutos, and hands them to the "collector" to help his brothers a little in their injured pride.

Thus proceeds our new "nationalist" campaign, both in print and in communities, sustaining itself by belaboring "assimilation," that which the priests of the new idolatrous "nationalism" point to all the day long in communities such as "Vozilizchki." "Be sure to realize, you Jews of Vozilizchak, that you cannot depend on 'assimilation;' you have no alternative, therefore, except to bow down before the idol of 'nationalism.'"

These worthy lords, however, confuse two distinct concepts, "equality" and "assimilation," hoping thereby to mislead the popular mind. They conspire to slay the aspiration for justice, equality, and the recognition of human rights—the dangerous enemy of their beloved "nationalism"—by fraud and misrepresentation. They try to pass off "assimilation" as striving for equality, whereas in actuality it is the true accomplice of the "new nationalism." The priests of this new nationalism hope thereby to gain automatic support for their cause from the rejection of "assimilation" (actually its sister), and continue to vilify the striving for equality, which is itself as far removed from both assimilation and the new nationalism as is truth from falsehood.

It is true that as a reliable support for the Jews, "assimilation" is weak, a staff of a bruised reed. But this is not to say that "nationalism" is any blessing either. In fact, it suggests that "nationalism," as desired by our new leaders, is itself a curse. For do you know why, really, the "assimilationists" were kicked off the platform in great disgrace? Because the assimilationists were not aspiring to justice, because they were not striving to make widely known and accepted the justice of the weak and persecuted! They aspired only to stand in the place of "the great," in the place of the Junkers,[80] and to be persecutors with them. Is it not logical that the humble poor man who longs to be a Junker, and who forces his way into the Junker office to ask pity on himself in these words, "I beseech you, oh Junkers, compassionate sons of compassionate fathers, be gracious and merciful to a pitiful man who longs to stand on a par with you, and be so kind as to bestow some of your glory upon him!"—is it not utterly reasonable that, as a reply to his request, he receive a good and proper Junker slap across the cheek together with these words: "Beggar, you are overcome by the desire to be a Junker, and so by your own admission accept the Junker way? Here, then, is a small Junker sample of what one of the lower class, such as yourself, can expect in the way of treatment at the hands of the Junkers whenever he be forced to stand in their province!"

After being scornfully driven away from there, without having satisfied their own desires for themselves to be Junkers, what did the more clever of those assimilationists do? They returned to their people and began to clamor among themselves, "Nationalism, Nationalism, Nationalist Organization!" in order to get their fellow Jews into their own clutches and become Junkers in their own house. This is the true explanation of the condemnation which our nationalist lords in unison heap upon the assimilation facing us. They have come to entice us to accept upon ourselves their nationalist rule, and are in effect saying this to us: "We really are deserving of your accepting upon yourselves the yoke of our Junkerism, in appreciation for the curses which we launch against assimilation, and in recognition of the great love we have shown you in leaving the ranks of others and coming here to be Junkers over you." For it would appear that the worthies vowed solemnly to manage, somehow, to be among those who ride upon the backs of their fellow humans, either by riding upon the strong, healthy backs of "Karl" or "Michte," or at least by riding upon the scrawny backs of "Israeliks," should other riders of "Karl" and "Michte," already firmly planted, toss them over their shoulders and drive them away.[81]

---

[80] Junkers were the land-owning aristocracy of Prussia and Germany. Tamares regularly uses the term to designate a militaristic, exploitive ruling class.
[81] The full force of Tamares' astute analysis of the oppressive-exploitive elations among the subjects of these authoritarian regimes is fully developed in Chapter

After this analysis, it seems to me that our eyes should be opened somewhat to the deceptive act which has been presented before us for some six years, an act in which two travelling sisters, identical twins named "assimilation" and "nationalism," have made a great display of belligerence, with the latter cursing, spurning, and scratching her sister, "assimilation," mercilessly before our very eyes, that by virtue of this we should be willing to accept the quarrelling which she brings into our midst.

After these words it is possible to recognize the true worth of the nationalist answer to our people, the answer that permits our nationalist lords to glorify themselves over the people, and also to recognize whom they really intend to benefit by it, the people or themselves. More precisely: the Jewish sentiment within them or the ruling sentiment with them? Their Jewish sentiments or their sovereignty sentiments?

What does it benefit the Jewish community to be associated with the evil group that purveys such solutions? It is for the Jewish community to reply to them as follows: Go to hell, both with your assimilation and with your new nationalism. All this devilish fussing of yours about assimilation and nationalism is of concern only to those who aspire to become Junkers or who have the souls of Junkers; but for the masses of the house of Israel, no good can come of it. Furthermore, Junkerism is in no way whatsoever the mission of Israel.

The mission of Israel is both to await, and to help bring about by its great influence, the coming of that happy time when the right to a secure life will not belong only to Junkers, but will belong equally to all humans, whether Junker or not. More exactly, when the recognition will be fixed in the hearts of all that Junkerism does not depend upon princely garb or a sword fastened upon the loins, but rather that every one created in the image of God who knows how to respect others created in the image of God, is to be regarded as a Junker. For two thousand years our bruised and persecuted people has carried in its arms the Torah, the Divine echo of world morality and justice, and has suffered much on its behalf. It has not suffered this in order to achieve, at last, the happy moment of sneaking into a Junker coat for half an hour, to taste thereby the flavor of going about with neck outstretched, and the sword beneath the coat rattling on the pavement to proclaim: Clear ye the way for the flaming Jewish sword which revolves around assimilation and nationalism.

In short, it is for the Jewish community to proclaim clearly:

Five of *The Commjnity of Israel and the Wars of the Nations*, "The Freedom of Torah and the Arrogance of the Sword," on page 162.

"I have put off my coat;
how shall I put it on?
I have washed my feet;
how shall I defile them?"
—Song of Songs 5:3

Now that the bow of our might and our political arm has been broken these two thousand years, and we have already arranged our way of life in order to exist without a Jewish state; now that our people has already suffered political demise, and the soul of our people has already been privileged to shed the gross body of political pageantry and the burden of kings and officers, yet still fly about in the land of the living, even after the removal of the political body, to live the spiritual life without the gross needs of the flesh; now that our people has already been privileged to present before the world the great vision, that it is possible for a spiritual people, lacking all the material trappings of a nation, to outlive by far those people that have at their disposal material might and power: how, then, shall an eternal people such as this, purified now these two thousand years of the bodily dross, want to return and begin all over again, like those nations that suffer process and change, to return and again embody itself in the gross matter of "statehood," with all its politics and its host of intrigues, thereby staking its existence on a perishing entity, on dust that vanishes?

Now that our people has already been tried in the crucible of affliction these two thousand years, and has suffered in every possible way, including blows at the hands of the hoary political teraphim of others; how, then, shall we not receive instruction, so that our hearts cease panting for those idols of terror which the grosser nations exalt? How can it be so easy for us to dismiss our chastisements, and the blood of our wounds that has been flowing for so long? Shall we regard the blood as ownerless water spilled upon the ground, and neglect the wounds completely, without so much as raising them as an ethical example before all the peoples of the world, that their hearts may know some compassion, and so come to reject their idols of terror, and that all of them may come to bow before the God of justice and mercy?

How shall it be so insignificant in our own eyes to permit the blood of our wounds to resemble the blood of a beast of prey which was stricken and wounded because of its wayward scheming, and which, upon being cured slightly from the blows, hastens back to its work of clawing, roaring loudly after prey in every street?

No, and again no! We neither want, nor will we accept, any consolations or cures that are "political," "territorial," etc., etc. We want none of these cures that are defined in the dictionary of the masters of teraphim and sorcery. These are prescriptions that, apart from their everlasting vanity and worthlessness that is well known to every one of the initiated, have also this feature: they convert into vanity and nothingness all the blows and bruises that we have suffered until now, retroactively reducing all of that to naught, without rationale. Like a beaten dog have we suffered until now! Therefore we utterly despise, and reject, prescriptions such as these that come to dismiss our chastisements and the suffering of our Exile, that come to make us lowly in hindsight, and which claim that for two thousand years we were driven about, lowly and without a country or government, before finally being privileged to gain one small piece of "territory" by great imploring and pleading. Should this be cause for delirium and enthusiasm, that at long last we are privileged to become the smallest of the small among them? This passes all bounds of absurdity!

Our sole cure and consolation is the purification and cleansing that we received in the crucible of affliction, and the spirit of humility, the spirit of "the great morality" that the Exile planted within us. This spirit is, indeed, worthy of being held tightly by us. Never to be let go, it is a treasure worth all wealth; it must accompany us in all our ways, as a perpetual lamp unto our feet. Even when we go to seek relief for our oppressed condition, we must seek only a cure for our bent statures, not for our bent spirits. We must seek to make our backs tall, not our hearts lofty. In simple words, this is the desire not to be trampled on, the desire for equality and the recognition of human rights, not the aspiration to be aggressors included in the aspiration to sovereignty. The aspiration for equality will not be found either in assimilation or in nationalism, nor in any of the other hellish deceptions of our day, for all of them have as their goal the denial and burial of the rights of individual human beings, and the handing over of the individual person as ransom for the fraudulent concepts. The genuine striving for equality will be found only in justice and uprightness, in the recognition of the rights of humans simply because they are human. In this striving for justice, there is no need for us either to thrust ourselves into the midst of alien, idolatrous worlds, as assimilationism urges, or to drag these alien idols into our own world, as nationalism urges. For the striving for justice and compassion is "very nigh unto us, in our mouths and in our hearts, that we may do them" (cf. Deuteronomy 30:14). These are found in our Sacred Literature, the glorious champion of justice and righteousness, which we teach diligently, and in the crucible of suffering and the affliction of the Exile, which softened our hearts and planted in us feelings of compassion for, and participation in, the sufferings of others.

It therefore falls upon us to sit in our place, within our house, to cling steadfastly to the fortress of our Sacred Literature, the mighty defender of justice, and to aspire toward, and actively strive for, the spreading of justice until it becomes the possession and inheritance of the entire world. From this there comes a powerful rejoinder against those empty ones, who deny the Jewish people any further mission in the world by arguing that our one mission, to spread the knowledge of "the Oneness of the Creator," has already been fulfilled. This idea, they say, is now the property of the entire civilized world; our mission is now completed, and the time has come for us to step off the stage. The foolishness of those who assert this consists in their seemingly not knowing that "not the teaching but the deed is primary."

What value is there in the idea of "Unity" having penetrated the minds of many of the nations if, as with the well-contented, sleek, and satisfied, the Divine illumination has not penetrated their hearts, which still remain full of oppression and haughtiness? What value is it that all the mighty of the world build great temples "unto the heights," where they bow the knees, and lowly bend before the God of heaven, if their bowing is not for the purpose of humbling themselves, to recognize the sovereignty and power of the God of Heaven, so that their hearts not be lifted haughtily above their brothers and sisters? If all this be but for the purpose of humbling others, to magnify their own awesomeness and glory by appearing before the congregation as appointed representatives of heaven, of what value is it? In addressing the lack of a contrite spirit and a heart of flesh, a feeling heart, there remains much, indeed, for the well-contented and well-fed nations—who busy themselves meeting and making covenants with God in great temples overlaid with silver and gold—to learn from that "people driven and plucked." Because of the threat of death by the wrath of the oppressor, that people still must greet its Father in heaven, and arrange its Passover seders, in holes in the earth and in caves.

It falls upon us, then, to sit in our house, knowing clearly that our table is greater than the table of the worshippers of teraphim, that our crown is greater than their crown, with full trust and confidence that in the final end, our culture—the culture of the people of the book, "a people driven and plucked"—will vanquish all the Edomite cultures. Cruelty will melt before compassion, the mighty will don garments of shame before the consecration of the Kingdom of Righteousness. Then happy and well shall it be for us, and happy and well for all the world.

Part III

On War

Introduction to
The Community of Israel and The Wars of Nations

"A Jewish pacifist? Isn't that an oxymoron?" This common reaction is understandable even as it requires correction. The foundational text of Judaism after all is the Hebrew Scriptures whose varied contents include a number of battle hymns and celebrations of armed triumph. Especially well known are The Song at the Sea (Exodus, Chapter 15) and Song of Deborah (Judges, Chapter 5). Add to these numerous reports of armed clashes, throughout the Pentateuch and the Historical Books.

At the same time we also find in this Foundational Literature unsurpassed visions of peace:

> Nation shall not lift up sword against nation,
> Neither shall they learn war anymore.
> (Isaiah, 2:4)

> They shall not hurt nor destroy
> In all my Holy Mountain;
> For the earth shall be full of the knowledge of the Lord,
> As the waters cover the sea."
> (Isaiah,11:9)

> Not by might, nor by violence,
> but by My spirit, saith the Lord of hosts.
> (Zechariah, 4:6).

These and numerous other citations are also the Jewish Heritage from its most sacred texts.

How shall these various texts be interpreted? Which shall be emphasized? No religious tradition is static or fixed in its fundamentals; all evolve as life develops and adaptations and fresh understandings emerge. It is important to remember that basic Jewish texts such as Mishnah, Talmud, Midrash and others through the centuries also play a vital role in lived Jewish religious life. Quite remarkable for example are various Rabbinic interpretations of the triumphal Song at the Sea that convert the simple warlike meaning of the text to advocacy for a peaceful approach to existence.

It is not only Jewish tradition that displays such interpretation and development. Gandhi represents quite a striking example of this within Hinduism. If one reads Chapter 1 of Gandhi's most cherished pacifist text, the Bhagavad-Gita, one is in for a surprise. Here the God Krishna, embodied as Arjuna's charioteer, gives a surprising reply to Arjuna's misgivings and hesitations to kill in battle his own relatives. Krishna sternly responds by saying, Arjuna, you are a member of the warrior caste and it is your duty to wage battle irrespective of the persons you slay. Arjuna places this within the framework of, "the eternal cannot be slain, and that which is slain is merely temporal." In other words slay in good conscience.

By what interpretive means does Gandhi convert this to a pacifist doctrine? It is a question that deserves exploration parallel with the interpretive techniques of the Rabbis in converting the Song at the Sea to a celebration of peaceful means of conflict. At this point, we merely note that religious traditions adapt, evolve, and articulate fresh insights as they are lived and experienced in the world.

In short, to designate Rabbi Aaron Samuel Tamares as "A Jewish Pacifist" is not at all an oxymoron, but rather a recognition of this powerful peaceable current within the living stream we call Judaism. This is clearly manifest in this author's introductory remarks to Tamares' excerpts published in *Judaism Magazine* in Winter 1963 and Spring 1968. Stephen L. Weinstein also emphasizes Tamares' "ardent belief in pacifism" in his introduction to his exploration of Tamares' view of galut, exilt, in *Jewish Quarterly*, Vol. 76, No.2, Summer 1978.

What were the circumstances that contributed to Tamares' pacifism? We have his own testimony to the devastating pain of war that made an early and profound impression upon him. In his autobiographical sketch, he reports feeling deep kinship with the hopeless pain of a Polish neighbor, a mother whose adolescent son was killed in the Russo-Turkish War of 1877. Tamares, a sensitive eight-year-old, identified with the mother's inconsolable pain, and reports that this image was vivid for him throughout his life.

In his earlier Essay on Liberty and Sermon on Liberty, the passion of Tamares' denunciation of war and its minded, mechanical, passionless mass murder, was fueled by a keen sense of intimate personal loss and bereavement. At the time of those essays, World War I was a theoretical anticipation, not an accomplished atrocity. Even then, Tamares' language had a personal dimension while describing what we might call system issues. In this current monograph, the Community of Israel and The Wars of the Nations, Tamares now struggles to understand how such a calamity did occur. Remarkable is Tamares' employment of some profound Jewish concepts such as The Exile of the Presence, the accompanying Presence of the Exile, The Wars of Gog and Magog, and the Concept of the Messiah to illuminate and deepen our comprehension of surrounding political events. In comparing "The Freedom of Torah" with "The Arrogance of the Sword" Tamares actually engages in very subtle social analysis of what effective freedom means, and the social atmosphere necessary for its achievement. In discussing various freedom movements of his age, Tamares asserts explicitly the importance of self-awareness and self-recognition to the achievement of true freedom. Never is the individual human being—flesh, blood, feeling and spirit—absent from his frame of reference. Reading his essay of nearly a century ago, many a statement can illuminate some of our contemporary social struggles.

A striking example of this is his interpretation of the Rabbinic statement "If you have seen the kingdoms engaging in strife, look for the footsteps of the Messiah in the wake" (Bereshit Rabbah 42:4). By "Messiah" Tamares understands "a term for the redemption or liberation of the spirit of humankind for the expansion of ethical awareness and the knowledge of God in the world." Tamares associates this with Isaiah's vision, "nation shall not lift up sword against nation" and "the whole earth shall be filled with the knowledge of God." He then contrasts the peaceable, non-territorial life of the Community of Israel with the destructive violence of nations armed and at war, and suggests that in assessing the insupportable damage of increasingly destructive warfare, nations will of necessity look for alternatives to the present national sovereignties, with their accumulating record of belligerent atrocities.

Now it is also illuminating to read Tamares in relation to some contemporary issues. Reading Chapter 3 of this book while also reading "The Lost Menagerie" and "The African Paradox" in Alan Weisman's *The World Without Us* is fascinating. Here is Weisman portraying the lethal effects of humans on their surroundings and themselves, and here is Tamares struggling to understand the complex interplay of destructive anger and compassionate sympathy within individual human beings. Add to this the image of this shtetl rov heading each day to the Southern stretches of the Bielewieza Primeval Forest, and there pondering Rabbinic interpretations of Messiah and Wars of Gog and Magog. Facile assumptions of divisions between classic texts and natural surroundings are quickly demolished by this experience. Time and again I am startled by how totally contemporary Tamares feels, at the same time being distinctly a resident of a different time and space.

Tamares' deep appreciation of God's Presence within the conditions of the Exile is touchingly expressed in Chapter 4. After portraying a best-case experience of the Divine Presence, Tamares daringly argues that Exile should not be understood primarily as punishment but rather as purification. He itemizes the ways in which land, government, authority and officialdom reduce the Divine Spirit to routinized, formal ceremonies on state occasions. For Tamares, liberation from territory includes liberation of Spirit; his argument and examples are both subtle and substantial.

The perceptiveness of Tamares' analysis is keenly evident in his nuanced characterization of inner freedom, external compliance and hierarchy versus equality within human society in Chapter 5, "The Freedom of Torah and the Arrogance of the Sword."

Chapter 6, "The World Mission of Israel and Its Distinctive Identity," is a fervent affirmation of Israel's responsibilities to the world at large. The fulfillment of this responsibility requires primary attention and focus on perfecting the quality of life within the dedicated community. The purpose of this quality of life within the community is to show that human dignity and personal fulfillment are not ultimately dependent on political power exercised over geographical territory.

The summary of Chapter 7, "The Land of Israel," defines the relation of Jews to the historic Land of Israel from this perspective. It is again a distinct challenge to the common understanding of this relationship. This will be further expanded in Tamares' last published work, *Three Unsuitable Unions*.

The Community of Israel and The Wars of the Nations addresses the question of individual participation in war quite differently from many of the writings in the United States during the Viet Nam War. In both cases, there is an argument from tradition prohibiting the employment of destructive violence on the scale of modern warfare. In the United States, the focus was individual conscience against a system of national conscription. Tamares is contemplating the function of a dedicated community in the midst of national conflict.

Is Tamares, then, a "pacifist"? Exact definitions of this term would take us far afield. Instead, let us register the fact that Tamares articulates a powerful support for radical Jewish advocacy of non-violent means for securing human values. This is especially manifest in his remarkable essay on Passover and nonviolence, "A Sermon on Liberty."

In this general context of alternative approaches to questions of individual participation in organized warfare, Daniel Weiss' "Just Peacemaking and Ethical Formation in Classical Rabbinic Literature"[82] is another compelling challenge to our accustomed categories of thinking about this issue.

On a personal note, at the time of my rabbinic ordination in 1957, when I was struggling with the question of serving two years in the military chaplaincy or two years of alternative service during the Korean "police action," Tamares was a valued guide and a cherished companion.

---

[82] *Journal of the Society of Christian Ethics*, 32.2, Fall/Winter 2016, pp. 23-38

The Community of Israel and The Wars of the Nations (1918)

Foreword

> "Woe unto those creatures who see,
> but know not what they see."
> (Talmud Hagigah 12b)

It is the duty of every man of intelligence to inspect searchingly the events of the world, and to extract from them correct conclusions. What event in our world impresses itself so mightily upon us as the phenomenon of war? And what war was so severe as the last war? There is nothing comparable, therefore, to the value of the lesson to be gotten from it.

How astonishing, then, to see that this terrible contemporary period—which among various rulers of the world gave birth to pride, courage, and effrontery, thus enabling them to assume the responsibilities and terrors of offensive after offensive, of slaughter upon slaughter, of the Sodom-like devastation of region after region, for four consecutive years!—despite all this begot no mighty expression of judgment, no thorough evaluation by anyone of these deeds, and no correct conclusion or logical inference from these happenings!

With what was that half of mankind which remained at home concerned, while the other half, deranged, went forth to take cover in the thickness of the earth, from there to cast forth torrents of destructive, ruinous fire? And how does it respond to—that is to say, evaluate—this phenomenon?

"How does it respond?" As our eyes weary themselves with the pages of the newspapers, or our ears with the conversation of any group discussing world affairs, to our great shame it becomes obvious how banal and petty are the judgments issued on the subject of the wondrous deeds of devastation performed there on a field by Asmodeus.

It is needless to remark how utterly superficial is the opinion common among the narrow-minded, that German militarism bears the full guilt for the war—as though Allied Powers were engaged in writing tefillin at the time that the Germans were preparing for war!! Yet similarly superficial and insubstantial are the opinions even of those keenest to see the corruption surrounding the ideals of the Allies. For this they share: both seek to assign the responsibility for the war to one or the other of the belligerents, without realizing that by assigning the blame to this or that "side" they justify the war as such and strengthen its fever.

This, then, is the "thoughtful judgment" of the homebodies on the events of our time.

And what are the actions and deeds of this non-participating half, at the hour when the others are dying in parched holes and trenches? There is naught to say concerning the activities of those gross individuals whose souls are of coin, manipulators of the market, who at the very hour sit making millions with great pleasure. But even those socially concerned groups and parties which occupy themselves with social ideals, and which of late have regained some life after the shock which came upon them at the outbreak of the war—go forth to see, what spirit reigns among them? Every one of them eagerly resumes mouthing with gusto his ancient hymns and slogans, without any revisions in the wake of the happenings in the world; without, as it seems, their having learned anything at all from those terrible events, except this: now every one of them views with enmity the building of idealism from "the war to make men free." (In this respect they are exactly like the monarchist parties, who within the subjugated nations bide their time waiting for complete world confusion in order, as is their one dream, to build from it, and crown from among themselves a king to saddle upon their brothers.) Even the social-democratic parties have this as their one complaint against this war, that it has benefited only the bourgeoisie, and so they urge their fellow proletarians to deflect to their side the benefits.

In short, this entire half of mankind resembles a vulture hovering about carrion. For as the one half of mankind went forth to wrestle with the bitterness of death in holes in the ground—just so the other half, remaining in its houses seated around its well-filled tables, drew forth from those very cellars of death its food and drink. From its material portion there spreads the odor of carrion; and from its spiritual sustenance—the scent of the angel of death.

To complete this heartening picture, a picture of corruption of thought revealed by those whose connection with the war is not one of purity, must be added the stupidity of thought and feeling on the part of those who relate to it not at all. The relation of those who see with the eyes of a calf the world of the Holy One, Blessed be He, and its terrible events—they neither see nor feel anything whatsoever of the events around them. This is the relation of the "public" which fills theatres to capacity and splits its guts laughing at "hanky-panky," so widespread of late, or of the young people who of late fill the papers with their "congratulations" on the "engagements" of their cousins, trying to outdo one another in the extravagance of expression about "the blossoms" which they will strew along "life's path" for "the beloved"—of those designated to serve as fresh cannon fodder for the world in a few years, and who in the more immediate future are candidates for "children begging bread, and not a crust for them."

The Talmudic portrayal in the legends of destruction of the Temple—"One half fought three days and nights, the other laughed and sang, and neither knew of the other"—this, it seems, is the prototype of all wars among all peoples at all times. A portrait which has enclosed in it the secret of war: for if those who continue to celebrate, who with their equestrian neighing continue that senseless "life as normal," if their senses were not obstructed and closed, the other half could not go forth to the activities of its "normal way of life"—murder and killing.

But this behavior at the time of war, this benefit which accrues to every nation, this "normal" way of life as it were, and because of which war itself is seen as normal—this which was at one time also regarded as the desirable and normal way of life for our nation, is no longer at all desired by our people now in exile.

To our satisfaction it may be asserted that the aforementioned normalcy pattern is for us an imitation of the outside and that within the depths of every Jew there is a different attitude, an intelligent and ethical approach to the events of the world.

To give expression to this relation in print, to publish in the world the true Jewish position concerning the happenings in the world, which is also the truly neutral position—a position which illuminates the duplicity of politics, not from the point of view of other political deceits, but from the viewpoint of the Bible, the wisdom of mankind and the sense of its exalted mission—to proclaim this message to the world is the sacred task of every Jewish writer at this time.

I trust that, with the help of the Lord, in this present book I shall make a beginning for those who come after me in the completing of the task.

THE AUTHOR

(With the help of the Lord,
the month of Elul,
the year, 1918)

Chapter One

Theories of War

1.

The opinions and judgments of mankind concerning war have differed from generation to generation. In early times, when mystery held sway, war too was judged and assessed in terms of mystery. The entire nation, from one extreme to the other, knew "clearly" that "war was ordained by heaven." Its appointment, its purpose, and its proclamation were all decreed in the heavens, as was likewise the place of its occurrence. All the movements and campaigns of the armies here in the world below—all the ragings of the camps of the earthly kings, all the savage assaults here on earth by sisters behaving like beasts of prey—these were no more than the echo of fights occurring simultaneously among the hosts of the heavens, among the patron-angels of each king in the heavens above. And upon the very face of the firmament, evident to the masses of men through comets and eclipses of the sun and moon, were obvious signs and omens of the events to take place at the time of war.

This supernatural assessment of war was a valuable refuge for the war makers—the ruling classes and their attendants who officiated at these deeds of human slaughter—who could take shelter in it from the rage and anger of those led to the slaughter. It gave free reign to the vile intrigues of the destroyers of the world. This supernatural explanation was therefore exceedingly dangerous to the peace of the world.

In later generations, when reason grew stronger, and men began soberly to inspect the events of the world, the supernatural assessment ceased having so many disciples among the mass of men. In its place came the naturalistic, realistic theory, which said that war was the expression of hostility, of mutual enmity between different races and peoples, which took shape in their hearts, and from time to time, when the accumulation was too great, necessarily burst forth.

These naturalistic theories of the "enlightened" generation are not one bit better than the supernaturalistic theory of earlier generations, for this assessment too serves to conceal the principal perpetrators of war. When the blame is put on "the whole," one loses sight of the specifically and immediately responsible. Not only that, but this explanation, like the previous, denies completely the rule of the sin and stubbornness of different men—the manufacturers of its implements and the leaders of its campaigns—and makes of war a decreed necessity. Only thus does it differ from the earlier theory: one sees war as "decreed by heaven," the other as "decreed by nature."

So far as it concerns the success of the despotic individuals who send tens of thousands of men to their destiny, there is no difference if the material of their mask of "it is decreed" (with which they cover their faces) be taken from the "decree of heaven" or the "decree of nature."

So far as it affects the decay of the moral sense among men, I suspect that the materialistic theory of the "enlightened" generation does far more than the supernaturalistic theory of the "savage" generation. For the minds of the latter, despite their primitiveness, could not accept the horrible vision of war as a natural happening, and had to seek fantastic explanations, while the former, "intelligent" men, can understand the cruelty of war and all the rest of its abominations in a simple and natural way.

2.

Besides the aforementioned theories, the supernaturalistic and the naturalistic, share this characteristic: both assist the Demon of War—one unwittingly, the other almost by intention. Besides these two there is one further realistic theory which does try to trace the steps of the Devil of War in order to annihilate him. This is the theory of the social-democratic parties, which assert that in every war the blame rests solely upon the small class of the privileged which holds the reins of the people and rides upon its back. These masters are they who, with their political intrigues, kindle the fire of war; and they are the very ones to whom war brings agreeable results. To remove this malignant sore one must change entirely the social order so that there will be no upper and lower classes, no riders or bearers of the burden; or at least one must put bits in the jaws of the riders to limit somewhat their reign over those who carry. In that way, if the latter are put once again in the hands of the former, they will be delivered only for servitude and suffering, not for dying.

This evaluation of war surely contains much truth and justice, both in its analysis of the cause of war and in its proposals for the extirpation of war. For true it is that the principal culprits in wars are found among the ruling classes, who entice and incite the masses in their armies to assault the masses in the armies of the other countries. Even so, that mass which permits itself to be enticed and incited like the mad watchdogs of a despot is responsible for its own corruption and will not be forgiven its offense. For even real dogs, those which walk about on all fours, when incited by their masters to attack someone, will be greeted by the latter, and rightly so, with a clout on the head, and not with a blessing in tribute to their selfless obedience to the commands of their masters! For however much the ugly clay of war may be imbedded in the hearts of the "people" itself, yet those who busy themselves with this "pretty" material and moisten it, shaping it and making it ready for its goal and even bringing it to full activity—surely these are none other than "the ruling classes." Therefore it is undoubtedly very necessary to limit the power of these rulers over the people so that the latter be not delivered into their hands, like clay into the hand of the potter, for any folly or perversion which the hearts of the leaders may desire. By this the possibility of the evil of actual war would be greatly limited.

If it seems man's destiny that evil instincts will rule over him for yet many days to come—until that time when from on high shall pour forth the longed-for sprit of purity—at least let this evil in him express itself in a direct and natural way: at the desire and initiative of each individual in accordance with his own needs, and not by that contemptible and humiliating process of turning men into wild dogs who both dance and hate at the behest of their masters. At one moment the Englishman has no quarrel with the Austrian nor the Austrian with the Englishman; suddenly the order goes forth from the rulers to hate and attack, and the "subjects of state," the lowliest of creatures, suddenly are "filled with hatred" and attack and assault one another with great fury as each soldier tries to outdo the other in the intensity of his savagery, at the same time constantly glancing backwards to make sure that his commander and inciter sees properly his diligence.

The disgrace of this shameful image, this image of beastliness, must surely be removed from mankind, so that mankind may at least assume its natural image if it is not yet able to attain its Godly likeness.

In short, this last theory of war, the democratic, is serious in intent and offers desirable proposals for preventing the evil of war. However, it fails to abolish war at its root, and the basic cure for the malady of the world (as we shall explain further on) is not to be found in this theory either.

Chapter Two

Dreams of the "Messiah"

1.

One wintry evening, seated at a table in a corner of the academy of a small Lithuanian town, there in the semi-darkness held at bay only by the light of a small candle are to be found "Abraham the merchant" and "Joseph the baker." Before them on the table are two open Gemarahs. Yet it appears that they are not studying them, but rather are talking softly one with the other.

For now many years these two companions, night after night at this hour by this table, have met to study together with dedicated enthusiasm their set portions of the Gemarah. From this wonderful spiritual fount of the Jewish people they have drawn forth the consolations of God for all the discriminations and persecutions imposed upon them, and renewed and added to daily, by their persecutors, as well as for their many woes in earning their livelihoods, those parched "Jewish occupations," vexing all the day long. Within this purifying well they would each evening immerse and cleanse themselves also of the moral impurities of the commerce in which they necessarily engaged by day, but from which there accumulated within the depths of their "Jewish soul" much pain. Why, then, on this evening are their joyous voices silenced? Why have they forsaken for now their source of life?

Yet not so! Ascribe not foreign thoughts to them. These boon companions have not left their blessed spring: the sacred surroundings in which they sit: the well-worn texts open before them, carriers of enchanting ancient glories, their very visages at this hour—all these are witnesses to the fact that their conversations do not encompass mere trivia or money matters, but that their whisperings rather concern sublime things which are related to the open volumes. These companions have not abandoned these wonderful tomes, but have this particular evening substituted for the usual halachic issues haggadic material whose source is here, confidential legends.

Alarming events have happened and are happening in the world. Nation rises up against nation, and kingdom against kingdom, and the earth is filled with blood and fire. These dismaying events—which may indeed bring to the spiritual sufferings of the persecuted Jew some small relief, in that now he suffers in the midst of a world of suffering (and not, as previously, in the midst of a world of joy)—have by the same token increased his material sufferings without measure.

Oppressed and agitated by the distress which reigns in their houses in the wake of many woes which have afflicted their families: the pain of a son gone to war, the misery of a daughter returning to her parental home a widow, the misery of her children who stretch forth their hands for bread which is not; confused and frightened also by the agitation of the silent air, which is transmitted minute by minute from the farthest horizon and which once conveyed only news of passers-by or workers in the field, but which this day (the echo of the firing of cannon from the battlefield) seizes the attention of those sitting on the stoops of their shops in the central market place, witnessing as it does to the ever-approaching destruction, and with it, for the Jews of the city, the certain threat of being uprooted from their places, once again to take the staff of the wanderer—oppressed and agitated by all these painful things, our aforementioned two friends this particular evening leave their sigh-filled homes to flee for a short while to their house of refuge, their sanctuary, to spend there a few minutes in the company of their ancient friends, Abaye and Raba.

Yet notice! They come to the house, sit down at the table, open the Gemarahs, and attempt an issue of halachah. But try as they may to focus their thoughts on "learning," they cannot.

Their minds cannot bear, this particular evening, the keen disputations of Abaye and Raba. Not only that, but their hearts as well find no comfort just now in mere learning. "Learning Gemarah" can bring rest to the oppressed soul of the Jew in ordinary times, since the daily limitations and pressures he suffers as a Jew are so familiar to him that he bears them with hardly any pain except for the spiritual suffering due to their humiliation. And from this insult to his honor the Jew can find full relief in the activity of studying Torah. The mere opening of the Gemarah delights the mind and restores the soul of the Jewish people, lifting and exalting it far above the insulters, so that the detractors themselves become laughable along with their insults. Even the material troubles seem worthwhile in its eyes; it will give all in payment for this, its inheritance.

But the same does not hold for these recent tribulations which are not merely Jewish but general. Wickedness and folly have exploded, a flood of fire consumes, and nations and kingdoms go forth to the blaze. The explosion is of such intensity that it seems like a cataclysmic upheaval in the regular flow and normal condition of nature. The earth cracks, it quakes and totters, for its sin is grievous. To find consolation for this world upheaval; to give rest to the excited heart at this moment, which is hardly a moment of pleasure—it is altogether impossible to delight the heart of the Jew at this hour by the study of a legal issue in the Gemarah, but only through seeking the key which will resolve the doubts and wonderings lodging in the heart, only by arriving at the depths of the contemporary phenomena which terrify the world and all in it.

It was these solutions that our friends began to seek after finding themselves unable to study an issue of law. But despite this they remained in their places, their Gemarahs open before them, for they knew in their hearts that in the atmosphere of this house of study with these books, more than in any other place, there would be kindled within them that light by whose illumination they might find the true solutions to these mysteries. There they sit whispering, these two friends, speaking softly to one another: that these wars are surely "the wars of God and Magog," and that one may see in them "the footsteps of the Messiah."

2.

Behold, dear reader, I have thus guided you to a place where you may hear a new evaluation of the alarming events now taking place in the world. As for you, if you be a modern man, please, be not too hasty in mockingly dismissing from consideration this evaluation, saying "these babblings about the 'Messiah,' heard in the academies in Jewish neighborhoods whenever wars break out in the world, are most absurd; they yield only foolishness and nonsense to those who engage in them, and cause loss and damage to the world at large. For is not also this theory supernatural? And the supernatural evaluations, as was mentioned above, only serve to strengthen the power of the Devil of War and to increase his might." Yet for all this please do not be overly hasty in dismissing the judgment of this simple pair of Jews; for they did not invent it out of their own imaginations; it was transmitted to them from the early sages—from our own Talmudic sages. "If you have seen the kingdoms engaging in strife, look for the footsteps of the Messiah in the wake" (Bereshit Rabbah 42:4).

This sublime and ancient judgment, from whose perspective we have viewed 2,000 years, had within, despite its mysterious appearance, a naturalistic-realistic content which we shall present now in summary, and in the succeeding chapters at length. This content is disclosed as if by intuition to the eyes of these men of intellect, who by clear and penetrating observation see the ethical striving and the esthetic aspiration which must be realized in the end, be it sooner or later.

For behold, the "Messiah" in the legends of our sages is a term for the redemption or liberation of the spirit of mankind, for the expansion of ethical awareness and the knowledge of God in the world! The "Messiah" of the sages is, in the common allegorical expression so typical of the rabbinic style, the continuation and fulfillment of the brilliant and unmistakable vision: "nation shall not lift up sword against nation," "the whole earth shall be filled with the knowledge of God." In the prophets this spreading of the knowledge of God upon the earth is, as we know, conditioned by a living organism, the Jewish people, which is designated for the event; from which we learn also that in the legends of the rabbis the meaning of the "expectation of the Messiah" is this: the anticipation of the exaltation of the honor of the Jewish people and the shining forth of its culture, the Jewish culture, in the world. The dictum "if you have seen the kingdoms engaging in strife, look for the Messiah in the wake" thus contains a very realistic point, namely: at the time when wars break out among the nations, then all the lowly instincts of the citizens will cast aside their bondage, the beast in their hearts will emerge bare and unveiled, and the absolute bankruptcy of the general culture will be revealed—then expect the approach of the Messiah, i.e., the exaltation of the Jewish culture.

The naturalism and realism of this judgment of the rabbis, as thus explained, not only has not been refuted or disproved by the many wars and the attacks of nation upon nation—which have been repeated periodically during all the centuries since the formulation of this judgment, and Messiah has not come—but ever becomes more verified and certain. It becomes more certain by the lengthy existence of the descendants of the formulators of this doctrine, the Jewish people, whose members perpetually witness nation swallowing nation and then disappearing, while they remain—they have been, are, and will continue to exist. "Nations come and nations go, but Israel stands forever" (Kohelet Rabbah)." It is logical that this nation, which has been a constant eye-witness to all the events which have transpired in the world, is also suited to judge them. And the legends common among its children which pertain to these events—it is logical that they receive consideration.

I cannot assure you with certainty whether the minds of this pair of simple Jews, solvers of the riddles of the world, have grasped clearly the realistic content of the legends they recite or only the supernatural shell of the words; for they are simple Jews, accustomed to accept at face value the dicta of the rabbis, without seeking from them too many ideas. But even so, one may not dismiss the essence of their whispered conversation, the whisperings of small, simple children of parents who were great men in the world, and to whom applies the proverb: "The child's talk is either the father's or the mother's" (Talmud Sanhedrin 56b). In this case, if one cannot vouch for their intellectual understanding of the contents of the legends, for this one can vouch with absolute certainty: the inwardness of their souls inclines toward the pith of the sublime legends upon their lips. For that same tradition which places the words upon their lips trained and educated them, and by its spirit and emphasis their senses were cultivated and developed in them.

Therefore, dear reader, make you ears like funnels and attend exceedingly well to the whisperings of this pair of Jews sitting at night by the light of that small candle near their open Gemarahs, passing judgment upon the events of the world. Do not be dismayed by the mysteriousness of their words, for it is merely the characteristic speech of those whose very essence and existence (that is, the essence and existence of their people) is mysterious. And on the other hand, the subject under consideration, world-terrifying wars, is itself as if enveloped in thick clouds of mystery, and as though standing aloof and inviting a solution not merely prosaic. Yet within their words, spoken in hushed tones, is a realistic assessment of war, or rather, a realistic-mystic, which appears more correct than any of the "naturalistic" theories previously cited.

And within this true theory of the source of evil in the world may also be found that cure to remove the evil effects. In this too it differs from the other theories, which, as it were, diagnose the source of the plague but are unable to reveal the correct way to remove it.

Chapter Three

Supernaturalism and Naturalism in the Legends of "Gog And Magog" and the "Messiah"

1.

We remarked in the preceding chapter that the haggadic tradition concerning "the wars of Gog and Magog" and "the footsteps of the Messiah," which is rooted in our people and which is most especially discussed in the circles of the academies at times of war, contains within it the most rational appraisal of the happenings in the world. But precisely how shall the position of this tradition be explained, which associates wars with the expectation of the "Messiah," and which presents the Jewish people in the role of the envoy about whom the events of the world focus? To explain this matter we must probe somewhat deeper into the causes of wars.

Above, in Chapter One, we presented two different theories of war. One (the early view) sees war as a mysterious phenomenon whose causes are concealed in the darkness of the hidden spheres, beyond the province of nature. On this view, those who dwell on earth have no access to the deeper causes of war, and no ability to prevent its outbreak. The second (the later view) sees war as a natural phenomenon whose causes rest here in this world, within these creatures who indulge in the game of war. This "naturalist" view itself has two formulations. According to one, war is a psychological or a biological phenomenon: it is, psychologically speaking, the expression of hostility rooted in the hearts of separate nations and races, which from time to time bursts forth; or biologically speaking, the simple bursting forth of the beast in the heart of man.

The naturalistic outlook, from this view, almost like the supernatural position above, makes a permanent condition of these historical human mockeries known as "wars," and despairs of finding any counsel for preventing them.

According to the second formulation of the naturalistic outlook, war should not be designated at all by the term "phenomenon," whether psychological or biological; rather is it the artificial plottings and intrigues of a small group of men who hold power in the nations. On this view, there is at hand a simple and easy solution for preventing wars: namely, to take from these ugly men the means they have for realizing their ugly aims.

On first consideration we approved the naturalistic outlook in its second formulation, that is that it throws the primary blame for war upon the class that holds power. For however much the ugly clay of war may be imbedded in the hearts of the mass of people, yet those who busy themselves with this nice material, moistening and shaping it for their goal and bringing it to completion—these are surely "the ruling classes." Therefore it is undoubtedly necessary to limit the power of these rulers over the people so that the latter not be delivered into their hands, like clay into the hands of the potter, for any folly or perversion that the hearts of the leaders may desire. By this the possibility of the evil of actual war would be greatly limited.

Nevertheless anyone who suggests that simply through external changes in the arrangement of the world, through changing in this way or that the objective living conditions of people, the evil of war will be completely eliminated even in possibility—this surely is mistaken. It is the utmost naivete to believe that it is within the power of a small group of "rulers" to pick up and lead forth myriads of people to strange and savage deeds such as those of war, without the crowds themselves having within their hearts some slight inclination toward these deeds. Were the inner attitudes of the masses wholly rejecting of war, a small group of leaders could never swim against such a stream.

It is true that in the history of the world we have often found individuals swimming against this current. But these few were people of great and pure soul involved in furthering great and pure ideals, the strength of whose ideals sustained them in their efforts, and who swam against the powerful current "things as they are," propelled by the force of that most majestic and sublime urge, "things as they ought to be." In contrast, petty and frightened individuals like the ruling groups, engaged in tasks that have no rational support—how shall they be emboldened to swim against the stream? How shall they be enabled to put into action their vile plans?

From the foregoing, then, how can we not approve with all our hearts the serious intentions of the holders of the "naturalistic outlook" in its second formulation, who call us to war against war, and how shall we disagree with their suggestions? But in the matter of uncovering the root of war, it is impossible for us to assent to the decisions of this naturalistic group, which holds that war is, in its entirety, nothing but a manipulation by a plotting few, the rulers. Obviously here we must agree with the opinion of the first of the naturalistic schools, which holds that war is a natural phenomenon whose roots are imbedded in the hearts of the people themselves.

And in truth we essentially agree with those who maintain this position, that war is a natural phenomenon, but not for their reason. They see the reason for war either as the mutual hostility between different nations and peoples, or in the animal instinct in man as such. But these reasons are not correct ones, for neither the one nor the other is the natural cause of war. The former, the mutual hatred between different peoples and nations, is in no way natural but purely artificial. It is prepared and developed in the first instance by those very manipulators who afterwards weave war. For from that side of nature, which will you have: either man is by nature evil, in which case he is malicious toward all, and will show no mercy even to his loved ones; or he is not evil, and so will do no harm even to those remote from him. As for the second reason, "the animal instinct in man," either it is actively evil all the time or only from time to time, when something angers it. But note, are not these instincts the kind which erupt widely and suddenly, without any order, and without any means of stopping them instantly? But war is not like these, for war proceeds deliberately, with order and commands. An officer at this moment commands, "shoot!" And the next minute—"cease fire!" At this moment—"be wrathful!" And at the next moment—"halt the anger!"

Thus is negated the foundation and basis of the reason of the first naturalistic position, according to which war is a natural phenomenon. And now it seems as if we must wearily return wholly to that antiquated outlook which sees war as a supernatural phenomenon.

And I insist that indeed this is the case! We must return to that theory which views war through the lens of supernaturalism, because the strong evidence which we above brought against the "naturalistic" so compels us once again to inspect the supernaturalistic viewpoint. But not popular and misty supernaturalism which has not rational support or basis in reality, like the supernaturalism of the early unenlightened generations; but rather an intelligent and rational supernaturalism (and such supernatural mystery there is truly in reality). Supernaturalism designated by this name not because it conceals or hides in remote regions never seen by the eyes of any living thing, with strange images and visions which bear no resemblance to truth; but rather because it is hidden and concealed from senseless eyes to which are revealed only the external appearances of natural phenomena. But to those eyes which penetrate to the inner essence of phenomena, behold, the aforementioned mysteriousness is a perceptible reality.

The correct theory of war is therefore a synthesis of the views presented above (the mysterious or supernatural and the natural). That is, war is a supernatural-natural (or mysterious-natural) phenomenon.

We shall now explain.

2.

All the characteristics of the activities of men in times of war: the outpouring of poems, essays, and stories venerating and sanctifying war from writers and poets who sell their souls to Satan; the kind of "reverence for the government" which overpowers the residents of the country whose administration has announced war; the slogan "the holy war" which is spoken without hesitation by every one of the belligerents; and above all, the ruin which forces the poets of war feebly to designate the "homeland" by that shameful and all too appropriate name "altar," "the altar of the homeland," and the slain of war by the term "sacrifices"—all these characteristics clearly show that war is a kind of vestigial remains of primitive idolatry which has persisted among nations even in modern times. And while it is well known that all the artistic creations and phrases mentioned above are fabricated in the hearts of these imposters for the purpose of capturing the soul of the masses, it is equally well known that these invented notions would not be given expression by the misleading falsifiers, or listened to by seductively persuaded ears, unless they corresponded to some inclination of the heart.

Modern man has developed much intellectually, but in the moral virtues he has remained the same primitive savage, new only in that his barbarism has increased greatly. For behold, all the early idols and images whose proportion of nonsense exceeded that of evil have for that reason been abandoned; only that idol known as "the homeland" together with its worship known as "war" (whose proportion of evil far exceeds its nonsense) has not been abandoned by modern man but has been retained intact. And of course he has tried to refine and develop this idolatry well, removing insofar as possible the boorish shell of stupidity and retaining only the kernel of pure evil—an evil particularly adapted and conforming to the taste and "intelligence" of modern man.

In short, war is modern idolatry: of all the foolish worship of idols, that single remnant which the "enlightened" generation has chosen to retain.

The idolatry of ancient man, as is well known, did not stem solely from the foolish stubbornness of the human heart, but also from that yearning, deep in the soul of man, for some ideal; from the ennui which oppresses the soul when it has no concern or vision. And their foolishness consisted only in this: that their uncircumcised hearts chose for the nourishment of their souls unseemly beliefs and strange and confusing practices. It is like the proverb: "God created man in His image, and men go forth inventing idols after their own dispositions." And now it can be understood that even the idol of "homeland" or "fatherland" to which modern man pays homage, has been erected by the nations to fill the great emptiness in their souls which is due to their being constantly preoccupied with matters of country, of earth, and of egotism. Also thus may be understood their making for themselves this idol after their own image and likeness, from their own essence and their own ways of living.

Modern nations busy themselves in matters of civilization and social welfare with great hullabaloo: they sow and plant, build bridges, pave highways, manufacture, make fairs, etc. But the motivating spirit of all these activities is the lowest kind of egotism. All these occupations and activities are undertaken solely in the heated pursuit of wealth, possessions, and careers. The demon of destruction and annihilation, who oversees all these activities and structures established by his tool of gross egotism, stands behind them and completes them with an expression of mockery. But he, the demon of destruction, is one thing; and they, the nations, quite another matter: they sink more deeply into egoistic activities without pause. Their hearts become ever fatter, their feelings ever more obtuse, their souls emptier. This emptiness of soul spreads a thick darkness of dullness over the soul. And the "seers," prophets of doom who are themselves tainted inside by the "dark demon," in seeing his success, help unwittingly to strengthen yet more the darkness within. They also contribute to turning these dulled ones, who are searching for something to banish this dark senselessness, further toward the desired goal of the inspirer of these visions.

The nations provide theatres, circuses, sports, taverns. Crowds stream to these "holy places" night after night, finding in them the charms with which to banish the spirit of ennui. There they sit all the night, driving away boredom by means of various desires and sports which, combined with the quaffing of goodly quantities of alcohol, intermittently shake their grief. These means manifest well their effects: the grief becomes oppressive, and the slight disenchantment, after this therapy of a full night, yields its place to still greater ennui. The destroyer-demon, overseeing the activities of the egotists, watches with a sneer on his lips their daytime "worship," the civilizing work of social welfare, as it were. He then accompanies them at night to the taverns, standing by while they linger there, with always a blessing on his lips: "May tomorrow night as well be like this night."

Obviously the destroying demon could rest already content with this satisfaction of his aspirations, laughing as well at these petty idols that the nations have formed for themselves in their own images and likenesses. For even these small idols have the power to do no small damage to the lives of men. But why should the demon-destroyer settle for small triumphs when the perceptions and character of the nations give him the possibility of greater ones? Why be satisfied with the idol of the tavern, with petty and local idols of each individual city? Because of their pettiness, their glory and honor are not so great in the eyes of the people, and their influence not so compelling. Those who wish may visit these places of worship; those who wish may refrain. Additionally, the destructiveness of these idols is quite limited, extending only to the people themselves but not to the works of their hands which they have so laboriously established in the world. Why settle for petty idols of limited demonic destructiveness, when the demon-destroyer has its eye sharpened for mighty extermination: the annihilation of the people together with all their creations, like the devastation of Sodom, which returned the world to its prior state of formless void.

The dictum of the rabbis is: "any house in which no words of Torah are heard is bound to be destroyed." That is to say, any house not founded upon the spirit of humility where the teachings of Torah are applied, but rather in a spirit of gross materialism, is bound to be destroyed. This applies not only to a private house, but also to the founding of entire peoples and nations. Demonic destructiveness will not be satisfied with petty idols of the local taverns, of limited destructive range, when his hand can hew from the dispositions of people a gigantic carved idol shared by all in the land, of such magnitude that with it his blinding and seductive influence will be massive, and his strength sufficient to subdue beneath it everything—to destroy all with one blow.

The name of this great idol is "the honor of the fatherland," its shape determined by combining all the private egotisms found in the hearts of the residents of the nation. Its worship is the slaughter of millions of men in wars for the "native land."

Footnote: This comparison which I draw between taverns and wars has been anticipated in a confused way by one of those authors who sell the fruits of their pens to Satan, found in a patriotic Russian paper at the beginning of the war. In one of his fraudulent hymns which he composed to glorify the war, he reached such a degree of confusion that he began to praise the war because it educates people in "the ethic of abstinence, the discipline of renunciation." These are his confused words: "The nation, which up to now was carousing in taverns and steeped in pleasures of the flesh, at the announcement of war suddenly abandoned its mixed drinks and went forth to suffer and to risk its lives on the field of death." That is to say, this nation, which up to now was gluttonous, drunk, and whoring in the taverns, suddenly "uplifted itself" and went forth to do these very things in an outpouring of wickedness and drunkenness both greater in quantity and more intense in quality. Pillage, plunder, and rape occurred in all those places where battles were fought, as wickedness was set free in connection with those events. After filling their own bellies with cups of wine, men would fill the bellies of others with bullets and bayonets. Is this not an appalling "sanctification of the Divine?" In the deformed mind of this scribe, his twisted logic drew a straight line connecting the tavern to the war.

3.

This is the order of the development of our idol and its worship. The residents of a region have but one desire, the desire for wealth and property. This material egotism, which aspires to take possession of and hold all in its vicinity, by its nature brings with it the spiritual egotisms of pride and arrogance, manifested in the pursuit of illusory honor and in the desire to dominate others, to gain control and make them subservient. But such domination can be achieved only by the sword, and does not reveal itself fully except by the gleam of the sword, broken but glistening amidst drops of warm blood.

For from the most ancient of times the shedding of blood has had this special distinction: every kind of mockery and enticement has been connected with it, helping and receiving help from it. "The early magicians and sorcerers would pour out blood and collect it in a pit, there to draw for themselves the contaminated spirit of magic" (Ramban's commentary to Leviticus 19). And the modern backsliders shed blood to draw from it, for themselves, the contaminated spirit of pride and arrogance; to make, over blood shed, an eternal compact with the special cruelty of oppressors; and to set upon themselves, by the gleam of the flashing sword amidst the blood flowing by their hand, the enticing splendor of dominion and sovereignty.

In a word: the sword is that single idiom by which hollow man can express his being and essence, the sword anointed with blood—the excellence of the empty man!

But the small sword of a private individual—how much blood can it shed? And how much can its limited flashing impress a proud eye? For the inner emptiness of the egotist, who has no feeling of inner, essential worth, but whose esteem is gotten only from outside—this emptiness is so extensive and deep an abyss that it can absorb limitless mockeries and seductions. Therefore every individual boastful-indolent consents to contribute his individual haughtiness and self-aggrandizement to a general pool, the "national;" to unite all the private swords, making of them one staggeringly large and gleaming sword to hang upon the thigh of the gigantic idol called "the fatherland." The dimensions of this idol, which they themselves erected, and the glittering of his mammoth sword, blind them. They invest this idol with all their pride and haughtiness, and through its glory they esteem themselves, not seeing or understanding that this idol of their pride will convert the private citizen into a permanent bondsman crushed beneath the feet of his priests in time of peace, and into a lamb for the slaughter in time of war. For truly, all pride is nothing other than abjectness; all those who love to dominate the weak do not themselves object to being slaves to the mighty; and all who express their being by brandishing the sword do but proclaim their own lowly nothingness.

Yet the abject lowliness of spirit, which causes the inhabitants of a country to grovel beneath the feet of the great idol, has its compensations. Soon it bestows that ostentatious delight yielded by the waving of the sword at its neighbor (the national idol of some other country), which to each one of the inhabitants seems as if he is the one brandishing the sword, and as if all the great glistening splendor of the thousands of swords waved by his friends—the soldiers of his nation—flashes forth from his very own sword.

The aforementioned idol, in waving this great sword, casts its bolts in both directions and achieves thereby two distinct ends: half of the fear and awe falls upon the neighboring people, and half the defilement and ugliness upon its own people.

In this way the idol of "national honor" becomes the center, the "heart" which both receives and gives honor to all manner of wickedness in the land: All the mean drives of every private citizen for spoil and domination pour their venoms into the heart, and from it—from the thoughts of blood, power, and territory in this heart—the poisons return, and sweep away in a yet stronger stream all the inhabitants of the land. All the private horrors committed daily in the lives of individual men, from the cruel gluttonies by which the powerful bit by bit squeeze and drain their fellow men who are less powerful, to the dramas of dueling and other violent murders—all these receive their nourishment from the general heart. All the cruel images of private lives are merely smaller copies of the great portrait of cruelty which stands in the shrine of the public idol, "national honor." "If you see oppression of the poor and violation of justice and righteousness in a 'nation,' be not surprised at the matter, for the very high protect it...."

For since man is a social being, the individual spirit is hewn and carved from the general, and the individual would not dare commit these scandalous actions did not the general practice offer him support, were not the sword the pride and glory of the people as a whole.

In the beginning this idol, the heart of wickedness, is the principal cause of a people's being led astray morally, to descend to the very lowest level of depravity. And afterwards, when their measure is completed and their hour has come to drink from the cup of retribution, behold, this very idol itself (the heart also in the payment of their recompense) is the chief cause of their being thrust from the land of the living to hell!

For at last it became loathsome to this idol to display gratuitously its altar, "the altar of the homeland;" and so it contrives causes for disputes and intrigues, whips up dances of war, and invites its "subjects" to offer it their heads and entrails. The "subjects" eagerly arise and with desire run to the slaughter house. True, they cry and sigh at the time they leave home, but we note that this crying does not prevent their unanimously going on the business at hand.

For two opposite dispositions rule within them at this hour: the natural characteristic of the animal, and the mysterious-seductive characteristic of the man who has perverted his way. The pure animal quality in the man cries and complains bitterly at this going to slaughter. But unlike a true animal, the corrupted man cannot determinedly stop himself from going, because in the chambers of his heart lodges the mysterious-seductive inclination and waits in ambush to exact from him at this moment payment for all his former sins. To achieve this goal, this urge creates in his imagination visions of glory and honor connected with the black vulture of war, which spreads its wings over his head; and in weakening his spirit of resistance to entering this majestic pit of destruction, these visions thrust him into the very jaws of the vulture.

Thus does the "subject" or "citizen" go forth to death, a lowly creature; and though the pure animal in him cries out and objects, the perverted man in him triumphs and leads him to hell.

As a proof that the citizen's going forth to the slaughter is not wholly due to external coercion, but also to an inner irrational-enticing urge, this fact may serve: this very man whom we saw only a few days previously shedding tears with his wife and children at separating from them—behold him now! In the field this "crier" runs like a panther and tries with determination to excel in the manly deed of plunging a dagger into the vitals of other men who have no quarrel with him nor he with them, solely in order to "find favor" in the eyes of his superiors who command him, and to receive from them a piece of round metal, the "medal of heroism."

Admittedly there is much of the animal quality of the horse in this activity of the "dedicated subject." The horse too rejoices when it senses war, lifts its mane, and takes pride in the privilege of being saddled beneath the legs and thighs of he warrior riding it. But the man, perverted and foolish, who runs to devote himself to war, besides resembling the horse in his level of intelligence, has in the depths of his soul another horse of a different variety, an irrational horse commissioned for deeper and more remote ends: the end of carrying his rider, the sinful man, to the pit below.

Concluded are the descriptions of the ways of war and its causes. It has been explained and established that War is not a sudden occurrence of chance; neither is it a solitary link lacking all connection with other links in the chain of life. Rather it is the necessary result of the low dedication of the nations, and appears, due to psychological-irrational causes, after every evil period of history in order to chastise those who inhabit the earth. War is the great crisis of immorality which discloses in retrospect all the sins of the society and all the falseness which was plastered into the building of its civilization.

And the idol of "national honor," which stands by to proclaim the going forth to battle at the time of war, and which in times of peace, before the war, dwells in the midst of the feverish activity of the civilization, publicly preparing all the weapons of war with such impudence and ease that one would think by this it, too, was participating in the work of social betterment—this idol is the "demon of destruction" which grabbed Noah when he planted the vineyard (that first substance for fulfilling the desires of the flesh) and said to him: "I shall join with you, but take care that you not infringe on my portion; for if you do, I shall kill you" (Midrash Rabbah Genesis 36). This "demon" accompanies all who work for civilization in a gross spirit of egotism, and little by little prepares the means for utterly demolishing both them and all their works.

This mysterious law has never been, and will never be, change by any external revolution or by any manipulation of the objective conditions of the world; but only by an inner revolution of the heart which will open the eyes of men so that they may know and recognize what is the true glory of man. For so long as man's inner spiritual world is not made fit, no amount of correction and change in the social order will help in removing at its root the evil of war. By these external changes in the arrangement of society the occasions and strategies of war will, of course, also be changed. Instead of wars between nation and nation or people and people, there will be wars between one professional group and another; and instead of bullets of steel there will be born new missiles, so that we may yet be privileged to see man kill man prettily, without steel at all. But the essentially beastly attitude toward the shedding of blood will not be destroyed so long as man's hearts are not made fit and egotistic corruption continues to be the ruling spirit in all the activities of men. For until that time the "demon of destruction" will not cease to occupy that seat from which he concocts schemes to destroy that which men build, by inciting them to attack one another. And if the schemes and plots of this "demon" are no longer able to be "political" (for the present political forms may be changed by changing conditions), there will be classes: class attacking class. And even if improvements in the objective world were to go so far as to make all the inhabitants of the world members of one economic class, yet even this would not yield status for the soul or nourishment for the spirit. And the psychological lack of status and the spiritual emptiness would again burst forth violently along other paths, still seeking illusory honor by dominance and arrogance—yet new ways to keep hold, in one guise or another, of the inheritance of Esau, the inheritance of "by your sword shall you live."

It is possible to find strong fear in the principal promulgations of the democratic parties against the war, which has one refrain in every proclamation dealing with this issue, the strident and bitter complaint: "The war benefits only the bourgeoisie, and for the proletariat has no advantages." How far from the rejecter of war by our holy prophets, and how inferior, is this negation of war based on the complaint "What's my gain?" How far is this negation of war because of dissatisfaction with the division of the booty, from the rejection of war because of the abundance of concern and love for that created in the image of God, because of the abundance of purity and ethical beauty in the spirit!

Thus the rejection of war is the counsel which our great seers, in raising their sublime ideal of "nation shall not lift up sword versus nation," made conditional to nothing else: not to agreements of "appointees of the court of the Hague," nor to agreements of "the allied coalition" made by various manufacturers by munitions makers, not to stipulations of "democratic revolution or even socialistic revolution," not to requirements of any external change in world conditions—but only conditional to "the earth shall be filled with the knowledge of the Lord," the inner worth and glory of man.

The promise/assurance of the earth being filled with knowledge of the Lord, which the prophets expressed in simple and realistic terms but whose content (the sudden opening of the eyes of the creatures to the recognition of Divinity) is, for all that, mystical and miraculous—was clarified and made more comprehensible to reason by the rabbis. They expressed this realistic content in legendary terms, it is true, but with this import: that the dawn of light/enlightenment would come when the darkness reached its very limits and its terrible consequence passed all bounds. These are the legends of "the wars of Gog and Magog" and "the footsteps of the Messiah" which we heard this particular evening from the two Jews sitting in the academy and discussing their open Gemarahs. These legends contain a very naturalistic idea, that is to say, mystical-naturalistic, namely: when grandiose wars break out upon the earth involving nearly all the nations of the world (like the picture of the Gog-Magog legend), and the foolish pride of the sword entices them into this whirlwind of hell, the nations are devastated and men devour their neighbors, that what will emerge from the war will be the famous caricature of "two wolves consumed one another, till all that remained were their tails"—except that there only the tips of their tails remained, while among the nations only the heads of the tails will remain, i.e., the "leaders" who sat at ease in their palaces and made their hearts full of wine even as they sent forth their "subjects" to annihilation. At such time will be revealed the complete bankruptcy of the culture of Esau, whose pride is the sword and who is consumed by that very sword; (note that the Hebrew root of Gog suggest "pride and arrogance," and those of Magog "melting and dissolving into nothing"). Then the sound of the footsteps of the Messiah, the God of Jacob, will begin to be heard. Steadily will approach that time and whose history and way of life form the time of first contributing these sublime ideals to a desolate world have helped it preserve these ideals as its inherited seminal duty. These first steps of the "Messiah" from his hiding place into the world (i.e., his attesting the ideal of the hatred of violence and tyranny in a clear and definite way, and his establishing it as a revealing touchstone) he first attempted painfully in the Jewish world.

Therefore it falls upon the Jewish people to prepare itself, at the present period, to receive the Messiah. The preparations consist in this: that in every single corner of our people there shall spread and become acute the awareness of the sublime mission of our life, and that in all shall grow strong the emotions of love of Torah and love of the holiness of our people. Then it will be possible to have established in our midst a chief habitation of the Messianic idea and a proper basis for the revelation of this idea in a pronounced and tangible way.

Then and only then, when this revelation shall have a solid basis in the midst of one people, can its work of influencing the rest of the world begin. Even those who first proclaimed the Messianic ideal, the prophets, in their original program for the order of the expansion of this ideal in the world, did not suggest that the abstract idea hover in the air by itself, but that the prime cause of its expansion be the living and tangible example presented to all the inhabitants of the earth by the image of the Jewish people. "And it shall be, at the end of days, that many nations shall walk saying: 'Come, let us go up to the house of God of Jacob, that He may teach us of His ways.'" "Nation shall not lift up sword against nation."

In the following chapter we shall say a few words on the theory that within the pale settlement of the Jewish people is found "the habitation of the Messiah."

Chapter Four

The Exile of the Presence and the Presence of the Exile

1.

The events of history move rapidly in this world: nations decline and nations arise. Every nation in its heyday holds the world firmly in the palm of its hand: it plucks the wool without tiring, devours the flesh ravenously, and at the same time tries to breathe in its soul and spirit, believing absolutely in the just merits of this procedure....For while it knows no limit when it comes to material devouring, in the realm of spirit it does have its satiation point. So joyously exultant is it in the idolatries of "sovereignty" and "conquest" that it believes itself to be spiritually overflowing with "blessedness," to such a point that it is compelled to shower upon others its goodness and glory. Widely engaging in these two estimable practices—exploiting and plundering all men, and "teaching" and "guiding" all men—every ascendant nation for a certain time manages to boast and behave foolishly, until finally it descends from the pinnacle and its place is taken by another nation, also half despoiler and half "guide."

Through all this long history of succession of nations, one nation in the world trailed in the wake, Israel by name. Time after time it was cast about and driven from one country to another. Its ruck-sack, always ready at hand, was filled largely with books—books for the study of the Torah. Within the bundle of books were found also a small prayer book and a small wax candle. So soon as the wanderer had located a night's lodging, just so soon would he arise at midnight, find some corner in the inn, seat himself on a low stool, light the dim candle, open his tiny Siddur, and recite Tikkun-Hatzot/Midnight Prayers of Lamentation. In his reciting he would, while half hungry and half shattered, cry and bemoan his physical sufferings. But basically he poured out his heart because of his spiritual travail, because of "the Exile of the Presence." He would gasp bitterly and recite:

> "Then was I His only beloved
> And the Glory of the Most High was I called;
> Now to the depths have I descended,
> And my Most Beloved to the heights has ascended."

The "seventy nations" and the mockers see this tragedy and are content to explain it lightly and cynically: "For you, accursed Jew, it is fitting indeed to bemoan and bewail 'the Exile of Presence', for you are plagued, smitten by the Lord and afflicted, having neither Presence nor God."

For many generations the uncircumcised have showered upon us, in great quantity, the arrows of their scorn, intending thereby to establish within us "Exile" in the sense of forsaken by the Presence, until of late they have managed to hypnotize some of the feeble among our own people. In these last generations our hearts have ached upon hearing even certain of our fellow Jews, just as uncomprehending and uncircumcised of hearts as their non-Jewish counterparts, deprecating and dismissing the life of the Jew in Exile, scornfully spitting on "the Galut" by presenting it as the cause of "the lack of spirituality," and denying to the Jew in Exile all possibility of the finer life.

2.

For anyone with even a bit of a brain in his head surely understands the matter in quite the opposite way: the sorrow of our people over "the Exile of the Presence" is an indication, not of its remoteness from God, but precisely of it nearness to Him. The solitary beloved, in sitting and shedding tears of great longing for her lover Who for the time being is separated from her, by this surely does not prove that her lover has rejected her or forsaken her forever. And how much less does it provide even one shred of evidence that she, the beloved, has rejected her lover. Just the reverse. First of all, the tears are testimony to the fact that the soul of the beloved is still bound to the lover, and that without Him she cannot live. And this being so, her tears are no evidence that her lover has left her forever or even for any extended length of time. It could just as well be that the strength of her love and devotion is so intense that the separation for even a single hour is sufficiently painful to provoke tears of longing.

If this judgment be possible and logical when applied to tears of human love, which is not always mutual—for there are instances where she may love him without his loving her—then applied to the tears of the "the beloved," where both Beloved and Lover are spiritual (the Community of Israel and the Blessed Holy One), this assessment is not only possible but compelling. Since the Community of Israel longs for the Blessed Holy One, this implies that He also longs for it.

> Those who love Me do I love,
> And those who seek Me shall find Me.

Seated on the ground at midnight, the tears which "His only beloved" sheds night after night for "her Most Beloved Who to the heights has ascended," are a clear indication of the intense nearness and the burning love which exists between the beloved and her Lover.

The intelligent man recognizes the nature of those tears of woe shed by the elderly Jew at midnight, seated on the ground in some corner of his house, bent and alone, reciting "Tikkun Hatzot" and bemoaning "the Exile of the Presence": they pour forth from a mighty spiritual stream which dolefully wells up within him and which provokes in him a great longing for the Presence. But he who lacks the sensitivity to recognize the nature of the tears shed by the grandfather over The Exile of the Presence at the time of "Tikkum Hatzot" each weekday night—let such a one kindly take the trouble to observe the tears of this very same grandfather at the time of "Kabbalat Shabbat/Prayers for Welcoming the Sabbath." Let him but take the trouble to enter the synagogue on the Sabbath Eve and see the tears of joy and ecstasy which the grandfather sheds as he welcomes the arrival of "Sabbath the Queen," the arrival of the Divine Presence. Then his error will become apparent to him, his error in so misapprehending the tears shed by the elderly Jew each weeknight over the Exile of the Presence. For surely now he must be convinced that this mourner is not in any wise forsaken by the Presence, but quite the contrary: The Presence is very near unto him, so near that he actually receives and welcomes It each and every Sabbath.

He who misunderstood the content of the lament recited plaintively by the beloved, the Community of Israel, the previous night, a weeknight: "Now to the depths have I descended, and my Most Beloved to the heights has ascended"—let him please mark well the demonstrative hymn, "Come, oh love, to greet the bride," sung by the self-same beloved (Israel) with great passion this night, the Sabbath Eve. Let him note, please, that her Lover Who wandered so far off, even ascending to the heights, returns to her dwelling time after time to rejoice with her in the delights of love. Attend the ecstasy and exaltation of spirit with which that very Jew proclaims "Thou didst select us" on the Eve of Sanctifying a Holy Day, or the stanza, "Awake, awake, for your Light has come," on the Eve of Sanctifying the Sabbath. Note well the endless glow and satisfaction streaming from the face of the Jew on the Sabbath Eve.

> 'And God blessed the seventh day and hallowed it...'
> He blessed it with the light of man's countenance,
> And He hallowed it with the light of man's countenance.

3.

This joy and ecstasy—which even in Exile seizes the Jewish people each Sabbath and Holy Day Eve by means of the glorious and exalted prayers and hymns through which it expresses its soul—is the true mark of the sublime exilic creativity of the Jewish people. For although the Jew in exile was not especially creative in the material realm, for reasons independent of him, he was, despite this, most creative in the spiritual realm.

And his true joy in this creative task the exilic Jew expresses in his hymns and prayers concerning the tranquility he finds through his most pleasing mate, the Sabbath.

With these words we have laid the foundation for the assumption, readily assented to by all the initiated among our people who have penetrated to the inner spirit of people and its sacred literature: that not only did the Exile not remove from our people its exalted task and mission, to bear witness to the Providence which in the first instance established it as a people; but, on the contrary, it has in fact assisted it in this task, easing its work in assuming this mission. It is not at all as the erring would have it, that "Exile" has laid waste the creative power of the Jewish spirit.

This in general terms. We shall now proceed to portray the exilic creation in greater detail.

4.

Two thousand years ago, at the time of the renowned Revelations at Mount Sinai, the hour had arrived for the Creator of the Universe to give to the world His Torah, i.e., to give to the world below the Divine Emanations of Faith in and Cleavage to God (Emuna and D'vakut).

The Jewish People responded to His call by hastening to express its willingness immediately in these words: "We will obey and we will hearken." Therefore the Torah was conveyed to the Jewish People, creating a firm bond and covenant between the People and the Holy One, Blessed be He.

For the people the covenant had as its goal their becoming "a kingdom of priests and a holy people," i.e., their becoming a People each of whose individual members would have within his heart purity and nearness to God to such a degree that it would be, as a whole, a kingdom all of whose members were priestly and holy: every member serving nobly in the Divine sanctuary and comporting himself with the holiness befitting such ministering. The people had just escaped from the burdens of Egypt and had seen, with its own eyes, the absolute collapse into nothingness of material might and "national," "sovereign" pride; and it was itself situated in the midst of a dry, barren desert with neither "national territory" nor an established army...These factors made the hearts of many people ready to welcome the covenant. Their total removal from the tight trap of materialistic nationalism well prepared them to respond, "We will obey and we will hearken," to proclaim ecstatically their complete readiness to become "a kingdom of priests and a holy people."

But after this, when Israel came to the land of Canaan, seized it, spread itself like a leafy tree in its native soil, and established for itself a sovereign political life "like all the nations," there began hovering over its head the danger which Moses our teacher had warned against: "Lest when thou hast eaten and art satisfied, and hast built goodly houses, and dwelt therein… then thy heart be lifted up, and thou forget the Lord thy God, who brought thee forth out of the land of Egypt, out of the house of bondage."

The Holy Spirit began to be driven away and separated from them by the gross spirit of "political nationalism" which took their hearts. And as the Holy Spirit fled from the people, the imprint of the Torah also faded, the trace of the Divine ordinances they had received at Mount Sinai. Rather than the Torah eventuating in an Immanent Godhead dwelling in the midst of the children of Israel, a Divinity Whose abode was the heart, the heart of every individual Jew—rather than this, the children of Israel began viewing the Divinity as exclusively external, with Its abode in the midst of political protocol and propriety.

From that point on the children of Israel became "political," and the Torah became merely a kind of constitution, similar to those constitutions from "cultured nations" that we today know all too well: on paper, drafted and signed, but in practice, the complete opposite.

Corruption begets corruption. The corruption of the ethical sense, which followed in the wake of the invasion from without by the spirit of "political nationalism," soon brought them to request that a king be set over them also, "like all the nations surrounding them."

The prophet, representative of the Intimate Presence, cried out bitterly against the clamor for the appointment of a king, the clamor to make of the Torah "an official document." And the Holy One, Blessed be He, expressed His full participation in the prophet's sorrow by saying to him: "for they have not rejected thee, but they have rejected Me, that I should not be king over them." But to destroy them because of their gross cravings was not the desire of the Holy One, Blessed be He.

The Jewish People fulfilled its intention to be "like all the nations," and performed its part: it saddled itself with kings. And the kings performed their part: they involved the nation in cruel wars though absolutely nothing required it ("optional wars" in Rabbinic terminology), and thus the people were killed and killers, slaughtered and slaughterers, "felling with axes of iron," "measuring among the wounded one to be rescued and two to let die." All of it, the whole business, exactly as carried in the surrounding nations.

The Father in Heaven, the Holy One, Blessed be He, sat mourning the straying of His sons in the paths of the nations, but, as is His wont, He granted them freedom to follow their own hearts to the very end. But with the passing of time, the kings had their fill of the delicacies of "the nations," of the dainties of war, and then there came to their minds the memory of the God of Israel. One king especially was mindful of the Holy One, Blessed be He, one who in his childhood was a shepherd in the desert, after that a refugee hiding in the forests, and who carried within him two souls: one "kingly," i.e., mighty, fit to "lift up his sword against eight hundred, whom he slew at one time;" one saintly, cleaving to the Presence, which "did sound the harp at midnight, busying himself with the Torah." This king did remember the Holy One, Blessed be He, and decided to build a house in His honor.

At that point, when the "king" began concerning himself with a "house" for the Lord, the Holy One, Blessed be He, was no longer able, as it were, to contain the wrath long pent up in His heart due to the vain mockeries committed by His people through kingship, and He immediately rejected the idea: "Thou hast shed blood abundantly, and hast made great wars; thou shalt not build a house unto My name, because thou hast shed much blood upon the earth in My sight" (I Chronicles 22:8). The reason for the rejection according to Scripture is this: it is not for kings, wagers of war, to build houses for the God of Israel, for His ways and attributes are the complete opposite of kings' sovereign ways and wars.

5.

The work of building the Temple was taken out of the hands of the king who had engaged in the work of kings, i.e., the active waging of war, and was transferred to his son, the "peaceful king."

But a king, even if he be peaceful, is still a king. And if, by virtue of the numerous victories already won by him or his forefathers in subduing all the neighboring nations, he be slack in waging new wars which would demonstrate further the prowess of his sword (a process indeed very tiring and troublesome)—even so, that characteristic desire of royalty, to expand over all the surroundings, in no wise abandons him. But he can express it, now that the nations are subjugated, in more gentle ways: by extending a "humble" hand to his submissive neighbors and by going about with them "like a brother." He pays them a visit on their feasts and festivals, and invites them to his own feasting and celebrating.

This same disposition, to expand by means of intimacy, served this "peaceful king" also in building the Temple. In every item of its construction, from preparing the materials right through to composing the prayer for its dedication, he constantly looked to the kings and nations around him, as if the erection of the Temple were a collective project, his and theirs.

He rejoiced over the great palace he had built for his God, over the reverent spell which the building cast on his subjects and neighbors, over the throne greater that the throne of any king, over his own exceptional liberalism and generosity in living in peace and friendship with all the nations and drawing them near by "his great kindness."

This dwelling, and everything connected with it, was arranged just the opposite of what it should have been were it to realize its purpose, that of being a dwelling place for the Presence in this earthly sphere. This ideal of the Presence, resting upon and influencing the earth despite Its being high and uplifting, great and wide, embracing the entire universe—despite and precisely because of this, the realization of the ideal requires a contraction and a joining to a people chosen for this end. For, since this Ideal Presence is high above the heavens and wide beyond the earth, the hearts of men are too small to encompass It. Thus It requires for Itself one people which will concentrate on It, cherish It, and absorb It within themselves; then, from the splendor of that people, light will emanate to all peoples. But in the Temple which Solomon built, just the opposite happened. The Ideal Itself became so confined and debilitated that It Itself required fattening by thousands of cattle and sheep; and despite this and because of this, the arms of the Ideal family stretched and extended until It, too, embraced all the nations and went forth to join in the dance with them.

6.

Now, when that people which had accepted the Torah, the Jewish people, had taken possession of a land and was leading the political life, appointing kings and waging wars like all the other nations, and settling accounts with the Torah by enclosing it in a Sanctuary in the midst of such pomp and external display as one would bestow upon a deceased who would soon perish from all hearts and souls—at this time the nations came to realize that they really need not tremble so before the Torah.

Thus fared the Torah of Moses all the while that Israel sat upon its land, its king upon its neck, and the Temple atop both: famous throughout the world, its true followers now as if spread among the nations. In that measure to which the Torah extended over the superficies of the earth, to that degree did it become more superficial within the camp of Israel. In that measure to which some of its customs with external glitter, suitable for political officials, made their way in the world, to that degree did the Inner Spirit flee from the Jewish nation itself; and the materialistic craving for the tastes and temptations of the nations grew apace.

The prophets, men of great souls and inspired intellects, the Teaching of the Lord in their mouths, their hearts filled with the Intimate Presence from Mount Sinai—great was their sorrow over the foolishness of their people, and they stood warning the children of Israel that they were drawing ever nearer the precipice beyond which lay nothingness.

Not for this had the Holy One, Blessed be He, selected the children of Israel when He brought them forth out of Egypt and gave them the Torah at Mount Sinai, and certain it was that He would not tolerate forever their backsliding and turning aside from the mission assigned to them. Certain it was that He would soon lay hold of severe means to drive His people toward the goal He desired, shattering and destroying in wrath and fury all the crude contrivances and paraphernalia of alien "nationalism," from which were issuing influences damaging to and destructive of the Torah. That is, the Holy One, Blessed be He, would raze the palaces of kings, pull down the Temple, and exile Israel from its land.

Then, in those first days after the catastrophe, the children of Israel would suffer terribly; but from that darkness would shine forth a great light for them: from their bodily woes would be raised and established their spiritual world. Then would the Torah return to its proper lodging: in a parched desert was it given, and to the desert of Exile it would return. And there, in its traditional home, it would once more blossom forth in the hearts of the people. The nearness of God and the Intimacy of the Presence would return to them as in the days of old, as in the days of their departure from Egypt. In these words of warning the prophets expressed most pronouncedly the purpose of the destruction of the Temple and the Exile, of which events they did forewarn Israel continually. It is clear from this that Exile was not exclusively or even primarily a punishment for the past, but rather, and essentially, a constructive measure for the future: the return of the Presence to "Her place"—the hearts of all who are in a state of loneliness and solitariness.

The prediction of the prophets came to pass.

7.

The cessation of their pride in national sovereignty on the one hand, combined with strong feelings of loathing and rejection for the neighboring nations of those times, stirred within the children of Israel powerful longings for the God of their ancestors. At these times of longing there was born a strong urge to return to their source.

The returnees from Exile built the Second Temple by a scheme completely different from that used by Solomon in building the First Temple. Solomon stood inviting the nations from everywhere to come and take part in the building of the Temple, while the returnees from Exile made every effort to keep the nations far removed from all aspects of the project.

Even the idea of setting a portion of the subjugated Jews building a Temple "to whatever God promenades there in Jerusalem," originated entirely with the King of Persia himself ("the Lord awakened the spirit of Cyrus"); for it had not occurred to a single Jewish leader to appeal to the "gracious king" that the house of God might be rebuilt with the help of an alien king.

The kind offer of the king—the head "arranger" in the matter of rebuilding the Temple—to provide them with soldiers and horsemen for their protection on the way to Jerusalem, was refused by the exilic leaders with apparent humility but hidden sarcasm: "The hand of our God is over all those who seek good from Him; but His wrath and fury is upon all those who forsake Him." And to the other foreign volunteers who offered their services in the project, they replied simply and without further explanation: "It is not for you but for us to build a house for our God."

The contrast was felt most of all in the matter of the study of the Torah. For Solomon, the sacrificial worship was the principal activity of the house erected to God, and within it he offered such quantities of cattle and sheep—thousands upon thousands—that "the altar was too small to contain them all." For the exilic leaders, the sacrifices were merely incidental (a fact which will emerge clearly obvious to anyone who takes the trouble to inspect the sprit of the Scriptures with a perspicacious eye). It was practically a case of having to comply with the expectations of the Persian king, the inspirer and supervisor of the whole matter, who instigated the practice and also contributed toward it from his treasury. For the leaders of the people, the main purposes in erecting the Temple were: that they might thereby create a center for the study of Torah and the observance of the commandments, (for upon these they had set their hearts in returning to Jerusalem)—"For Ezra had set his heart to seek the law of the Lord, and to do it, and to teach in Israel statutes and ordinances" (Ezra 7:10) and that all the returnees from exile might collectively pour out, here in the midst of this holy center, all the tears of longing for their Father in Heaven which had accumulated in their hearts all those days during which they had been so far removed from His altar.

The concentrating of the People within itself, and the craving to live in intimacy with the Presence through the study of the Torah—the original intent of the giving of the Torah—earned itself, from that point on, permanent residence in the midst of Israel, and became a decree never to be transgressed, neither during that period of the Second Temple, nor in the time immediately after, nor for all time to come.

This is the ideal that was widely realized in the days of the Second Temple through the study of the "Oral Torah," the Oral Torah being both the partition which separates Israel from the other nations and that which strengthens its covenant with the Holy One, Blessed be He.

The Oral Torah, diligently studied and practiced, is the means whereby the Presence is brought to rest upon the heart of the individual Jew; and the giving to the Jew of this most precious gift for meditation—this wonderful, wise, and inspired collection of laws and legends in the Talmud—is also the expression of both the intimacy and affection of the Presence for him.

8.

This principle—the preservation of Jewish integrity (yihud)—was placed in the very foundation of the Second Temple, and because of it the vocation of the Oral Torah held the chief place in the spiritual life of the people; so much so, in fact, that the whole business of the Sanctuary and its sacrifices was reduced to second rank before it. "Greater is the study of Torah than the daily sacrifices" (Talmid Erubin 63a). And how indescribably less still was the value placed on the alien pleasure of "national sovereignty" as compared with the satisfaction of Torah.

Consequently, at the time of the destruction of the Second Temple the scholars were disinclined to wage a stubborn, all-out war, either for their political status or for the Temple—knowing full well that these possessions, which could be taken from them by the power of others, could not stand without such bloodshed, whereas their everlasting inheritance, the Torah, no power on earth could succeed in taking from them. And when Rabbi Yohanan ben Zakai was given the opportunity to salvage something by his influence, he asked for no national concessions, but only for "Yavneh and its scholars"—a refuge for the Torah. He asked nothing from the besiegers which was in reality theirs, for the granting of such a request would have been an act of grace on their part, and so would have created the expectation of perpetual gratitude. Instead he requested from them something which, whether or not they were willing to grant it, would in the final end remain in our hands.

Take note. The Second Temple was destroyed. The Higher Providence had found, apparently, that the good influence which dwelling in the land had on the spirit of the People—its being sanctified by the commandments connected with the land, as well as its taking upon itself the promissory seal of the "Covenant of the Parts" (Genesis 15:13-16), in these ways strengthening the bond between the People and its Heavenly Protector—such influence had already done its maximum to insure that, even though far from the land, the good effects of the land should not thenceforth cease among the people. The sacred memories of the land, and the turning toward it at the hour of prayer, would suffice to preserve its influence upon their hearts. And their further actual dwelling upon the land as a "kingdom" would bring, from that point on, greater spiritual loss than gain. For even those few remnants of the gross, outer shell, those mere fragments of the material paraphernalia of "nationalism"—i.e., even the dimmed example of the power-political life which still held sway at the time of the Second Temple—served to prevent the true inner Substance of the people from being revealed, which was its mission yet from the time of Mount Sinai. Therefore did Providence cast down even the vestiges of the paraphernalia of that "nationalism" and sweep them from the path.

Then did the Jewish people sprout wings truly free, rising to the uttermost heights, building for itself, in the great, spacious heavens, a buttress on the skiffs of the wind, far from the reach of the earth-dragon—that dragon which stands ever ready to make spectacles of the nations and monarchies: spurring this one against that one, stirring that one against this one, establishing "countries" and overturning them, enlarging "nations" and swallowing them.

At the hour when Titus the wicked packed all the vessels of the Temple for transfer to Rome by "ships of the sea"—then did our people take the Inner Substance of those vessels, the Holy Spirit, and carry it to its ships plying the air of the heavens, and establish there "the Heavenly Jerusalem."

Wherever Israel was exiled, wherever the people were sent, even though thousands of parsangs from Jerusalem, two images accompanied them: the image of "Jerusalem, the holy city," which the people would engrave on the tablets of their hearts, sealing therewith the memory of "the love of her espousals" with the Holy One, Blessed be He, in earlier times, in the days of her youth (cf. Jeremiah 2:2); and the image of "the Academy of Yavneh," which provided a living copy for every place of settlement as they established, everywhere they went, a House of Study in which they could continue their life with the Holy One, Blessed be He.

In these tiny academies the life of the couple, the Holy One, Blessed be He, and the Jewish people, was established in most wonderful fashion. The Holy One, Blessed be He, found greater contentment in the air of Torah in these tiny schools—unique to Israel and uniquely uniting Israel to Him—than in His former spacious mansion where they fattened Him with burnt offerings of living flesh, even while the boundaries distinguishing Israel from the rest of the nations became indistinct.

And the House of Study performed its work of perfecting the people in a wonderful way. In the Academy, on a diet of "cakes of Halachot/Religious Ways," the intellect of the Jew was sharpened. In the Academy, on "fruits of Aggadot/Religious Legends," his feelings were refined. And the two together—Laws and Legends—cast their scent, the scent of the Intimacy of the Presence, from the Academy into the homes of the Jews. By this means all the Jews, wherever on earth they were scattered, became in recognized measure "a kingdom of priests and a holy nation." And in the Academy the Jew renewed his strength, by which he survived all his pursuers, and so the presumption was confirmed: that the Jewish nation was the work of God.

9.

Thus were "Exile" and the "House of Study" two wonderful catalytic agents for the Jewish people, for by means of them it progressed in the task which the Lord had assigned it at Mount Sinai. And these two catalytic agents were interdependent. Academy without Exile would not have survived, for its light would have been extinguished by the thick shadows of sovereignty and state; and Exile without Academy also could not have existed, for its subject, the people in exile, would not have survived. That is to say, a people without a Torah—and many such peoples suffered exile—yields to the indomitable power of its conqueror and becomes assimilated within the invincible ruling nation. With this the Exile ceases, and with it also the correction and purification of Exile. The result of such an exile is merely that the exiled people is removed from its own Molech idolatry and transferred to the Molech idolatry of another. When Torah and Exile are joined, great wonders are born in the soul of their bearer.

"The Holy One, Blessed be He, said to them, 'My children, if the words of Torah will be near you, then I shall call you intimates;' as it is written, 'the children of Israel, the people of His intimacy'" (Deuteronomy Rabbah VIII,7).

10.

Until very recent times, so long as the recognition of the Exilic mission was strong among Jews, there was found hardly a single murderer among our people, not even as an exceptional case. But in recent times—since certain shallow ones among us have begun to cast aspersions on the Exile, by the same token also abandoning the study of the Torah—there have already been several isolated incidents of Jews launching fearful sieges, just like true citizens of a political state. But every exception merely confirms the rule. The Jewish community is still permeated by the recognition of its Exilic mission, and so its soul has remained uncontaminated by the poisonous corruption. And since the individual soul is an offshoot of the collective soul of its people, the desires of the heart of every individual Jew are still drawn to the side of holiness.

Justly, therefore, does the Midrash say, in reckoning the ethical balance of all that happened to us as a result of our losing our land: "Said the Holy One, Blessed be He, 'When it was destroyed'"—i.e., when the kingdom was destroyed and the root bearing gall and wormwood plucked out—"'you raised me for me righteous men; and when it was established, you raised Me wicked men'" (Song of Songs Rabbah).

11.

And thus it was that between two fires—the flaming light of Torah within our Houses of Study and the flaming eyes of the wolves outside—for two thousand years there was ceaselessly cast a singular and unique culture, one without parallel anywhere in the world: a culture soft as wax in material interests and hard as iron in matters of the soul.

And this culture grew, and developed, and presented before the whole world a people wondrous and legendary in its very surviving, and wondrous and legendary also in the quality of its soul and its way of thinking: a nation with ears attending and senses awake to every good idea; a nation which, if humanity sometime be ordered to make an ethical journey to bring redemption to the world, shall without doubt march at the head.

The purification of the soul of our people in Exile, and its being made receptive to every inspired idea—through which came about the possibility of understanding the previously proclaimed prophecy of our prophets, "nation shall not lift up sword against nation, neither shall they learn war anymore," not as prose resounding in the air but as compelling and perceptible logic—this purification was itself the Exilic creation of our people, and this was the very secret of our survival in Exile.

The sublime hymn, "Awake, awake, for your Light has come," sung ecstatically on the Eve of the Sabbath in synagogues wherever Israel is dispersed, is the spirit-in-song of our people's Exilic creation; and as night approaches to elevate the seventh day to its station as the Sabbath, the crowning glory of all Jewish creations, the hymn proclaims of its creator, the Jew, that he has not stopped making his Divine creations from the material of the commandments and the Torah of his God, nor will he stop such creating.

May the erring in spirit now realize that the lament of our people over "the Exile of the Presence" is no proof whatever of our people's having been, in Exile, emptied of the Holy Spirit; but, on the contrary, it is an indication of its being abundantly filled by the flow of the Holy Spirit. Thus even while our people laments the Exile of the Presence, and fervently longs for Its extension over all the world, it at the same time rejoices and takes great pride (for in this it may well take pride) in its Exilic Presence.

Chapter Five

The Freedom of Torah and the Arrogance of the Sword

1.

In the preceding chapter we explained how Exile prepared our people to receive the prophetic promises. We explained that the Exile transformed the Official Divinity which reigned in Israel so long as it lived a national, political life, into an Intimate Divinity; and that it planted the nearness of the Shechinah in the heart of every individual. By this intimacy with the Shechinah, the Jew's soul was made pure and his disposition sensitive. And purity of soul and sensitivity of feeling are the two chief qualities which impel the creation of the ideal, "Nation shall not lift up sword against nation," and which will also make it a living reality in the world.

We shall now draw attention to another quality which the Exile developed in our people, a characteristic which is also a powerful factor in the realization of the above mentioned ideal. I refer to the attributes of freedom and self-recognition or self-awareness, which the Exile has rooted deeply in the Jewish soul.

"Exile" and "Freedom" ! Undoubtedly the words will seem laughable in the eyes of the "negators of the Galut" among us, in the eyes of those gentlemen who will not for even one minute remove from their noses the hypnotizing spectacles of the powerful non-Jewish surroundings, through which they are grown accustomed to seeing only graciousness and glory among the non-Jews and only defects and deficiencies among us. For at the very head of their chart contrasting "they" and "we," prepared with the prior intention of disparaging our image, one finds the well known issue of "freedom" and "submissiveness." That is, how straight and erect is the soul of the established citizen, and how very great is his pride and his self-recognition. And in contrast to him, how bent and lowly the soul of the exile, the Jew; how despised and worthless is he in his own eyes.

Now these gentlemen rest their findings on a "tangible" fact, one to which they can actually point their fingers. They have taken note of the appearance of submissiveness given by the alien, the Jew, whenever he meets a solid citizen of the country, and have compared the comportment characteristic of each of the two at the time they meet: noting that the former stands with head bowed, speaking entreatingly, while the latter stands with head high, speaking impudently. From this they would establish that the latter is indeed free and respected while the former is merely a despised slave.

Now we who bring forward the notion widespread among all the initiated, that Exile planted freedom within our people, are by no means unaware of the appearance of the meeting described above. Yet despite this we strongly maintain our opinion for, as we shall explain presently, the fact referred to in no way touches the issue before us.

But before analyzing this occurrence of the citizen confronting the alien, we must first make clear that our position does not apply indiscriminately to any alien whomsoever, but exclusively to the Jewish alien. And this virtue of emancipating the spirit which we ascribe to the Exile, we do not claim holds for every case of Exile, however dark and ugly, but only for that Exile which is "black but comely," for that Exile which has with it Torah, for that Exile where the Exiles carry in their packs copies of the Bible and the Talmud, for that Exile which stirs within them a strong desire to meditate continuously on these books and which prepares the furrows of their hearts to receive well the influence of these books.

We now find ourselves making judgments about the Torah. But about which Torah? About the Torah of the Exile, i.e., that Torah which is deeply engraved in the souls of the Exiles. And so now, in opposition to those gentlemanly negators of the Exile who previously summoned their "tangible" fact as proof of their opinion, we, who affirm Galut and see it as an emancipator of the spirit, can also adduce one very powerful piece of evidence. This is the theory of the Mishnah: "'And the writing was the writing of God engraved upon the tablets;' read not 'engraved' (Hebrew harut) but 'freedom' (herut), for no man is free except one who engages in the study of Torah." (In other words, when the words of God are truly engraved on the tablets of the heart, they endow their possessors with freedom.)

This mighty dictum of the Mishnah, which not only relates the matter of freedom to Torah but decisively rejects all other kinds of freedom except the freedom of Torah, surely establishes at least this: that the concept of freedom is not something shallow or superficial, but rather a deep issue which requires considerable reflection; and that freedom in the modern sense, heard on every lip today, is not only far from the real meaning of freedom but quite another matter altogether.

2.

In all modern discussions of "freedom" and also in the propaganda of the parties fighting for freedom, this word "freedom" is always accompanied by the word "self-recognition" or "self-awareness." Now in essence the linking of these two words is correct. But the current propaganda, not having penetrated at all to the content of the words, has stumbled on the truth quite by accident, and so joins them only by superficial externals; and because of this its presentation of their interrelation will not be as it should.

For "freedom" according to this system is something one must "fight for," and "self-awareness" according to this system is neither less nor more than a part of the courage and daring required for the war—required to put spirit into the enslaved to seize the sword, rise against his oppressor, and so free himself.

In short, freedom according to this banal concept is something which needs to be gathered from the "outside." Even socialism, which is so far advanced in its ideas of liberty and freedom as to have formulated its well known proclamation, "freedom is not given but taken," despite this also agrees that freedom is held in the hands of others and that it must be released and taken from those others.

All the while, true freedom (explains the Mishnah, which has penetrated deeply into the matter) is man's inner freedom. True freedom hence rests in man's own hands. That is to say, when a man's eyes are opened to recognize his own essence and self, he is already free, and he needs no further declaration of independence or formal emancipation from others. "Self-awareness" is, therefore, not the mere preparation for freedom, but the very freedom itself.

But this also must be realized: the self-recognition of the Mishnah is not that of the modern propaganda. The latter's recognition is of independent pride and daring, resting on no base or reason other than that of "ability:" I am permitted to free myself and I must free myself because I am able to free myself. The Mishnaic self-recognition, on the other hand, does indeed include the recognition of dependence—on Him Who spoke and the world came into being—and it is clearly conditional to man's attaching himself to his Creator and making evident his form and image, the Divine image within him.

And since this attachment comes about only through concern for Torah, correctly did the Mishnah assert: "No man is free except one who engages in the study of Torah."

In the light of the foregoing it is possible to summarize the matter thusly: the order of acquisition of "freedom" and "self-recognition" is, according to modern propaganda, the opposite of what it is according to the Mishnah—and the difference is entirely to the credit of the latter. According to modern propaganda, since freedom is something external held by others, one must fight for it, taking strength and removing it from their hands. And "self-recognition" is of a self independent of others and self-dependent, whose essence is not characterized by anything external and whose existence is not assured by anything external. According to the Mishnah, the very reverse: freedom lies within the human spirit and requires no taking from the hands of one outside the self; and self-recognition is of a self indeed dependent on something else, but on something which, strong as a flinty rock, insures its existence: dependent on the eternal idea of "the resemblance of the form to its creator," and "in the image of God made He man."

This difference in the order of acquisition stems from the essential difference in their conception and goal. The goal of the modern propaganda for freedom is to free the bodies of the enslaved from the oppression of the masters, while the aim of the Torah propaganda for freedom is to free the souls of the enslaved from the defilement of the masters. The modern propaganda in inspiring the enslaved to fight for freedom arouses their wrath primarily against the impure deeds which the oppressing masters commit over the heads of the enslaved; the Torah propaganda arouses their ire primarily against the impure deeds which the oppressing masters compel the enslaved themselves to commit.

(N.B. In none of the preceding or the following do we even refer to that propaganda for the freeing of "countries" and "kingdoms," eagles" and "flags," which moves so gently among the nations through the plottings and intrigues of the diplomatic chiefs; for the vanity and deception of such "freedom" is so well known that there is no need even to speak of it. Throughout we speak of freedom in its most tangible and real sense, as in the propaganda of the Social-Democrats.)

Farther, according to the social-democratic propaganda, "freedom" means freeing the labor of the workers from exploitation by others; and "self-recognition" means recognizing the right to the fruits of one's labors. When one receives the fruits of one's labors, no matter from what source, then "freedom" is attained. And so, when repatriates are promised a large bonus, they return gladly to the work of their masters, even if the work be in the Krupp industries, in a factory preparing weapons to shatter skulls. The modern propaganda in this case is right: to achieve this kind of freedom one must indeed fight for it, for this freedom truly does lie in the hands of others and requires extracting from them.

For this kind of freedom the name freedom is not at all appropriate, for this is not soul-seeking but profit-seeking. The word profit has here been substituted for the word freedom, just as in the case of the other word, self-recognition, the words "recognition of one's own power" have been substituted. Here, consequently, there is no assurance that the emancipated will not afterwards turn subjugator, or that he who recognized his own power will not then oppress others. Here there is no assurance that those emancipated from one slavery will not soon fall prey to another. And the means themselves by which the above "freedom" is to be achieved—swords and spears—prophecy ill for the future of that acquired with their help. For is not the sword the expression of arrogance, and arrogance itself a sign of inner lowliness and nothingness? So that a sword resting on the thigh of a man suggests that the man himself rests on his sword—and so rests on something utterly vain and perishing.

3.

The only freedom deserving of the name is the freedom referred to by the Mishnah, the freedom of "one who engages in the study of Torah," the freedom of the Divine Image in man. And the freedom of the Divine Image is not so concerned about the exploitation of the body as about the exploitation of the soul. The Divine Image is not dismayed when the oppressor forces it to perform hard labor but rather when he would force it to worship idols.

The Divine Image is not degraded when the oppressor forces it to carry stones to the top of some wall, but rather when it is forced to throw stones at some head.

Hence the freedom of Torah is not unduly concerned about the bodily oppression of its bearer. To be more accurate, it is in fact very much concerned and angered by this, but it does not find it correct to wage stubborn wars on this account. Yet despite this it will fight, and fight with great stubbornness, against the oppression of the soul of its bearer.

"It will fight with great stubbornness"—i.e., this great stubbornness is its instrument of war.[83] For no other weapon (such as swords and spears) is recognized by him who engages in the study of Torah, not even in a war on behalf of that most sublime freedom, the freedom of the soul. Especially is this so since the freedom of the soul lies within the possessor of the soul, whereas brandishing of the sword is an activity which presents the matter in dispute as something lying out there needing to be taken by the sword. So in this case, such an activity would be entirely inappropriate.

This freedom, freedom of the soul, is the absolute freedom; and it is also the freedom which endures. This is the freedom of which others may be certain that from its possession no bondage will result for them; and whose inheritors may be sure that it will not finally, in the end, abandon them. For if it once shine forth in their hearts, never again will its light be extinguished.

It was this freedom which our people constantly and increasingly possessed throughout two thousand years of Exile. While its body was being first plucked and then drained by the ravishers, without their meeting any resistance, its soul grew even stronger and freer. This was thanks to the Presence of Torah, which nested in the hearts of the Exiles, and which stood courageously against the oppressors whenever they tried to subdue the soul.

---

[83] Cf. Gandhi on satyagraha. "Persistence" may be a more accurate translation.

This freedom began with Hananiah, Mishael and Azariah when they announced the following to King Nebuchadnezzar: "If it be for taxes and imposts, you are king over us" (we submit before you); "but if it be for the worship of idols" (to defile our souls), "you and a dog are as equals!" (Midrash Numbers Rabbah, Beha'alotecha) Or, in the alternate reading in Midrash Song of Songs: "But if it be this that you ask, to bow before your image, the command itself and the barking of a dog are as one before us!" And this freedom was maintained throughout all the later ages of persecution by hundreds of thousands of martyrs among our people who, with their cries of "Hear, O Israel," as they willingly went to the stake, engraved on the hearts of our people such a deep and profound love for the Torah that it will never be erased. "'For love is strong as death'—the love of the persecuted generations for the Holy One, Blessed be He" (Midrash Song of Songs). By their deaths, they made the Torah forever alive among our people, and by their martyrdom they rooted in our people that absolute freedom in whose eyes "the oppressor of the soul" and the "mongrel" are as one.

This unique and sacred chapter of our martyrs who went to the stake without seizing the sword, if indeed caused by the status and life conditions of our people, may still be seen as symbolic of the essence of that freedom to which our people aspired all the years of its wandering: that freedom which does not require procuring by the sword from without, but which is found within the person himself, that freedom which no oppressive or murderous hands can steal.

It is impossible that a people reared for two thousand years on the example of freedom presented by Hananiah, Mishael, and Azariah—regarding Nebuchadnezzar and his dog as alike at the time he decreed bowing down to him—should not have this freedom burning intensely in the hearts of a few chosen ones among its members. Moreover, in the hearts of all its members there should surely be found at least one spark of this freedom, even at this time. The spark should be there already at birth. But even more assuredly will this spark be inflamed in the Jew's heart each time he visits the House of Study and hears the sound of the reading of the Torah and the selection from the Prophets—those founts from which the Jewish soul draws both cleansing and strength, both purification and pride.

The accusation which Haman levelled against the Jews before King Ahasuerus, saying (according to the Targum Sheni), "One day in seven they rest, go to their synagogues, read their Scriptures, declaim their Prophets, and curse our kingdom and revile our sovereign," which amazes all those readers who know the custom of our people today (and certainly the custom dates from early times) which is just the reverse, blessing the king in the synagogue every Sabbath morning after the reading of the Torah—this accusation should not, in the light of our words, be at all astonishing.

For the villain senses instinctively the influence toward inner freedom exerted by the reading of the Torah and Prophets in the atmosphere of the synagogue on the Sabbath. In this atmosphere, filled with the Intimacy of the Shechinah and with the additional souls of the Sabbath, this influence on the congregation toward inner freedom resulting from the reading, was itself the most powerful of curses on the despotic kings and officials of Persia who loved to express their full impudence by forcibly defiling the souls of their subjects. Thus when that wicked man heard the Jews blessing the king on the Sabbath directly after reading the Torah (for such is their custom in order to insure peace among men), he responded like those poisonous rattlers which, when the sage tries to bring them near incense to assuage their wrath, become even more heatedly venomous. Just so did this villain become incensed to the point of wanting to destroy the Jews, and charged them with the sin of reading the Torah and Prophets just before blessing the king. In this accusation he was in effect complaining: What value, what value is there in the blessing of the king, in the blessing of the despot which comes forth from their mouths, after the curse upon despotism which comes forth from their culture and their education? What possible effect can the blessing of the ruling despot have in a synagogue where the air is filled with curses upon the reigns of tyrants?

From that aforementioned spark of freedom this known fact also results: all the kneeling and bowing of the Jew (even the smallest and most humble Jew) before the mighty is not sincere but merely conventional. In his bowing before the mighty, the Jew acknowledges only the former's power to strike him a blow good and true, but in no degree whatsoever does he acknowledge the "divine-man" within him. He humbles himself only before the flesh of his arm, not before his spiritual image. Indeed, the tyrant's spiritual image is utterly contemptible, and as nothing in the Jew's eyes. "In bowing before your image, you and your dog are as one in our eyes!" What stronger proof have we that this was the inner attitude of the Jewish heart—regarding as naught the spiritual image of the violent and mighty—than this fact: never were the latter able to force our people to abandon their religious beliefs, even in the face of all the persecutions throughout the ages. It would not have been quite so easy for our people to have summoned the stubborn resistance which they displayed against the mighty, had they not been constantly supported in their terrible sufferings by this clear assessment of the true spiritual image of the mighty.

4.

Up to now we have clarified well enough, in a theoretical way, our position that our people includes within it the true freedom. We shall now proceed to analyze the "tangible" fact brought by the "negators of the Galut" as a proof of their position, that the Jew in Exile is an enslaved and lowly creature, whereas the citizen of the land is a free and proud creature: the fact that when the citizen meets the Jew, the former stands with neck haughty and the latter with head bent.

In reply to this "proof," there is the following to be said. First, the act of standing humbly before the lords of the land belongs in the category of "If for taxes and imposts, you are king over us," in the category of those material goods relinquished by our people after it saw its political bow shattered, and came to realize its true purpose and mission in life. At that time it renounced and set aside such things as needs of secondary importance, and therefore not to be warred over. What new do the lordly negators of the Exile reveal, therefore, when they tell us that the Jew willingly presents, along with his other taxes, the tax of tipping his hat before the mighty? It is hardly news that the Jewish people is not, for example, a professional class waging war beneath red banners in order to abolish taxes or increase wages; for it does not see in the abolition of taxes or the raising of wages the achievement of happiness.

And what indignity have these lords found with the exiled Jew's behavior when he encounters the citizen? The fact that the Jew willingly tips his hat to the mighty, happily paying this material tribute, does not in the least prevent him from saying to this same mighty one immediately afterwards, either in word, thought, or deed: but if you want to try forcing my soul, you and a dog are as one in my eyes.

Secondly, in presenting the act of Jew and citizen meeting, the aforementioned lords commit a simple deception. They point the finger at a single line, the borderline between the two peoples, and hide their eyes from the great areas which lie further back on either side of the border, the whole internal lives of the respective groups. It is true that on the border where the two peoples meet, the citizen appears erect and proud. But let us venture one step inside the boundary, to the inner world of the citizens among themselves, and there you will see how pressed and pinched, bound and bent is the stature of that citizen alone by himself, how hunched and displaced his human form in his own world. For that whole world is like a high ladder with many rungs, this one above that one and this one beneath that one; and every single one of its "citizens" finds his head situated beneath the tail of the occupant above, and his own tail above the head of the occupant beneath. In such a manner, each one is, with respect to his tail, a master... and with respect to his head, a slave! Every one of them must consequently worm his way along, crawling like a reptile before his higher up and striding like a bear on the one beneath.

For this is the way that the culture prescribed by the sword crushes and breaks the souls of its trainees: by making each of its trainees half arrogant and half base, but not one whit a free man. By this it makes them fit and ready to fulfill the goal of the sword—to be dragged forth with ease on the day of need, into the midst of the whirling orgy.

In contrast to this, now survey, if you will, the internal scene on the other side, within the border of the Jewish world. There you will find reigning, in contrast to the world outside, almost complete equality. In the Jewish world you will not find the wealthy so lording it over the poor, nor the great over the small; and neither will you find the poor and humble so prostrating themselves before the great and wealthy.

For this, indeed, is the way of the culture shaped largely by the teachings of Torah: standing watch to make sure that the Divine image does not become blurred, and trying to prevent the division between great and small (which reigns so intimidatingly in that other world) from assuming the form of lordship and slavery.

Hence the citizen mentioned above, in his own world half master and half slave, at once arrogant and base, when he goes for a walk down his own street, seeking there some satisfaction for his arrogant half—i.e., hoping to meet a citizen of lesser status who will bow and humble himself before him—may, before finding such a sought-after man, himself be compelled to humble himself ten times before others of higher station whom he may chance to meet on the way. But in contrast to this, if he continue his hike just a bit further and come to the "street of the Jews," there appears before him a peaceful, inviting plain, easy to trample without opposition. There appears before him a whole world of those without "rights," whose greatest figures must humble themselves before the smallest of small in his world. There his pleasure in strolling is complete, for his arrogant desires can be fully satisfied as soon as he meets the first Jew; for the latter's figure quickly bows before him (in obedience to the Exilic command not to be too scrupulous over external-bodily humilities), and his own figure assumes twice its usual height.

The shallow see this incident on the boundary between the two peoples, and immediately ascribe freedom to the world of the citizen and subservience to the world of the Jew. But they ignore all the rest that goes on within the respective worlds. They ignore the fact that in the world of the solid citizen there is found only arrogance, not freedom (and the arrogance itself resides only in the lower half of the citizen, from which of necessity it follows that in his upper half there resides base lowliness). True freedom is found only in the world of the Jew. For true freedom is found only in a culture shaped by the prescriptions of Torah; in a culture prescribed by the sword one can at most have arrogance.

Those "negators of Exile," who see "freedom" and "self-recognition" only among the citizens, have obviously confused "arrogance" and "haughtiness" with "freedom," and the "recognition of strength and power" with "self-recognition."

Freedom can only be inherited by an Exiled people with Torah. And this freedom, as is well known, is one of the chief factors leading to the abolition of sword-waving. For even the sword-waving of that private, gratuitous "War of the Years," was itself the expression of the inner emptiness and degradation of its brandisher, who tried to salvage his honor by these inglorious means.

As for the sword-waving which goes on in "national" wars, where the individual is dragged in without choice, how much more in such cases is it based on slavery (and on the real slavery: the defilement of the soul of the enslaved). The rooting out of such sword-waving can come only through inner freedom.

And all the sublime visions of the prophets are especially directed at wars of this latter kind. It is not written, "man shall not lift up sword against man," but rather, "Nation shall not lift up sword against nation." For it is this sword, the collective sword forcibly placed in the hand of the individual against his will, which presents the greatest danger to the world today; and it also surpasses by far all private abominations.

Finally, learn from the foregoing this as well: that our people, the Exilic people of the Torah, carries within its bosom the seeds of the prophetic ideal, "Nation shall not lift up sword against nation;" for it includes within itself both the foundation of freedom and the basis for the soul's refusal to perform evil in the face of whatever command.

Chapter 6

Israel's global mission and its separation from the world

1.

Having discussed in great detail in previous chapters the meaning and the measure of the exile and having attempted to elucidate why the exile is an elevation of Israel's status, rather than a descent—we have now arrived, without further ado, at the splendid gates of our global mission, the task which was appointed to the Israelite nation by the prophets, namely "to be a light unto the nations."

Regarding our mission, three stages have come to pass during our exile: The period of time of abundant feeling but little discussion; the period of abundant discussion but little feeling; and the period that was distinguished by neither speech nor feeling, but rather by humiliation and ridicule...

"The period of abundant feeling but little discussion" was an extended period of time (analogous, in fact, with the length of the entire exile), when the Jewish people were of one mindset and one type (this period lasted until the end of the previous century among the nation in its entirety, and persists among the majority to this very day), with some superficial variation depending on the time and the place.

During this long period, the cognizance of this aforementioned mission burned steadfastly in the hearts and minds of the entire nation as a natural and simple yearning, which didn't need to be articulated, and also as a humble feeling, a feeling emanating from the depth of the soul, remaining hidden in the heart, unaccustomed to gallivanting and parading in the markets and thoroughfares.

This awareness that "we were a light unto the nations" did not diminish or fade, even as the greatest of the Israelite sages (i.e., sagacious in Torah) encountered philosophy and secular sciences, the product of the fertile minds of gentile sages. Despite the fact that the gentile sages of yore showed formidable aptitude in their pursuit of wisdom and invented many ingenious novelties, from which the foundations of all scientific industrial advancement derives, and despite the fact that the Torah sages respected these fields of knowledge and demonstrated a serious interest in their pursuit, despite all of this no depreciation of the value of our holy Torah was ever discernible, and thus there was no diminishment in the way we saw ourselves as compared to the nations.

When it came to our Torah, they knew without a shred of doubt, that the Torah was more valuable than all the other forms of knowledge, from an aesthetic perspective as much as from the light it cast upon the world.

"From an aesthetic perspective"—for after all, other forms of knowledge are tethered to the earth, and the way in which they develop must ultimately derive from a sensory and cognitive process, which usually takes place without regard to distinctions of creed and language, though some nations do develop in this way more slowly than others.

The Torah is, however, a celestial wisdom, the emergence of which was "miraculous," indeed *sui generis*, and was brought into this world through the agency of the Jewish nation for whom the heavens parted and lit the lowly earth with a celestial light, the light of the human soul, the light we may refer to as "holy" ("You should be holy, for I am holy"). And the reservoirs fashioned from this light, from biblical literature, remained in the world, forever itinerant, supplying the matter for the greatest art of all—the art of "holiness."

And as a light to the nations, the light of all the secular sciences is cast only upon the world, upon all things human. This category includes the human being himself and the light that shines upon him. But it shines upon him only as one link that links all the rest of the inhabitants of the universe, not upon his soul. In effect the light which shines upon him makes him a dark and materialistic being, a prosaic creation. The Torah, however, spreads its light upon the human being as an entity distinct from all else; and with this light that it shines upon him, it transforms him into a bright and incandescent object, a poetic object.

Therefore, the secular sciences, though they may overflow with bounty, cannot fill a man's soul, and his life would remain vulnerable to assimilation (these sciences would cast him in the melting pot with the rest of the universe's inhabitants). All of his existence would be desolate and rather boring, and the entirety of creation would be untended and abandoned. Therefore, after the world was built, beautiful and alone, with no person to look at it and derive pleasure from it, the Torah came and created the human being, or more specifically the person's inner soul, and gave him an advantage over other creations. The world now had purpose. Life gained an unparalleled spice and was adorned in holiday apparel forevermore.

For this reason, no uncertainty insinuated itself into the heart of the nation throughout the long years of exile regarding the value of Torah as compared to the other sciences; nor did they, immersed as they were in holiness, doubt their own worth as compared to other nations, who spent their time with the secular. Neither the nation's sages nor the nation needed to ostentatiously display their mission to the outside world in order to justify their existence.

This was the long period in which there was a lot of sentiment regarding our status as the light unto the nations, but little discussion, and this lasted all throughout the exile, and continues to this very day amongst the majority of our brethren.

2.

The present period—of little sentiment and much discussion—is what shall be spoken of anon. In the previous century, the industrial revolution advanced in heedless leaps and bounds. In other words, the abstract sciences did not themselves advance so much, but perhaps not so little either, and the basic wisdom and the theories that the sages of yore had laid as a foundation, were used as the basis for a great deal of practical experimentation by modern day scientists. Some of the experiments were a straightforward application of theoretical tomes, and some were more elaborate and ingenious. Scientists combined the known theories with others, and through this synergy created wondrous machines. These machines enriched all branches of industry and filled the land with motion and great sound. The nations in whose countries the automatons vibrated were filled with pride, and the government of those nations were filled with authority and the urge to dominate as they built their machines of war.

These developments catalyzed by the industrial revolution amongst the known gentile nations frightened the weak of heart among our Israelite brethren, dwelling as they were in the moth-eaten spiritual environment of those peoples, regarding the value of our own exiled nation, which had no tools to manufacture such mighty armaments. And the latter individuals started to reconsider their conduct and search minutely amongst their possessions in order to find some sort of passport so they could show the nations a testament justifying our existence.

They searched and of course found the well-known testament. And with it they say, "O nations do not imagine us to be merely simple wanderers who lost their land and sovereignty because of our weakness and inability to fight for it, we are not a discarded and useless tool… lowly creations that are not good for any important task… rather our dispersion among you was part of God's oversight, so that we may become your teachers and spiritual guides in the knowledge of God."

This was the time of which we spoke, of little sentimentality but much verbal ado (in other words much outwardly directed braggadocio), which has been referred to in recent literature as "the time of the attestors."[84]

This period, however, which unfolded among specific nations and un-

---

[84] A note on the use of attestors, testament, and mission: Tamares frequently employs word *"te'udah"* throughout these final chapters. His two most common uses of the term are the references to *"ba'aley te'udah,"* which I have translated as attestors, and *"te'udah"* by itself which I have either translated as "mission" or "testament" depending on the context. The reason for this translational choice is based on both semantic and circumstantial considerations. The word *"te'udah"* is understood as a derivative of *"ed* - witness / *edut* - testimony. I translated *"ba'aley teudah"* as attestors, because this group of people saw themselves as teachers and transmitters of Jewish knowledge to others. This usage does not, however, effectively convey Tamares' intention when he speaks of Israel's *"te'udah,"* which is both inwardly and outwardly focused, and thus more aptly expressed by the word mission, not just transmission to others. I still employ the term "testament," when it is contextually apt, especially in places when Tamares' is speaking about *"ba'aley hate'udah."* -T.Y.

der known spiritual conditions was short-lived, and very soon afterwards, the Zionist movement began to coalesce. The latter movement created for itself a distinct literature, and through this literature catalyzed a change in our testament, claiming that "it is the sentiment and the message of the testament which is to be ridiculed and derided." For, as we know, the first rhetorical act of Zionist literature (we speak here of "political" Zionism) when it emerged into the world was to cause a deluge of ridicule to rain upon our testament, a deluge which has never really ceased. Zionist literature caricatured these "attestors" and transformed them from the very beginning as a rhetorical device to serve their means. And whenever early Zionist writers wished to dismiss an undesirable opinion and silence the author it was enough––or so they thought—to label the person who articulated this opinion as "an attestor."

For as we mentioned above the attestors were weak in one particular way: paralysis seized them when they were confronted with the industrial progress of the world's nations, and they were moved to manufacture a certificate of Kashrut for their benefit. This inferiority complex is indeed worthy of sage rebuke. They deserve a slap on the face from our Torah scholars, who would say to them: "O infantile ones, O fearful men! Our forefathers did not see themselves as diminished or inferior to the nations, even as compared with the nations who developed the foundations of knowledge and science, for they knew (the very fabric of their beings confirmed it) the truth of the Rabbinic adage: Though God is indeed generous toward Japheth, He dwells in the tents of Shem" (Yoma 10)––and you diminish yourselves before modern day nations, titans of industry, who simply applied the theories and made them practical. You are therefore not genuflecting before higher wisdom, but before power and wealth. And if so, your accomplishments are pathetic, as are your attempts to ingratiate yourselves to the nations as teachers and spiritual mentors. What wonderful teachers of divine knowledge you are with these beautiful insights…

The weakness of the attestors, which is evident in the reason they sought this role in the first place, allows one to ridicule them regarding the absurdity of their approach, namely that their shame and ineptitude vis-à-vis the nations would be remedied by fulfilling the dreamed-of role of teachers and mentors… as the parable goes, the wife of a luckless man who was chastising her husband said to him, "If you are failing at everything, you could become a teacher!"

The right to ridicule the attestors is given to the nation as a whole since their Jewishness is alive and well, but not under any circumstances is this right given to Zionist literati. The weakness these intellectuals evinced vis-à-vis the lords of the land, which in the attestors' writings had only begun manifesting, developed in Zionist literature, to the point of forcefully contending that a nation without territory is not a nation—they decided that a person should not be judged by his own merit but rather by his earthly possessions, opining that our nation is not even worthy of being teachers. Their hazing of the attestors is to be understood, therefore, not as ridicule for their impotence but rather these literati scorned the shred of courage that they, the attestors, still possessed, namely that they still believed they could succeed at one thing—as teachers. For according to Zionist literature our nation in exile is completely and utterly impotent. Their ridicule is what our sages would refer to as "kicking someone while they're down." The Zionist derision vis-à-vis the attestors is more cynical than any our persecuted nation has had the misfortune of witnessing.

As you can tell, I have veered off topic, and dipped into the raging polemic against the "attestors," which was necessary to introduce the subject I wish to elaborate upon. For in the course of my discussion I will be prone to criticize the methods of the attestors, and I must distinguish myself from political Zionist literature, so that my critique is not understood as part and parcel of their derisiveness.

And now let us return to the subject at hand.

3.

As I elaborated upon in detail in previous chapters, our mission to be "a light unto the nations" is not less likely to succeed in exile—it is more likely than ever.

One should not, however, understand our testament (articulated in previous chapters) as entirely straightforward—namely that the reason we were exiled from our country and scattered among the nations was that so we would mentor them in the spiritual sciences, as the attestors of the period and countries referred to above would have it. The reason for our exile, however, was that we would first be a light unto *ourselves* and internalize the lesson the exile was supposed to teach us, and only at a later time and as a corollary, would we be "a light unto the nations." In other words, at the right time the gentile nations will open their eyes and observe the intrinsic worth of the eternal nation (the Israelite nation) dwelling in their midst and emulate their conduct.

Our testament "to be a light unto the nations" does not require of us to actively mentor these nations *per se*. In fact, the testament should not occupy us continually, even as a subject for rumination. For as I mentioned above, the enlightenment of the nations is their business, not ours. In other words, the nations must take the necessary steps and our job is to maintain equanimity and spiritual steadfastness. It was for this reason and for this reason only that our nation was shown favor. We were shown favor so that our spirit would be strong and hale and so that we would fulfill the purpose for which we were created, namely, to be a light unto the nations. This knowledge should be employed as a source of energy, inspiring us to become perfect in every way, since knowing of the genius intrinsic in oneself does not confer a blessing if it is hidden away in a secret place in the soul, in the crevices of the psyche, revealing itself fleetingly in thoughts, and rarely on the tongue and lips… its diffuse vapors disappearing… In short, our testament "to be a light unto the nations" is not a practical matter, but neither is it an idle thought. The aspect of our exilic testament that *is* our active responsibility is to enlighten ourselves.

Our testament "to be a light unto the nations" does not place any burden of responsibility upon us to act or direct any thought toward the gentile nations; rather this light should be internally focused (like the light of the menorah in the tabernacle whose candles were all pointed inward), and our light to the nations will inevitably appear when they finally open their eyes and observe the splendor in our world.

Our instruction to the nations is not a simple matter of appearing before them and teaching them directly in the descriptive manner; rather it must be indirect and practical, of the "do as I do" variety. Thus, our mission to be a "light unto the nations" (as our prophets predicted) is closely related to another prophetic promise, that we be "standard bearers (examples) for the nations."

This type of practical pedagogy is what our nation understood to be their task, contrary to the attestors who simply wished to teach descriptively.

Between these two visions of our mission is a deep chasm of difference, both ideological and practical.

Firstly, these two visions differ in how they see the exile. According to the attestors we must enlighten the nations through descriptive instruction without intermediaries; in other words they opine that we should essentially be teachers and not apprentices, and thus don't see the exile as beneficial in any way to the Jews themselves. And since the exile is not beneficial, it must be detrimental, at least to the people of Israel who have to bear it. The beneficiaries are the nations of the world (the attestors view the idea of exile, i.e., dwelling among the nations as essentially worthless). Our great accomplishment, the belief in one God, which we acquired while we lived in our land and sovereign territory (a state conducive to mental maturation according to these negaters of exile), our ancient wealth of spirit, is therefore wealth that doesn't enrich those who possess it; it is our burden to bear and the world's to enjoy. As those entrusted with disseminating the idea of oneness among the nations we are cast upon the earth as desolate wanderers, enduring physical privations, but also spiritual privation (and our wisdom rots away, like the landless youth in the parable quoted by the attestors); in order that our spiritual wisdom doesn't entirely dissipate for lack of an anchor, we are commanded to spread it to the four corners of the earth.

The correct understanding of our mission to be a light unto the nations, however, is that we teach about God by example. The exile is in fact, the opposite of what the attestors conceived: It is primarily a school to refine ourselves, not the nations. In the exile we are apprentices, and indirect mentors showing the world a live example of how one is to fulfill the divine ideal.

This considered difference in attitude toward the exile completely changes what it means to be faithful, as we shall discuss below (Israelite's distilled faith is a concept which the attestors love to trumpet); which in turn leads to a practical difference in how Israel the teacher is supposed to comport himself vis-à-vis the students, the gentile nations of the world.

According to the attestors' pedagogy of description and summary which relies on straightforward instruction, our nation must try to draw nearer to the nations and accommodate them as much as possible. For it is one of the great rules of instruction that the teacher must try to penetrate the spirit of his students and conform himself to the way they see the world; in this way the students are more likely to understand what he's trying to teach. The way in which this would play out is that we would begin as teachers but end up as students learning their ways… our nation would no longer be unique and even the Torah we'd be trying to teach would be altered.

If we teach practically and through mentorship, however, which is the core of our mission, the opposite will hold true. Our nation must therefore distance itself from the nations, who are its students, and remain aloof in every possible way. Only then will our nation survive and preserve its unique qualities so as to transmit them to the rest of the universe. For if our nation behaves any differently, our nation will perish and our mission to the nations will die as well.

4.

All the changes listed above ultimately derive from one principle shift, and that is how one understands the "knowledge of God" which the prophets promised we would spread in the world.

If "knowledge of God" is to be defined as inquiry and philosophical meandering regarding the prime catalyst and accordingly the beautiful religion or distilled belief is no more than the belief in oneness, and this is what is disseminated as "knowledge of God," then the Israelite nation does not need to remain so separate and aloof from the nations. Belief in oneness does not require a special people. This type of belief may be found in a world without Jews.

And you could also say that the principles of this belief have already been adopted by the majority of gentile nations which call themselves enlightened. And also the little that is left to teach to these nations seeking to achieve the complete oneness of the Israelite nation, or more aptly the privileged recognition regarding this specific idea of oneness, is starting to spread, and is more apparent in the writings of gentile intellectuals every day that passes, and this refined oneness is gradually revealed among them.

Spreading knowledge of God in this way is didactically useful only to professors of theology in their cathedrals and ministers upon their altars, while the rest of the world sinks to the 49th gate of impurity. This type of outreach to the nations is entirely tenable according to the dreams of attestors, for it will be well-received by the nations. Experience has taught the nations that they needn't fear the refined monotheism as they did at Mount Sinai, for the present belief does not pose a threat to their bellicosity and nationalism. The success of their endeavours has even been more pronounced after adopting many of the teachings of this distilled monotheism, so much so that in their eyes there is no reason not to adopt the little that remains…

The pride of these gentiles will not be offended enough to refuse such instruction from a "kike." Firstly, when they gather him into their house, the instruction shall change so completely, that it soon won't be apparent that he was ever a Jew; and secondly, a needy tutor, having been subsumed into a wealthy household, does not in any way detract from the grandness of his master. For the so-called instructor bows before his host and gives the latter precedence in every conversation (especially if he is of the type that fauns before the rich… as those who negate the exile do).

"Come to us then, dear kikes," the nations shall say. "Come instruct us and shelter under our roof, and be teachers or whatever you want to be, but at the very least come into our house and let us know you… let us know your refined religion, much of which we have already digested… now we are willing to further accept it. We are willing to accept what remains of your beliefs and your bodies as well. Your destiny has come and gone, kikes, now depart from the podium!"

This type of scenario is quite possible if one understands "knowledge of God" as theological or religious inquiry.

True knowledge of God, however, as the prophets understood it, is related to intimacy. The knowledge of God that the prophets urged upon humanity is correctly understood as nearness to God, as is alluded to in the verse "they yearn for closeness to God" (Isaiah 57). Closeness to God is not the same at all as a pithy argument in an academic article, or the concept of "cult" (Gottes-Dienst) in a book of prayers. The latter were conceived in order to bring one aesthetic pleasure, but the soul itself is not nurtured by these and cannot develop to its full potential. Some amusement may be derived by contemplating this concept of closeness to God but real intimacy with God will not be attained.

Knowledge of God as understood by theologians and ministers is not synonymous with closeness to God. The holy prophets who urged knowledge of God did not do so in order to invent some amusing pastime, but rather to elevate humanity to the pinnacle of their moral destiny, to transform human beings into gentle and pure creatures, who choose only good and who utterly abhor evil.

The cleansing of the human soul, that and only that, is what is meant by "closeness to God," and indeed closeness to God is a necessary step in the achievement of this process. For it is impossible for the human soul to be cleansed without engaging with the God of the Bible or the *Shekhinah* of the Torah.

Indeed, the prophets made the achievement of this ethical pinnacle contingent upon knowledge of God (destined to occur in the end of days): "They shall do no evil, neither shall they be corrupt, for knowledge of God has filled the land."

For "knowledge of God" means "closeness to God," or more specifically: the moral ideal of being at one with the divine presence in a setting devoid of negative inclinations. So until the time in which the pleasant-holy sense of morality will encounter humanity as a whole (as the prophets have ordained), and that time has yet to come, the Israelite nation, the people exquisitely sculpted into this tender material through their travails and their Torah and in whom are ingrained so many of the prophetic ideals, must make sure to zealously maintain their aloofness and separation from the nations.

For it is through this separation of the Jews from the nations that spiritual pleasure is set aside for the sake of the nations at the end of days, for the Israelite nation will be the backbone, nay the wellspring, of the moral resuscitation of humanity. And up until this time our separation confers upon the universe a measure of good, since it ensures that at least one corner of the world is free of the sickness and filth that threaten to overwhelm the world as a whole.

5.

What may be surmised from our arguments is that our nation does indeed have a pan-global mission, a mission to fix the world. Our duties do not consist of disseminating the tenets of the true religion throughout the world as teachers, but rather in looking out for ourselves and maintaining the vitality of the Israelite nation as it exists in this world. We were not exiled in order to teach or instruct but rather to be apprentices and further develop. We have not come into this world in order to disseminate an aesthetic veneer of a distilled religion; rather, at least for now, we seek to cleanse ourselves through the Torah. Influencing nations will be a natural corollary.

In point of fact, we are unable to become religious instructors, for we do not possess beliefs or traditions which fit these concepts as the nations understand them. For they understand them in an abstract and foreign way as separated from life and removed from human concerns, as a belief which may be accessed from time to time when a person is moved to pray or genuflect. We, however, have the Torah, the Torah which is referred to "as the Torah of life" and as such is inexorably intertwined in the fabric of the day to day existence of the Israelite nation. This symbiotic relationship was divinely preordained. Just as the Torah's function vis-à-vis the world was evident to the creator as He formed the universe, so too was the destiny of the Israelite people, who were intended to be a living embodiment of the Torah which was created specifically for them.

It is known that in prophetic and Rabbinic literature the Torah and the people are one. We needn't bring quotes from the prophets, for their words regarding this hendiadys are so famous; but we will bring a short selection of the numerous Rabbinic adages on this matter.

"Six things preceded the creation of the world, the Torah, Israel etc…" "Israel's conception preceded everything" (Midrash Genesis Rabbah, Bereshit). "Who was created for whom: Was the Torah created for Israel or was Israel created for the Torah? Was it not the Torah for Israel?" (Midrash Kohelet). "They were a nation that made peace between Me and My world, for if they hadn't accepted the Torah I would have destroyed My world, indeed they are the people who make the edifice of creation whole" (Midrash Genesis Rabbah, Toldot).

All these Rabbinic dictums are indicative of a deep and abiding belief in our nation's vitality at the beginning of the exile, at a time when our apprenticeship was just beginning and we were learning how to be close to God. The Rabbis understood that it was through our nation and our nation alone that the Torah's teachings found an outlet.

All of these rabbinic citations are proof of the sages' farseeing and incisive realization at the advent of the exile long ago, at the beginning of our apprenticeship in the field of "closeness to God." The sages astutely recognized that in our nation only among all the nations of the world one finds a true reflection of the Torah's content.

For the Torah's content is synonymous with "closeness to God," or in other words, the dignity and refinement found only in the Jews of the Diaspora, colloquially referred to in the language of the people of bygone years as "the Jewish focal point," or, by the modern term "Hebraic Culture" in our most recent literature.

The modern terminology is quite apt. For it is true that our beliefs and traditions (which are the beating heart of our nation) are not in the same category as other world religions, nor are they a philosophical or scientific entity which may be analyzed with the tools of theological rhetoric: These beliefs and traditions are a unique cultural phenomenon—a way of life that is utterly distinct from any people or nation.

This is the secret of our nation, the focal point, which countless of our brethren have yearned for, sages and simpletons, orthodox and liberal. If our belief system were merely religion, the free-thinkers among us would not yearn for it, and if it were a fragment of abstruse philosophy, the *hoi polloi* of Israel would not cleave to it so ardently. Our belief is not this nor that, it is "the Torah." The Torah which is referred to as the Torah of life: the Torah which is the font of the special and wondrous life of a people, and therefore the yearning for it is so great among those who consider themselves part of this nation.

And since our belief is the Torah and the Torah is the embodiment of our nation's holy life—we are completely unable to function as religious instructors at this time (as long as God has not cleansed the nations from above) in the way that the attestors imagine is possible.

If our nation were to become teachers of a refined and polished creed, dressing in white collars and reading the thirteen principles from a shiny leather-bound book of catechisms; if our nation were to become religious instructors (the inevitable result of adopting the way of the attestors), in the mould of the Jüdischer Religions Lehrer in the German schools, unneeded and unwanted, except to appease the hearts of Jewish parents as they read the children snippets of "prayer" so that they will willingly sacrifice their children upon the altar of Germanization; or like the Field-Rabbi whose job it is to pray with the Jewish soldiers before going into battle, or to grant them atonement and promises of an afterlife when they are injured, pulling the wool over their eyes when it comes to the follies of war; in this way and for this purpose the nations would surely accept us.

Our religion, however, is not of the white-collar variety of the *Religions Lehrer* or of the dinner-jacket variety of the spiritualist. Our religion has been sculpted through persecution and exile and woven upon the same loom as our life, which has been very different from that of every other nation. And our Torah, the Torah of life, aside from it having been developed for thousands of years into a form that is inimitable by the nations of the world, is not coveted by the nations, nor is there any desire to emulate the ways of our Torah.

This refusal to accept our Torah is actually quite fortunate for us, for it is a sign that we tread upon a path preordained. We require that that Torah's initial attributes, those same attributes apparent at Sinai, endure (while the nations of the world are mired in their pollution), as the Midrash states, "God offered the Torah to every nation, and none wished to accept it."

6.

If we desire to contemplate our unique aptitude mentioned above, namely, "closeness to God" as it is referred to in our Bible, or more colloquially, "the Jewish focal point," or alternatively "Hebraic Culture" as it is referred to among the literati, we must ask—how did this aptitude come to emerge in the hearts and minds of our nation? And what are the tools by which this aptitude was sculpted and refined? We needn't look far.

"The unique Jewish focal point," the attribute which has come into focus over the course of thousands of years, is now staring us right in the face. In tandem with the Jewish focal point are the learning of Torah and the singular traditions, which were observed by Jews throughout this entire time period.

Phenomena which always occur in tandem indicate a connection between them, even if *prima facie* it is not evident. The two phenomena, referred to above are, however, clearly connected in an intimate synergy: the "Jewish focal point" was refined by means of our nation's singular traditions, but primarily through the unique font of the Torah. We have thus revealed the tools which helped develop our nation's singular spiritual aptitude. And the catalyst for this soulful immersion, this refinement of the spirit, is also quite clear: It is the exile, it is that we are "strangers in a strange land."

This means that in order to maintain our exceptionalism and defend our "Jewish focal point" we must strive to hold fast to our hearty traditions: simply put, to follow the Torah's precepts. And above all we must continue studying Torah and Talmud, which are the building-blocks of the wall between Israel and the nations.

The toll that Torah study imposes upon us is entirely worthwhile since it distinguishes us from the nations, and this would hold true even if it were onerous and not exhilarating. And it is indeed exhilarating and provides untold benefits to the soul. This tax is, therefore, not so much a tax, but a pleasure. If the gentile nations establish clubs dedicated to the sharpening of the mind, such as chess clubs, which have no higher purpose beyond pleasurable striving, and are ultimately egotistical—shouldn't our nation be ecstatic in its delightful and precious pursuit of Torah study? Intrinsic to this pastime, beyond the fun (and the pleasure of learning Torah is intrinsically fun and may be undertaken even when one is alone contemplating a book, and it is not like other games which require a partner wherein the pleasure that is to be had is beating the other person, which is a victory for man's evil inclinations), is its wondrous relationship to the fixing of the world. For through this pleasurable pastime, the uniqueness of our nation is defined and bolstered, and as they refine their "closeness to God" they prepare the contours for the moral resurrection of humanity in the future.

Up until this point we have spoken of the preservation of the sculpting tools with which our art, or our holiness, was perfected. We must also give credit to the catalyst which honed this tool, namely the exile, and etch its importance into our consciousness.

For recognizing the importance of exile is a necessary condition of existing in this world as a distinct entity as a "people who dwell alone and take no heed of the nations."

If we assume that the exile is in fact a spiritual adornment and a potent catalyst for the enhancement of the national soul in general and of the individual's soul in particular, then we as a nation can be sure that our self-worth is secure. We will continue to live the way we have in the past and sustain our legacy into the future. If we assume, however, that the exile is contemptible and harms the soul, what is our history worth, and what hope have we for our national future?

I said previously, "if we assume that the exile is not a weakness, but a strength and potent catalyst for the self-improvement of the national soul…" But is there any reason to cast doubt upon this assumption? Is the opposing assumption really worthy of consideration? Can we really give credence to the assumption or opinion that a people in exile is totally worthless, and cannot be called a nation according to the reckoning of national organizations? For the assumption that a nation without territory is not a nation is tantamount to saying that a man without property should no longer be considered human.

Lords and property owners do in fact think this, but do the unpropertied masses actually agree with them?! Yet among our brethren there are fools who actually accept the assertion of territorial nations that lack of territory is indicative of overall worthlessness.

The reason that such fools exist among us is understandable. If counted individually, the unpropertied are a big part of society, and in some places, such as cities, they are the majority—and thus they consider themselves important and do not consent to being labeled as worthless. Our landless nation, however, is exceptional among national entities. All the nations of the world who are defined as such have some place to call their own, some unique territory upon the globe, and thus in their opinion "nations" which lack territory cannot actually be considered nations. This convention is so normative among the masses that its power is immense and rests heavily on the individual. How then (the weak-minded among us argue) can we, the only "landless" nation among all the nations of the world, stand up to this international convention?

Let us, however, consider once again the comparison to individuals. Who are those who typically follow the majority opinion without much consideration? The answer is people of little or medium worth, those whose intellect tends toward banality. Gifted individuals of considerable intellect, however, will never blindly follow the majority opinion. In fact, they will generally be quite suspicious of a popular opinion since it often proves to be worthless, and will not be afraid to swim against the current, if they think that that is the correct course of action. So too, are nations, nations who are spiritually gifted, whose books have achieved canonical status throughout the world, should not hold the banal accomplishments of other nations in high regard, and more specifically they should ignore the popular measure of national self-worth, wherein nations are defined by the territories they inhabit and a person's worth is measured by the land he possesses.

Swimming against the current is one of the most ancient distinctions of our nation, from the days of our first ancestor, "Abraham the Hebrew" (as we find in Mirdrash Lech Lecha): "All the world is on one side of the scale, and he's on the other side"; (and in Midrash Genesis Rabbah, Vayishlach): "Regarding God it says, 'and God shall be alone and ascendant,' so too with Jacob, scripture teaches us the verse 'Jacob was left alone.'"

7.

The stand of our forefathers against the world should serve as inspiration to us to also stand against the world. If our first forefather did not lack in courage to stand against the world as a personal *sui generis* choice, should we his great great grandchildren (who with God's help are a nation) fail to march aloof before the national entities of the world?

Our view of what constitutes a nation or a country as it contrasts with the view of the other nations of the world should not be seen by us as swimming against the current. For the nations are, from their perspective, correct in valorizing the concepts of "country" and "kingdom" and we, the Jews, are correct in exhibiting disdain toward it. Our different perspectives resemble, in many ways, the attitude displayed toward money by two groups, commoners and intellectuals. In general, commoners and simpletons who don't value anything except for material possessions, are anxious about their property more than those who are learned or otherwise distinguished. This distinction was remarked upon by the Midrash in an adage attributed to a rich commoner addressing Rabbi Shimon Bar Yochai: "O Rabbi, you value Torah; among us, however, if you do not have money, there is no one who values you."

The same is true of the matter at hand: The people who don't have the Torah are dependent upon an external receptacle, in other words, "a kingdom" or "territory" for their nationalism. It comes as no surprise then, that they worry so much about the integrity of their territories and attempt to protect them to the best of their abilities. If the whole world cleaves to this way of thinking then preserving this external receptacle is for naught, for inevitably it shall be replaced.

The Jewish nation which has the Torah has time-tested proof that it can subsist without a territory or country for longer than it had the dubious distinction of territorial sovereignty. Our nation has the Torah, a celestial territory which is so much better than any earthly terrain.

Our nation has the Torah, and upon reading the Torah one can quickly discern that dependence upon territory for self-definition is not a sturdy crutch. The nations may or may not be overly-concerned regarding this unsteady crutch (and when they are concerned matters are even worse); but their power is never eternal, and there will come a time when they will cease to exist. Nationalism dependent upon territory, nationalism without Torah, nationalism for nationalism's sake (they will eventually realize), is simply not worth being worried about, though this does not give one who covets another's territory dispensation to occupy it.

Russian history tells of Prince Vladimir, who in the 10th century, after deciding to cast aside his idolatrous religion and adopt a new one, invited representatives of each faith so that he could choose the most worthy of them. He dismissed the Jewish representatives after asking them the supposedly pithy question, "Where is your country and kingdom?" After they answered, "God was angry at us because of our sins and scattered us among the nations," the prince retorted, "If God himself has spurned you, how can you teach others? Do you really wish that we too should occupy your unenviable position?!" This same dialogue is recorded about one thousand years beforehand in an interaction between a heretic and R. Joshua ben Chananya (as is recounted in the Talmud in tractate Chagigah), except that in the Talmud R. Joshua has an answer. The heretic's retort that Israel was a nation "spurned by God" was thrown back at him by R. Joshua who said, "God is still punishing us." The difference between the two accounts is that in Russian history the gentile has the last word, and the Jew has no answer, and in the Talmud it is the Jewish sage who offers the ultimate retort to the heretic. What the Talmudic sage meant was that the destruction of our sovereign state was a national penitence meant to cleanse our soul, so that even in death we are alive. For the staff of the Angel of Death has no power over the Israelites, because of the Torah and our closeness to God who looks after us, whereas all the rest of the nations die natural deaths when their kingdoms cease to exist. This historical account of Vladimir and the Jewish representatives is very typical, as is the emphasis upon the two worldviews, the gentile worldview and the Jewish worldview and the conflict between them.

The nations know from their experience that the sum total of their national vitality is dependent upon the territorial integrity of their country, and when they lose their country, all they can expect is national demise. Basing themselves as they do on this premise, they cannot understand the fundamental nature of the Jew who continues to wander the world without an independent state, and thus they regard him with disgust and fear lest they end up landless like him. For this reason they persist in banishing him and deriding him with insults to the tune of "return to the dust from whence you came." This resembles Prince Vladimir's retort, "Do you really wish that we too should occupy your unenviable position?"—implying that the Jew is but a shade wandering destitute and attenuated among the living. The Jew, however, knows from his own experience that his national identity is actually quite secure. Indeed, he may choose to respond, if he wishes, to their derisive catcalls which come from a place of insecurity. If he understands their insecurity well (as opposed to those nations who understand nothing), he comprehends that if and when they "fall" to the level of the Jew and become landless, their name shall no longer remembered, and they will be utterly obliterated. This fate is inevitable.

8.

Even a cursory examination of the singular purpose our nation is destined to fill, namely, the purpose of spreading Torah, can cause the hypnotic power of nationalism to dissipate, and we can gaze without fear into the eyes of the nations who are so proud of their territories and monarchies.

Even one who is weak of heart and cannot completely prevent this prideful hypnosis of the great territorial nations from permeating his consciousness with the help of the Torah's richness on its own—a richness known only to us and not to the nations who lord it over us—can employ a much simpler calculus known to all, including those nations that will quickly cause this cloud of uncertainty to disappear. All he needs to do is recognize that the pride and greatness of nations is insignificant when compared with our longevity and our marvelous history—longer than that of any other nation.

This source of pride, which is indeed the opposite of pride in the strength of one's arms, is completely justified, for it celebrates the miraculous existence of a travel-weary nation, which sanctifies God and circulates pleasing odours throughout the entire world. We, therefore, are permitted—nay, we are obligated—to stoke the fires of this pride in our heart to warm us against the frigid air blowing from the prideful nations.

As the midrash says (Toledot): "There are two prideful nations in your belly: The first is proud of the world he will inherit (i.e., that which is eternal), and the second is proud of the sovereignty he will wield."

In this pride we feel for the eternity of our nation, we can easily counter any nation which smugly prides itself in the splendor of its kingship and the glint of its sword…. we can counter any claim these gentile nations may have by employing a simple straightforward calculation, the same calculation as the millionaire, when a representative came to demand that he share his money with "the commune." The millionaire then proceeded to calculate how many people lived on earth and then gave this representative the very meagre share to which he was entitled…

In the same way the ancient Israelite nation can counter anyone who comes to them boasting of the splendour of their kingdom, and calculate the large number of nations disdainful of the Israelites who have long since perished, and through interpolation the many nations who will, with God's continuing providence, continue to display this disparagement. Bid them, then, adieu and accord them the respect that is due to them and the greatness of their kingdom (just as my midrash taught me to be mindful of power in its moment).

I repeat once more that we have the option—nay, we have a holy duty—to stoke the embers of this pride, for it helps foster our successful abstention from intermingling with the nations. For our aloofness is a strength and in no way detracts from our moral mission to fix the world. Our pride is thus, at least intermediarily, a boon for our moral task. For our mission to fix the world is dependent upon remaining distinct from the world, and the courage to remain aloof is in turn dependent upon recognition of our own self-worth. In fact our pride is not only an intermediary in the pursuit of our mission; in a way it also contributes directly, for as was mentioned above, this type of pride as opposed to the malodorous conceit in one's strength of arms, brings an aromatic air into the world and cleanses it from the stench of nationalism, at least to some degree.

9.

All the discourse and ideas related to above regarding Torah as the crown of the exiled nation, the diadem of its hale latter years, could function as a great bulwark against the threat of assimilation that seeks to insinuate itself into our homes by means of the hypnotic patriotism cast upon us by the nations. In earlier times, which were referred to as peaceful times, when the nations of the world ostensibly dwelt in peace under the fig trees and vines, they created what people, for lack of a better term, call "culture."

But what can be said today after a war that has engulfed the world in fire and tragedy such as had never before been seen? Now, when European culture has broken its neck and its nakedness is revealed to all; now, when it rolls into the chasm together with all the pride and glory of territorial nations; now, when the utter devastation of the wealth and glory of nations who depend on their sovereignty and territories has become apparent; now, when the awful fraud of their spiritual and material life has been exposed; now, when their pastimes and their ideals (including their nationalism) are revealed as bankrupt.

The man-flesh that the cannons consumed during the war reveals after the fact that the luxury they indulged in during the years of peace, the fat which these sovereign nations who depended upon their kingdoms and territories consumed, was in fact the fattening before the slaughter...

The way these nations are carried to the slaughter like bound sheep (even free nations such as America and France) demonstrates what kind of freedom they actually possessed, freedom of which we the "first class" citizens of other countries are jealous.

The "jewification" of these nations, the way they flee from their gods of war as sheep without a shepherd, wandering from place to place, cast aside upon the road with their wives and their little ones, with their old and their sick, as the snow piles up, is reminiscent of how Jews were banished from Moscow and many other places. Their jewification sheds light on the value of territorial integrity and the ephemeral joy of a homeland one can return to. This jewification completely undermines their claim of a mighty civil society, which they would have the Jews join whether they liked it or not.

The nations now cast aside all their labors and concentrate on manufacturing bullets and pillaging what their brethren have produced, and if it can't be pillaged, burning it. This casts a harsh light on how "right" they were when they prided themselves on being the builders and settlers of the world.

The trenches that the nations dig like mice and rats, burrowing there for years, rolling in filth, lice, disease and corpses—and for what or for whom? For the sole purpose of shedding more blood; crawling in rat-holes so they can ambush their enemies. What a reflection on their refined sense of aesthetics, of which they were so proud...

The sea of lies and intrigue with which the nations prepare their tools of fire for as long as the war lasts sheds light upon the value they attach to "Warheit" or truth. This truth that the nations, the first-class citizens, throw in the face of the Jew, and to which he is obliged to pay lip service to save himself from persecution. This is the same "truth" that a certain German philosopher was so enamoured of, the contours of which were so vast and so peculiar, that when it came to practical ramifications, it descended into the realm of the absurd. For example, if a man was fleeing from murderous enemies and took refuge in some house, and his pursuers came to ask where he was, his host was urged not to lie to them and say that the man was not there, according to this philosopher…

It becomes evident through the mists of their "pure" air, this air tinged with the smoke of warfare that has filled the universe, that this peculiar story their prophet of truth used as an example is an inadvertent hint regarding the ultimate destination of this cherished "Warheit." This European Warheit is nothing more than the "love" or hook that the pursuers cast upon those who flee, lest they manage to elude their long knives. From the "Warheit" that their philosophers legislate, a straight line is drawn to the fists of their aggressors. Warheit is what causes these aggressors to feel justified when they jump upon the Jew in anger, calling out: "Jew thief" after he sleeps in a city which he was forbidden to enter.

The rape of nations, and their transformation into cannon fodder for generals and leaders who drive them from place to place against their will and who rule over them against their will, sheds a harsh light on the value and security of their nationalism and their belief in king and country, and the unsteady bulwark they provide.

What a great comedy of liberation, a farce in which one takes nations which were once called by one name, and calls them by a different name, changes the color of their flags and then takes them to be cannon fodder elsewhere. And they call this liberation. These liberated people then celebrate their liberation with an idiotic frenzy, and do violence to innocent wayfarers, casting a harsh light on the great intelligence of the nations with this farce.

But why do I outline the fractures the war has caused in the material and spiritual lives of territorial and nationalist nations, when these fractures are so many that they become difficult to describe? Let us therefore say in short that wars in general and this final war in particular have revealed the nakedness of the universe to its very foundation and should completely extinguish the false fire that emanated from the false joys of these territorial nations.

Our nation no longer requires talismans or spells against this superficial hypnosis with which these territorial nations sought to mesmerize us, for this fata morgana, this mirage, has died ignominiously as it deserved.

Now instead of our nation and culture being the supplicant before the people of the world, begging them in a shy and reticent voice that they may dwell among them, now after the apocalypse (see chapter 3) our nation and its culture are transformed from supplicant to proud and victorious. The shy and reticent voice shall be transformed into a loud and mighty roar. "Jewish" Jews were never embarrassed before the nations of the world, even before the war when all was supposedly well. But now after the war that humbled the greatest of the gentile peoples—Jews, even the most superficial of them, shall never again be ashamed or embarrassed before the nations.

As Midrash Genesis Rabbah says: "Whenever Esau's light shines, Jacob's is not apparent (to the superficial among us); when Esau's sun sets, Jacob's [light] is revealed."

10.

And thus our nation shall be transformed from a supplicant to a champion, and shall emerge from this world war with a victory wreath. For in this war no nation shall emerge victorious except for the Jews.

And thus it has been since the dawn of time, no side of any war emerges victorious from the field of corpses and broken shields—no side, that is, except those who remain neutral and eat the fruits of the warring nations. This world war demonstrates this better than any: The two sides take bites out of each other like wolves until nothing is left but their tails and only the neutral nations benefit. But because this is a world war and there are almost no neutral nations, except for one (which does not participate in this bloodsport and has no part in the politics), the Israelite nation. In other words, this implies that the Jews shall be the beneficiaries of this world war; they shall reap all the fruits of the conflict and gather the bounty.

Neutral nations are often opportunistic with regard to war: They stand aside, their eyes glowing with avarice (like a vulture who smells carcasses) and try to surreptitiously stoke the fires of hell, gaining directly and quantifiably from the war (in other words, their bounty leads them to see war in a positive light) as they empty the pockets of both sides. Our nation is neutral in another way, neutral but sad at the hellish game being played. The bounty our nation shall gain from the war will (p.67) have a negative quality to it. It will be bounty derived from the negation of war and which leads to less waging of war; it will be spiritual bounty. Our victory will be a moral triumph over all nations.

And as is customary, following the war the winner "annexes" his conquered territory and presents the loser with a series of demands. Our nation, the only victor in this world war, shall therefore also make its annexation demands from a subdued world. These demands, however, will be of a different variety befitting her very special victory—the moral victory.

The first idea our nation should claim for itself after the world order has been overthrown is the idea of exile. This is opposed to the common sense Zionists, who learnt from the shattering of national altars the need for our own altar, and is opposed to the aspirations of the lords whose eyes turn to the "liberation" conferences which shall convene following the war, and who think that after the war they shall give us back our homeland of yesteryear (in other words, the construction of more altars). We should instead aspire to possess our exilic *terra firma*: We should be allowed to live wherever we wish and cleave to our own culture, a culture which is independent of land, kings, and lords.

The fulfillment of this aspiration is also dependent upon an outcome that is directly opposed to that of the political Zionists, which is to transform our nation into materialists; they would have us wear the thick and coarse territorial overcoat and make us dependent upon it. The political Zionists' aspirations are dependent upon the conferences following the war. Our aspiration, to make the Jewish soul independent and free of this territorial burden, does not depend on any outside agency. If we learn the great value of our Torah and our exilic lives, our existence in the diaspora becomes etched in stone, and no one will ever be able to erase it. Recognizing the value of our Torah and our exile described above was never more vital, for the nakedness of the world order has been uncovered in the apocalypse, and it has been revealed to be morally and materially bankrupt, rotten to the core.

Let us, therefore, claim the idea of exile. Instead of asking the nations of the world to give us our historical homeland back, we shall ask them—nay, we shall inform them politely that they should stop counting us as part of their polities and their history. In other words, we will remain "natural" citizens of their countries and evince a certain fondness for the environment in which we were nurtured. We shall wish the citizenry well, sharing with them a closeness that we don't share with citizens of other countries. Indeed, this natural state of being a subject is one which all Torah-focused Jews in every country they reside embrace with the best intentions. We will not, however, be subject to their historical countries, or in other words subjects to the history of their countries, wherein political history is the idol, and the political maneuverings connected to it are the paths of knowledge and wisdom... Regarding this type of subjecthood, Israel says: "I adjure you O nations, do not draw me to you, for I cannot sustain this closeness, and you will not succeed in your attempts to bring me in. Moreover, you have no right to be angry at me at my refusal to dedicate my life and soul to your idol of historical nationalism, for I do not bow to my own nationalist idols. And thus we ask and inform you, honored neighbours, that you should stop trying to hitch us to your historical carriage, for we do not ask you to help us build our own territorial-historical altars."

Zionists like to recall the adage uttered once by a great Christian sympathizer, "If we would allow the ancient Israelite nation to return to its homeland, they would construct a most magnificent edifice." (This very generous utterance brings to mind the famous story: In a certain country everyone was born a hunchback. Once, a straight-backed person visited this land, and seeing this deformity, thought to himself that the inhabitants of the land would see him as the perfect man. When the local population saw him, however, they keened and shared in his misery: "What a twisted individual you are. We must operate upon you and make you a hunchback.") This generous Christian should have said that if the nations truly recognized the value of Israel's continued existence in the diaspora and allowed them maintain an independent existence, they would be contributing to the most magnificent edifice in the world. For the edifice would be truly wondrous and helpful to the advancement of humanity. The cornerstone of this edifice would be the idea that "it is not the place that makes the man, it is the man that makes the place." This is the foundation of human rights, for it emphasizes human dignity over mere property.

But since the nations have not contributed to the construction of this edifice (the Jews have, though they have not seen fit to announce it to the world), from this day forth, after the ravages of these apocalyptic wars, the construction of this edifice shall be bravely trumpeted by the Jews themselves.

For these wars which destroy the nations of the world and reveal their triviality and their nothingness have already succeeded in removing the last vestige of shame attached to our exilic situation, and once our exilic situation is no longer a source of shame, all of Judaism's detractors disappear, and the biblical prophecy is fulfilled: "Who are you that you should fear from human beings who are like straw?" and "Do not fear, for you shall not be shamed, and you shall no longer remember the disgrace of your widowhood."

From this day forth, our very vital nation shall no longer feel constrained (by words but mostly by deeds) to reveal the secrets of its innermost heart in a voice that shall reverberate to the very heavens.

11.

These are the clarion notes that Israel should trumpet before the nations and these are the secrets it should reveal to them:

1) First and foremost our nation should announce that it has appropriated the idea of exile, and recognizes that dwelling in foreign lands without sovereignty is a natural state which helps nurture the growth of its world mission. Thus, all derision that is levelled at us is for naught, since exile is nothing to be ashamed of; rather it is a source of pride.

2) Following our appropriation of the exilic idea, we must reveal to them that between our world and their world lies a deep and terrible chasm, and their conduct and aspirations are not the same as ours. The aspiration of the gentiles is to ascend to the pinnacle of "manhood," and ours is to reach the heights of "glory." Or perhaps more correctly they strive for immortality

and we strive for [real] manhood. The means to achieve their success is the sword, whereas as ours is the book—ours is the study of Torah.

The nations who don't have the Torah cannot cast their swords aside (until the preordained time in the latter days), for the sword is an expression of their selfhood and their badge of honor.[85] We the Jews, who have the Torah, possess a more pleasant badge and cannot help being dismayed at the sight of the sword and its acts of destruction. Is it even remotely conceivable that a pious Jew would challenge one who scorns him to a duel... or that he would hesitate to cast aside an aggressor's invitation to a duel for fear of being accused of faintheartedness?

In short, it should now be known to you, O nations of the world, that betwixt our world and your world lies a deep and terrible divide, and just as you take pride in your world, we take even more pride in ours. As the Midrash states (BeShalach): Isaac bequeathed two inheritances to his children: To Jacob he bequeathed his voice, and to Esau his hands; and just as Esau was proud of his lot, Jacob was proud of his.

3) You, the nations, may surmise from this confession that the accusations that we are a nation within a nation are largely true. In other words, though it is a terrible lie that we have our own agendas that are in conflict with the pursuit of happiness and success of the rest of the nations of which we are a part, it is true that ultimate goals of the nations do not spiritually sustain us. Our sustenance is derived from the spiritual kingdom which we inhabit.

4) After revealing to you this secret, another secret becomes apparent: that the other accusation that is levelled against us—namely that we are cosmopolitan—is also largely true. Though we are cosmopolitan, it is not in the sense of greater or lesser loyalty to our homeland, but rather that we don't feel close to the land of our birth except in a natural sense, and not in an idolatrous sense, believing that the country should serve its inhabitants rather than the inhabitants, the country.

5) Furthermore, we shall confess that the accusations levelled at us,

---

[85] The tradition of dueling, where one who was offended would invite the person who offended him to a battle is a corollary of the broader national wars, which are not just capitalist schemes or class warfare as most people think, but also an expression of misplaced national pride. The rulers just provide the matches with which to light the fire and they are ready to cook. Thus, the prophet who spoke of the ideal of blunting one's sword had knowledge of the ways of God as one of the conditions: "He shall teach us his ways." Only learning Torah can help banish war games. "For they shall not learn war any more"—war shall no longer be what they study nor a subject in which they seek proficiency: It will no longer distinguish them.

that all Jews in all lands feel as though they were one nation—is also true. And the terrible accusation that is a corollary of this, that when war breaks out, a Jew does not willingly point his gun at another Jew from a different country, this is also true. Moreover, it may be said that a Jew does not willingly point his gun at anyone whoever they may be, for we all have the same father in heaven.

6) In the course of this declaration, we should correct a small mistake in the statements made by generals, such as the Russian General Stav, who believed that one should appease the Jews, and thus announced that Ze'ev or Vladimir the Jew acted in an exemplary manner in the course of a particular battle and earned a medal. This formulation is erroneous, and any reference to Judaism should be erased: Only Vladimir excelled at the art of war, and not the Jew within him, for what interest does Judaism have in war?

7) It has been said that German officers refused to shake the hand of their Jewish colleagues, who had become officers due to the exigencies of war, since the latter are not Aryan enough. We thus say to these same German officers that the Israelite nation bears no grudge, since they, the German officers, were not the ones who pushed them into gentile enclosures and forced them to become officers in the first place...

12.

And above all we should announce to the nations of the world that they should give up their attempts of assimilating us and eliminating us as a nation. For their labor shall be for naught, whatever means they choose to employ.

If they shall choose barbaric methods such as persecution and material deprivation, blood libels, and the like (which were common in the less cultured Russia, ignorant of the more sophisticated ways in which one gets rid of Jews), which are meant to ridicule us before the nation, and ultimately convince us that we are not worthy, these methods shall surely fail. For though these methods are meant to ridicule us, they ultimately backfire and are deemed ridiculous and repulsive by us. Ultimately this is the best weapon against assimilation. Everywhere where we are treated in this way there is no intermingling.

If, however, they shall choose modern barbarism (culture), as their method and grant us civil rights, with the intention of dulling the sheen of our Jewish identity, this too shall fail. A definite sign of their intentions is the requirement to send our children to be educated in the national school system and forbidding us from founding our own schools. Those who attempt this modern barbarism will not succeed either. For they too are abhorrent to us, no less than their uncultured brethren. The gentiles who drag our children into their schools and shove their polluted countenances into our faces exposing us to their coercive culture are more abhorrent to us than the gentiles who would expel our children from their schools…

But even if one may find completely liberal gentiles who seek to assimilate us in an entirely straightforward and upright manner, without any coercion or violence whatsoever, by giving our nation the freedom of choice; and if our people would choose to live a humble life separate from the nations, these gentiles would not impede them in any way; and if we would choose to join them they would welcome us with open arms and accord us a place of honor in their world. In these bastions of complete freedom of choice, these liberal gentiles would seek to convince us of the truth of their ways and hasten our assimilation.

If such gentiles were to be found (fortunately none yet exist), we could not but love and appreciate them, and these feelings of appreciation could very well impede our attempts to remain resolute and refuse their offer to join them. Despite this difficulty, our nation will have sufficient courage to rebuff those who extend their arms in genuine friendship, but who nevertheless seek to assimilate us. They (as opposed to those who would coerce us and whose closeness to us is no more than a wolf sensing its prey) shall be rebuffed calmly and with genuine regret instead of disgust and gritting of teeth.

How can I leave my world which stands eternal and join you in ephemerality? says the Israelite to this hypothetical gentile. As Midrash Kohelet states, "nations come and nations go but Israel stands eternal." Though you accord me high status in your world, how does it compare to the Torah and its values, and how resilient is it? Is it as resilient as our Torah which is forever sovereign? How can a person leave a position of honor in a great kingdom for a similar position in a more modest kingdom?

I said that rebuffing these liberal nations would be done calmly and with genuine regret. This attitude only applies to the mode of expression, for these nations shall not be content with a coarse rebuttal. The act of refusal must be categorical with no room for doubt, in the same vein as the sage of Tractate Avot, who answered a person who greeted him while he was travelling (it is quite likely that this person was of the non-coercive variety), and said to him, "Rabbi, if you come and live with us I shall give you one million pieces of gold." The sage answered him decisively, "Though you may give me all the precious stones in the world, I will not live in a place where there is no Torah…"

These genuinely liberal nations are noble and deserve our respect. We do not wish, however, to be assimilated.

And they have no right to be angry at our refusal; for they, the nations, held us at arm's length for hundreds of years, imprisoning us in the ghettos and forbidding us to walk in their streets. It is most difficult to impart to these gentiles that our imprisonment was not because we were unworthy or unsuitable to mingle with high society, but that we actually had no desire to do so… that they may have locked the Ghetto from the outside, but we also locked it from the inside. We can let them know this by not scurrying out into their streets the minute the lock is removed from the Ghetto door. If it took them hundreds and hundreds of years for even a small spark of divinity to stray into their world, then they can wait a little longer until this spirit shall be revealed to them in its fullness and majesty as it is described in the Bible.

Moreover, our courage to leave these gentiles empty-handed should not falter, for we know that our uniqueness is good for us and good for them. For only when we dwell side by side can we influence each other both materially and spiritually, and not when one is subsumed by the other—in other words, when we are absorbed by them—because that would ultimately lead to ruin, and the world will have lost its moral compass.

For if the Bible, the sage Jewish book, were to disappear from the world, the light of the cosmos would be forever extinguished (this the nations admit). So too, if the nation which was the means by which the Torah was brought into the world were to disappear, it would be a moral catastrophe of epic proportions.

In summary, our nation shall announce to the world that they should cease and desist in their attempts to bring us into their fold. For none of their strategies shall work, not the barbaric barbarism of the barbaric nations, nor the cultural barbarism of the semi-barbaric nations, nor the legitimate strategy of according us a place of honor, which the truly liberal gentiles may attempt. For what is this honor worth when compared to the honor our Torah affords us and our miraculous survival in the great diasporic desert?

"The nation say to them: "Return to us O Shulamit, cleave to us, join us (Shulamit represents Israel, and the tone of the following dialogue proves that these are the upright gentiles, who wish to assimilate us by "kosher" means) and we will make you leaders, hegemons and dukes. Israel answers: "What do you see in us, in Shulamit? What honor can you truly give us? Can you give us what God gave us in the desert as it says, "You are both pleasant and beautiful when you follow my precepts, I will fulfill all your wishes" [From a poem recited prior to the Torah reading on Shavuot]…"[86] "Your greatness is insignificant compared to the great things that He does

---

[86] Numbers Rabbah 2

for me at every opportunity."[87] "Do not yearn for the table of kings, for your table is greater than theirs."[88]

13.

All these announcements and pronouncements which hitherto had remained hidden in the heart of the nation shall now be stated publicly (not so much in speech but mainly through actions). From this very day, from the time of the apocalypse of Gog and Magog, we shall utter our message on every street corner. Though we are but few, we must not be ashamed; there is no one before whom we must be ashamed. If those at the helm of every nation taking part in this war who stoke the fire of this conflagration, who spew their poison and filth in public and then parade in the streets without the public instinctively shying away from contact with them, like the animals who avoided Cain after he did his dirty deed, why should we be deterred and ashamed? If the few and the mighty were not ashamed to bring a deluge upon the world, why should we be ashamed to make an ark and seek refuge in it?

We should not be ashamed because our nation has a record of swimming against the current from the very first, as we noted above. Was it not Abraham who shattered the idols of his father? If our ancestor the first Hebrew found it in himself to swim against the current alone, is it not incumbent upon his descendants to do so as a nation? If our ancestor dared to swim against the current at the very beginning, before our future as a nation was assured, is it not incumbent upon us to follow his example, for we have thousands of years of rich cultural heritage, living proof that Israel was fashioned by God into a nation.

If, when our nation was formed, those who were privy to its future needed to rely on their belief in the mysterious, this is no longer the case: The mystery is now revealed. Today the concept of eternal Israel has been transformed into something natural, or perhaps we may say, natural and mysterious. And the concept of "natural mystery" is something that can be accepted even by those who are not inclined to believe everything they hear.

Let us now parse the tradition of "eternal Israel," which until now was hidden in the shadowy corners of the nation's heart and regarded as a mysterious belief. Let us now parse it and transform it from a belief into a perspective, a lens, through which we may consider the natural mystery, evidence of the divine kernel at the core of our nation. By contemplating this we will be granted the courage to continue to nurture the uniqueness of

---

[87] From "Akdamut," the poem recited prior to the Torah reading on Shavuot.
[88] Mishnah Avot 6:6

our nation and swim against the current into the future. Whether there are many Jews in a place, or but a few, or even if there is only one Jew in a city full of gentiles—if he has his Bible and his Talmud in his hand (the books that have made him so wise, have amused him so much, and have awakened his consciousness, delighting him with accounts of his ancestors' exploits, the great pillars of humanity, the rocks from which he was hewed)—he possesses companions without equal which help him resist assimilation into the great populations which surround him, just as his ancestor Abraham did not relinquish his identity. There is great symbolism in the legal decision of the Shulkhan Arukh (Orach Chayyim 55), regarding prayer quorums which may be considered complete if a minor with a Torah scroll in his arms is present, the book compensates for the age of the minor.

Indeed, it was in this way that the first Israelite expressed his innovative spirit and swam with mighty strokes against the prevailing current, as is recounted in the Midrash and reflected in the biblical verse quoted below. The Midrash recounts that Abraham shattered the inanimate idols and images of his father Terach. And the biblical verse describes how Abraham cast aside the cultural idols, when he left "his land, his birthplace, and the house of his father" (the locus of cultural idolatry, or patriotism). In the same way, his granddaughter the Israelite nation should cleanse its inner self from false beliefs, from hoaxes, and from all other forms of tomfoolery which are prevalent among the nations who live impure lives, so that the biblical adage, "for there is no magic in Jacob" shall ring true, and Israel shall be worthy of the biblical sobriquet, "a wise and discerning nation." Moreover, our nation must banish from its midst ignorance and stupidity because they can only aid and abet evil machinations—for the essence of our nation's uniqueness and its ability to swim against the ugly current of world order is evident in our people's nationalism which is not dependent upon these fonts of evil, for it is a nation without land, without kings and without its own officials. It persists in this world by following the edicts of Yehonadav son of Rechav who said (in Jeremiah): "You shall not build a house, nor shall you acquire one, for you shall dwell in tents all your days, so that you shall live a long life upon the land where you reside."

It is apparent that the prophet didn't choose these final words of Yehonadav coincidentally in his castigation of Israel and his call that they follow the true path; rather it was because this lifestyle was one that would perfect and refine the Israelite nation—and indeed their refinement is largely dependent on whether they follow this testament.

When Israel swims against the current by being a nation without a national homeland, a nation in which a spirit lives and thrives without needing a territorial receptacle for its nationhood, our nation becomes a marvel for all the world to behold. From this nation's midst, the Torah, pure and perfect, emerges and ameliorates the human situation. The adage, "the courageous man should not brag of his courage," neither should a castle owner boast of his castle, "for it is only in wisdom and knowledge of God that man should feel himself lucky" encapsulates the triumph of man's freedom of spirit inherent in this way of life.

14.

At this time we are vilified and despised by the nations for the example we set, and they name us "cursed Jews" ("wandering Jews" and "cursed Jews" are synonyms, universally recognized by all nations), but we are not dismayed by this. For as long as God has not conferred upon the nations any spiritual purity, they are right to excoriate us with such epithets. From their perspective, we are truly cursed and deficient in blessing: blessings such as, "You shall live by your sword"… benefits such as possessing altars upon which one may sacrifice and utter prayers such as "Let them rest in peace"…

From their perspective the nations have reason to deride us; and though they deride us it doesn't harm us in any way, for their derision is a validation of our essence. If warriors and creators of blood and gore call us cursed, it is in effect a sign that we are "the seed which God blessed."

And they shall persist in their vilification of us as long as they offer moral justifications for waging wars—in effect validating us with warped tongues—until at some point we shall begin to influence them against their will (for their anger is a sign that our influence is beginning to undermine them…). Eventually they shall validate us explicitly, and shall say, "Come and let us climb the Lord's mountain, to the house of the God of Jacob, and He shall teach us his ways!" At this time the end of days which was promised by the prophets will have arrived.

Needless to say, our degree of influence upon the world is dependent upon our own efforts to improve ourselves as exemplars, first as apprentices in exile. But then, when we have excelled as apprentices, we can be teachers and guides with no ulterior motives.

Thus, when we make a concerted effort to sustain our nation and its culture, we ultimately serve the universe in its entirety. For then we become an example of a nation which has achieved a sovereignty that is part of human destiny.

For this reason, maintaining our nation in exile as exemplars is our universal mission. It was not to disseminate our ink and parchment among the nations that we were scattered, but rather to nurture an exilic nation as an example for the world: A living embodiment of Torah exegesis. For there shall be no perpetuity to the Torah in the world other than as a part of Israel in exile.

The dissemination of our bookish learning requires that we be scattered, but exile and estrangement which are a corollary of being scattered are unnecessary and harmful according to the "ink and parchment" view. According to this way of thinking we must try to achieve closeness with "the students," and become one with them. But the opposite is true if our goal is to nurture our exilic nation and become a living commentary to the Torah. If this is our goal, we must be exiled and estranged in order make ourselves distinct from the nations of the world.

For the sake of our universal mission (for the sake of Tikkun Olam), Israel must be distinct from the world!

Chapter 7

The Land of Israel

1.

In previous chapters we discussed the advantages of the exile. It may seem extraneous to mention that though living in exile may be beneficial, no severance of the Jewish ties to Israel is implied. Despite our criticism of those among us who disparaged the exile, it should not be understood as a critique of the yearning for the Land of Israel referred to as "Zionism."

This yearning in its new and practical form, in the emulative sense, namely, "let us be like other nations," which has developed in recent years among the political Zionists—Zionism understood in this way should be spurned and discarded according to our book. This Zionist aspiration is a product of the pity our modern Jewish brethren felt for their nation, shivering without her garment and orphaned from nationalist idols. They (our modern Jewish brethren) took it upon themselves to wrap her in her coat, and cause her to be dependent upon it; they pushed her to revive the false deity of nationalism and cast our nation as a sacrifice upon this deity's altars. This aspiration may be discarded, as we have argued. For we have proven that there is no reason to pity our nation's naked state, for she is not shivering without this nationalist garment... nor is there reason to pity her orphaning from this nationalist idol, for orphans who have buried such a father... it is better that he rest in peace, and never again see the light of day...

Israel, however, is not only a physical homeland, a land which was once alive and is now dead—there is grave doubt if it is indeed worthwhile to revive such physical homelands—Israel is also a spiritual homeland. Israel, for the Jew, is not only the birthplace of his people, but also, and perhaps especially, Israel is the homeland of the Torah—the cradle of the Jew's godly culture. A homeland, which is, therefore, immortal: which has not ceased being vital for even one moment of the exile. For it furnished his soul and his being with its holy memories, and with it as a shield he withstood the pull of immersion among the nations and he did not fall into the gaping maw of their corporeal nationalist idols. This spiritual homeland helped the Jew dwell distinct in the land of the gentiles and catalyzed the creation of his lofty exilic culture.

Israel in this sense is the Israel that our nation yearned for ever since it was exiled, and it is this Israel that causes the best of our brethren, time after time, to inspire their coreligionists to return to it whenever they could manage, and live in Israel and settle there once more—a holy nation in a holy land. The Jew will always seek to return to Israel and live there; Israel is vital and extant in his memory and in his very veins, it is this Israel which he has preserved in his memory at all times, it is this Israel that he yearns to see with his eyes.

2.

Between this ancient Zionist yearning and the new Zionist yearning lies a chasm of difference, both in theory and in practice, both in the reason for this yearning and in its goals.

In theory the political Zionists yearn for a land upon which our kings trod, whereas our nation yearns for the land upon which our prophets trod.

For remember the lofty lesson from the Midrash (on the Book of Judges): The Holy One Blessed Be He said: "In this world you asked for kings, and the kings caused you to be killed in battle. Saul caused them to be decimated upon Mount Gilboa and David brought a plague upon the nation. When Israel saw what these kings had brought upon them, they began screaming, we do not require a king, we want our first king back, God is our judge, God our king shall save us. God answered, upon your life, thus it shall come to pass, as it is said, 'On that day God shall be one and his name shall be one'"—this lofty parable serves as a guide to the Israelite people and all of their national aspirations.

The political Zionists yearn for the land upon which our forefathers fought and died… whereas our nation yearns for the land upon which pitch and sulfur are scattered upon all wars.

The political Zionists yearn for a land upon which miracles will be performed from this moment and into the future, for they became cognizant that upon this land in the days of yore, Maccabees once fought like lions, and now they wish to save face before the nations who glorify their lion-hearted warriors, for without this military prowess they would wish to be buried, God forbid, in shame... Our nation, however, yearns for a land upon which the miracle of the small tin of oil was enacted for their ancestors sake, the tin of pure oil which burnt for seven days and which humbly endures, which lit a flame that the mighty currents of worldly Greek culture and corporeality could not snuff out.

The political Zionists yearn for a land upon which our nation shall be "a nation like all other nations"—whereas our people yearn for a land upon which our distinctiveness from all other nations shall be further emphasized.

Just as the theory diverges, so does the practice, and the practical ramifications of these divergent theories are significant, as well as how one manages propaganda, both internally and externally.

The Zionist yearning in its new form wishes to submit Zionist proposals upon the tables of the diplomatic conferences that follow the wars... and it is happy and proud of this work... the old aspiration wrinkles its nose at these activities.[89] This new Zionist aspiration, as it is presented to the nation, seeks to win the hearts of the people with false and misleading tricks such as a national anthem to the natural world of the homeland, which will allude to the blue skies above the mountains of Zion (those same would-be lyricists dwell at this very moment in Yehupetz [Kiev], though they sing of the Jordan...). It is because of this that I refer to them as false tricks, for all poets of patriotism are poets who go out into the world and don't say this is a nice tree, but say, our country in which this tree sprouts is nice. They are thus prone to spouting hyperbolic claims about the beauty of the homeland, saying that there are no blue skies like the skies of the homeland. Misleading I call them because of the propagandist goal of these political paeans to nature. For these political paeans about nature invite the listener to conclude that it is worthwhile to fall in battle and become a rotting corpse upon a field on behalf of this beautiful land, on behalf of this homeland (or in reality on behalf of the rulers of the homeland) which has such iridescent blue skies... the old aspiration for Israel wins hearts through truth, when it sings to the people of a blue sky, which truly doesn't exist anywhere in the world, spread out over the Judean hills. Those same skies from which God spoke do not require anyone to become a rotting corpse.

All these differences ultimately derive from a fundamental divergence in

---

[89] And for even the non-political Zionists, who can't bring themselves to think negatively of the political struggles (the work of wallowing in the dust of kings and ministers) because they think that perhaps some recourse will be found for their aspirations through this type of maneuvering, the ultimate goal is what leads them to tolerate the means but not to justify them, and definitely not to see them as holy.

aspirations. The new Zionist aspiration was awakened when its adherents believed they were perishing nationally and as humans, and started to think of themselves as dead—the old Zionist aspiration, however, continued to beat strongly in the heart of the nation which felt itself vital and alive in exile.

And because of these divergent causes, the ultimate goals of these two aspirations are different. The new Zionism hopes to revive in Zion what ostensibly died in exile: Namely, they wish to create in this Jewish homeland and in the heart of Jews, this coarse feeling of sovereignty, of which they had been divested in exile. The old Zionist aspiration wishes to revive and nurture in Zion that which is alive in exile, and make it even more vital in the land "whose air gives life to souls,"—namely, the old Zionists wished to cultivate the humility of spirit and the intimacy with the divine presence that grew strong in exile. For our nation discerned that even the memory of Zion was helpful in nurturing this spiritual harvest, and it followed that it would rise to ever greater heights in the actual Zion after the exile which preceded it.

In summary: Israel was precious to the Jews because of their love for the Bible. Consider the glorious pedigree of this land: it was upon this land that the creator first kissed the Israelite nation, where he conferred his spirit upon the best and brightest among them, and put in their mouths kingly words, words taken from the heavenly treasure chest of wisdom, which had never previously been heard at any time or in any place.

Israel is precious to the Jews for it was there that the Bible originated; Israel's history is recounted therein, and Israel's ultimate return to the land is prophesized throughout. Indeed, the Jew sees the exile as adorned with a golden vein of prestige, for it is a biblical exile. The Bible prophesized the coming exile, and also designated it as the means of uplifting the Jewish soul—and for this reason that same golden vein of prestige is discernable in our desire to return to the land, and the yearning is great. For this too was prophesized by the Bible, and it is our destiny in the latter days, because it will mark the culmination of our apprenticeship, our time for personal growth in exile, and indicates that the time to ascend on to the world stage and teach others is at hand.

If the sage Menashe ben Yisrael was able to convince the English authorities to open the doors of their country to the Jews by claiming that the Jews must remain scattered throughout the world for the Messiah to come, for thus it is written in the holy books, then it follows that for the Jew himself it is a sweet and precious prize to return to the Land of Israel and found a global cathedral dedicated to spreading God's wisdom, which according to the holy books is a later stage of this same process and the culmination of the period of dispersion.

3.

And thus we have arrived without intending it at the famous Zionist catchphrase, "the spiritual center." For it is our opinion that out of all the aphorisms and slogans disseminated by the Zionists of this generation, this particular catchphrase succeeds in capturing the essence of the Zionist aspirations in the nation's heart. For is it not true that since time immemorial all the great Israelite visionaries dreamt of the holiness and spirituality inherent in Zion?[90]

This slogan successfully translates the old yearning for Zion into more modern language, using a new term without sacrificing the content of the old aspirations. The rest of the slogans modern Zionists have adopted seek to change both the terminology and the content of this ancient yearning, and thus will never find their way into the nation's heart.

For in truth, the main reason our nation would like to return to Israel is to develop it as a spiritual center from which Torah will overflow and reach Jews, wherever they may happen to live. They want to return for the sake of the Torah that shall come forth from Zion and replenish the Jewish diaspora.

The concept of Zion as a spiritual center is well-established; more specifically, this book attempts to elucidate that this spiritual center in Zion will not only be the agent of change but will be affected as well (as long as its establishment is wholly human, and the edifice is one we construct on our own as an exclusive center for our nation; in other words before a heavenly temple descends from above in the latter days for the benefit of all the nations). Not only will Zion influence the exile, but the exile will also influence Zion. The implication of this is that the material that comprises "the Jewish genius," shall be imported from the diaspora and shall be meticulously sculpted in Zion. For it is the exilic soil that is the most fertile ground for the nurturing and tending of the "Jewish genius," and Israel is the workshop where it may be sculpted to the greatest effect. In Israel clear winds blow, winds that caress those who labor at these endeavours and make their work easier. In the diaspora, however, icy winds batter and blast, and one must dedicate time and effort to mitigating their impact. The choicest of pearls grow in the deepest seabeds, but they are fashioned into beautiful gems in land-based workshops.

Therefore one can say that the relationship between the spiritual center in Zion to the diaspora is akin to that of a developed country rich in factories but poor in natural resources and a country that is rich in materials but lacking the knowledge to process them (like the relationship between

---

[90] Cf. Tamares' later rejection of this position in Section 21 of *Three Unsuitable Unions*, Infra, p. 226.

Germany and Russia), and thus transfers the materials from the latter country to the former country, where the materials will be processed and refined into expensive merchandise, which is then returned to its country of origin for its citizens' benefit. Thus, the influence exerted by the industrially developed country upon its neighbour is essentially giving them back what was originally theirs.

This way at looking at the symbiotic relationship between Israel and the diaspora is summarized in a pithy Rabbinic adage (Ketubot 75): "One of theirs is preferable to two of ours, and one of ours if he goes there is preferable to two of theirs." This is the way the "settlement of Israel" should be understood, and the Zionist endeavour should be guided by the spirit of this adage.

4.

It goes without saying that all of what was spoken of above was not meant to exclude Zionists of other types. The Zionist endeavour is meant to be inclusive, not exclusive. And certainly the nation shall accept anyone and everyone's help in rebuilding Israel, on condition that all those who wish to negate the diaspora shall only be secondary to the endeavour and that they shall not set the tone.

If the Zionist endeavour shall proceed in this way, namely that the entire nation's ancient aspirations will be the guiding force, and the modern Zionists who wish to eliminate the concept of diaspora shall play second fiddle; if these Zionists shall heed the injunctions of lofty "Judaism" as a guiding force of their endeavors, and the idea that our poor and desperate nation needs saving shall be relegated to the dustbin of history; if that faction of Zionist shall be marginalized, then matters shall proceed apace.

Moreover, there is a way in which one may achieve a modicum of territoriality whilst observing the commandment to settle Israel without it detracting from the inherent holiness and exaltedness of the endeavor. Namely, we should aspire to return to Zion primarily for the sake of the holy spirit that dwells there and view the settlement as biblical idea and as one of the Torah's commandments. But just as in every biblical commandment there is an element of Rabbinic interpretation, one must meld holiness with practicality here too. The Bible commanded the settlement of Israel to fulfill the loftiest ideal of holiness, but the intent of the commandment may have also been to provide the Israelite nation with an insurance policy, beyond the promises: "For I God do not change, and you the sons of Jacob will not be consumed"; "And though they reside in the land of their enemies, I have not forsaken them nor spurned them in order to consume them and break my covenant with them, for I am the Lord their God"—promises given to the

Israelites that they shall have a national identity with or without a territory.

Thus when the idea of a national home shall become a secondary concept for us residing in some small corner in our hearts, even its secondary status shall be mitigated by the Torah; in other words when the nation shall aspire to Zion since this is what its dear Torah wishes for it, knowing that the Torah's intention among other things is to provide our nation with a homeland as an insurance policy; when this idea is viewed through the lens of the Torah, it shall be cleansed from the filth that such ideas gather in this world. In this way our settlement of Zion shall not simply be a matter of procuring territory.

A good analogy for this is the commandment of seeking contentment on the Sabbath and the holidays which the observant Jew fulfills for God's sake, knowing all the while that God intended in his commandment that the contentment be of the spiritual variety, and thus in the course of the consumption of the food and the appeasement of hunger the foods shall be cleansed from their debasing coarseness, and the Jew shall eventually taste the fruit of the Garden of Eden. But woe unto him who takes the opposite course, and dives into the platter of holiday fish for no reason but to appease his hunger—regarding this type of behaviour Malachi said, " I shall throw the excreta of your holidays back upon you."

5.

The logical conclusion of our argument is as follows: When the objective of a national homeland will become secondary in the overall scheme of Zionist aspirations; when the Zionist idea will be carried upon the hale shoulders of an old and spiritually healthy diaspora wishing to return to the land of its forefathers with tremendous spiritual treasure acquired in foreign lands throughout the generations, "like a bride who was well-regarded in her mother-in-law's house but searches for praise in her father's house"; when all the other Zionist factions carried in the weak and trembling arms of a grandmother who seeks refuge (i.e., the factions who would negate the value of the exile) shall be cast aside lest they become the dominant voice; then the rest of the nation, including the most fervent (or more accurately, desolate) Zionists, those who cry "Give me Zion or give me death," shall benefit.

At the present time these aspirations are still a pleasant dream which gladdens the heart, and this is good; but so is the future when the objective shall be realized, and the great Israelite nation shall secure its small land known as the Land of Israel, and shall rebuild its ruins. This project shall resound with a mighty clap of thunder which shall be heard throughout the entire world. For despite the modest contours of our land and despite its meagre population, the greatness and quality that the immortal people shall bring to this endeavour shall ensure that they will dwell there in great honor and shall compensate for the dearth in manpower.

If, however, the Zionist aspirations shall stem from negation of exile under the assumption that the Jewish nation has ceased being vital and creative and is an empty husk; if this propaganda is successful then woe unto our nation, woe unto them in the present and woe unto them in the future, even if they successfully procure "Palestina" through political lobbying at the post-war conferences by claiming historical rights. Using these "rights" as justification, the usual suspects from the world of diplomacy are bringing a deluge of blood and fire into the world; they destroy nations and their nationalism and invent new nations to aid and abet in the destruction of the nations the diplomatic czars wish to discard. Even then, even if by haphazard chance our politicians shall manage to acquire this small scrap of territory no bigger a lizard's tail for a weak and downtrodden people—that is all they require, since the entirety of this nation's vitality (according to those who negate the exile) is encompassed in the spasms of this lizard's tail—it is a land in ruins given to a ruined nation which lost its vitality thousands of years before and has nothing with which to commend itself in the present except its past. For it is regarding this attitude that the popular aphorism maintains: "relationships with the dead beget trouble."

The Zionists of the factions who would negate the exile and cause our knees to fail, who would see us as though we were already dead, deserve to be derided in the same language used by Rabbi Yehudah, the Head of the Academy, and Rabbi Eliezer [Midrash VaYechi] as they were walking outside of Tiberias and saw a coffin being transported to Israel to be buried: "What good did it do him to die in exile and then come here to be buried?"—He who comes from abroad is as one who is already dead, because he thinks that his Judaism is dependent upon the land… his return to the land to revitalize his Judaism is ultimately a return to the land in order to buried…

****

Zion, the chosen land, shall not be built, nor is there any desire for it to be built, by anyone but the chosen people, chosen not only in the distant past but chosen at all times including the present time. This perpetual chosenness is the product of the fruitful circumstances of the exile. Say then that Zion shall not be rebuilt except by recognizing the usefulness of the exile, rather than negating it. Recognizing the importance of exile does not require any special insight at this unfortunate juncture. The darkness of wars, the delusional byproducts of "territorial" nations, which have swept over the entire world, have made it clear how precious a commodity an exiled nation is.

Through the semi-opaque clouds enveloping the study hall of a small town (to which I guided you and welcomed you at the beginning of this book) our eyes are drawn to the candle that burns before a pair of Jews with their books open who speak of the final war of Gog and Magog and the coming of the Messiah.

The semi-darkness that shrouds this pair of Jews, with their Talmuds and their modest candle partially dispelling this darkness—they are the symbol of this time, the blackness and mist that covers the nations, all the nations around us, and the humble taper that burns meanwhile in our Jewish world, closeted and distinct from theirs.

The Zionist aspirations must eventually go beyond the purification process of the diaspora, the purification process which created the legend of the wars of Gog and Magog, and the legend of the Messiah, and which will ultimately present the two as diametrically opposed… We should not believe that the wars themselves are Messianic but rather that they are wars of liberation, and this liberation is what we should aspire to, since they will liberate Zion… and in them one may see the fulfillment of the Biblical prophecies.

Zion should continue to develop within us that which we have acquired and nurtured in our exile. We have ceased to be like all the other nations, and we don't need to be given back the dubious gift which we have lost… Zion shall be the olive press wherein the spiritual olives which have grown in the fertile soil of the diaspora shall be taken, and there they shall be distilled and their oil shall burn with a light that at the end of days shall dispel darkness from the entire universe.

Introduction to Tamares on Zionism

It seems fitting that the final essay of Tamares' last published volume, *Three Unsuitable Unions*, addresses the issue of nationalist Zionism in relation to Hebrew language and culture. Published in 1930, the year before his death, it is a further assessment of issues he had dealt with in his earlier writings. The first brief essay revisits his critique of socialism as inadequate in linking the cessation of war exclusively to economic rearrangements. The second brief essay restates his critique of overly zealous, ritually focused Orthodox Jewish practice, again one of his earliest concerns. The lengthier final chapter is his final critique of political-nationalist Zionism as an unsuitable accompaniment to the renewal of Hebrew language and culture.

Thus his concerns come full circle: The three topics of this final volume are clearly portrayed in his autobiographical sketch as central concerns even in his earliest years. His outspoken criticisms of ultra-Orthodox "frumkeit" (hyperpiety), his early advocacy of Zionism, then subsequently his total break with it, prompted him at first to publish his newspaper and journal articles under a pseudonym. This final volume, like two of his other five published collections, is ascribed to One of the Passionately Concerned Rabbis, not to Rabbi Aaron Samuel Tamares.

Tamares both observes and is a contributor to the movement for the revival of the Hebrew language among Jews, although his more personal autobiography is written in Yiddish. All of his collected published works are in Hebrew and, I should add, quite an elegant, flowing Hebrew. His natural gifts of expression, combined with his fiery temperament, his deep devotion to Jewish learning, and his passionate love for the spirit of the prophets, are stunningly displayed in the eloquence of his Biblically-laced Hebrew. I have tried, in this translation, to convey some of his eloquence by a generous use of the semi-colon to retain the flow of his phrasing.

Tamares knows that many of his companions in this effort to revive Hebrew are active in the political Zionist movement. Some of them emigrated to Palestine as part of the Second Aliyah, 1900-1914. Tamares remained an active participant in the revival of Hebrew, even while knowing of its intimate association with nationalist Zionism. This final essay clarifies and explains the terms of his involvement, arguing strongly that this revival no way validates the political claims of the Herzl-led nationalist Zionist movement.

Tamares grounds his passionate criticism of nationalist Zionism in his fervent rejection of war and its spoils. He is outraged that the discourse of political Zionism validates World War I without any mention of its devastating human costs. This compromise of fundamental Jewish religious principles receives intense, yet precisely measured condemnation. The betrayal of Israel's mission to the world, carefully restated, requires that the revival of the Hebrew language not be dependent on affirming nation-state nationalism, with its attendant sovereignty, domination, and amoral, ethically dubious power politics.

Tamares was not alone in questioning this understanding of Jewish nationalism. The goal of an independent, sovereign, power-political nation-state as "the highest expression of Jewish national life and the culmination of Jewish history" did not go unchallenged among Jewish thinkers. The quotation, from *Zionism and the Roads Not Taken*, by Professor Noam Pianko, (Indiana University Press), an illuminating study of the Zionism of Simon Rawidowicz, Mordecai Kaplan and Hans Kohn, reminds us that many Zionists looked to "an alternative to nation-state nationalism that would reconfigure the relationship between nationality, sovereignty and international politics." Many today are surprised to learn that Henrietta Szold, the founder of Hadassah, the women's international Zionist movement, appeared before the United Nations in 1946 to oppose the division of Palestine into Jewish and Arab States, as did the President of Hebrew University, Judah Magnes, the philosopher Martin Buber, and other devoted, early Jewish residents of Palestine.

As one reads Tamares' appreciative portrayal of young Jewish pioneers working the land in Palestine without thought of national sovereignty, and his invocation of the Holy Land with its Biblical events, he would, I suggest, be better understood in relation to these figures rather than being seen as totally anti-Zionist. His prescient 1905 critique of traditional, sovereign European nationalism, fully validated by the carnage of that first World War, was an early, unusually eloquent outcry against the dangers of unrestrained national sovereignty. The League of Nations and the United Nations represent attempts at regulating, for the sake of human survival, the inherent dangers of political nationalism in the form of sovereign states. Rawidowicz, Kaplan, and Kohn, in their quest for alternatives to Herzl's proposed enthronement of European nationalism as the ruling force of a renewed Jewish relation to the historic land of the Bible, clearly share Tamares' unease with the nation-state paradigm for the Jewish people.

Tamares' clarion condemnation of such a goal as antithetical to the true mission of the Jewish people may, on first reading, appear extreme. Yet the reason for his rejection, the very nature of nationalist sovereignty as manifested in World War I, and followed, some years after his death, by World War II, is echoed more broadly even as I write today on the centenary of November

11th, 1918, Armistice Day of the "War to end all wars." The President of France, Emmanuel Macron "toured France's World War I memory trail...the killing fields of Verdun, the vast ossuary at Douaumont and the monument to heroic African soldiers at Reims. Each stop made the same solemn point: Nationalism kills." (*N.Y. Times*, Nov. 9, 2018) "Century Later, War's Demons revisit Europe" reads the caption on an article referring to "the old demons of chauvinism and ethnic division." (*N.Y. Times*, Nov. 11, 2018) Please, read Tamares' prescient outcry against this background in our own times, more than a century later.

As for his harsh anticipation of nationalist sovereignty at play in a Herzl-inspired State of Israel modeled after nineteenth century European ethnic nationalism, keep in mind such elements as these: a state-authorized Chief Rabbinate refusing recognition of the validity of a religious conversion overseen by as eminent an Orthodox rabbi as Haskell Lookstein; the continuing indifference in Israel, without any serious move toward exploration, of the Arab Peace Initiative of 2002, repeated in 2007 and 2017; and the recently passed Israeli law enshrining the right of self-determination in Israel as "unique to the Jewish people." For Tamares, the only surprise would be our surprise at developments such as these.

Could there have been an alternative to the nationalist Zionism that could also have addressed the unimagined atrocities of the Nazi genocide and the horrors of the Holocaust? This is a question that demands and deserves its own respectful, probing treatment in a context beyond the scope of this volume. Awareness of this question, however, should not blind us to the serious problems of classical European nationalism that Rawidowicz, Kaplan, and Kohn confronted, that Tamares, decades earlier, so passionately portrayed, and that Europe itself confronts anew on this hundredth anniversary of Armistice Day: the 11th hour of the 11th day of the 11th month, 1918. Is it not painful, and frightening, to realize that Tamares' impassioned outcry may be not only historical but all too contemporary?

—E.G.

Three Unsuitable Unions (1930) (Summary)

by
AHAD HARABBANIN HAMARGISHIM
("One of the Passionately Concerned Rabbis")
RABBI AARON SAMUEL TAMARES
(1869-1931)
from
SHLOSHA ZIVUGIM BILTI HAGUNIM
(THREE UNSUITABLE UNIONS)
(1930)

1.

Directly after the World War, when the corruption and devastation of that atrocity had affected the feelings of all Jews and inclined them to a renewed investigation and appreciation of their traditional culture, the movement to revive the Hebrew language and culture gained new strength. This movement could have raised high the ensign of Israel in the world, and could have contributed to those in despair; and the Hebrew language could still serve to unify Jews everywhere while transmitting those sublime values embodied in this tradition. It could help form a new heart within each individual, and could raise the Jewish people to that state of fitness whereby its universal moral force could make itself felt wherever Jews dwell.

But obviously the language could so function and the Shechinah dwell within it only if its substance were pure and worthy. The good wine which has accumulated within the beautiful flask of the Hebrew language has flowed from a great variety of circumstances and conditions over thousands of years, but always with one particular quality: that deriving from a Judaism which served everywhere as a living challenge to the idols of the earth before which the nations bowed.

2.

The need for this corrective function of Judaism has grown sevenfold as the wickedness and folly of this "enlightened" world have grown apace. At first the intention of the Hebrew language and culture movement was that the Jewish people serve as a living challenge to the abominations of the earth, a task for which all its teachings, customs, sufferings and experiences had prepared it. To be a strong and universal people, the reviver of the dispirited of this earth, swimming against the currents of the world while trying to rescue the scattered remains of humanity's ethical possessions from beneath the smoking ruins or the recent conflagration: this was the original vision of the movement. How tragic, then, that the movement has become associated with Zionism which, as interpreted by its political leaders, is the very reverse of the sublime willingness to swim against the violence- and persecution-filled currents of the world today. For political Zionism aspires entirely to swim with the stream and be assimilated to the nations.

The Zionism of today, whose leaders love to gain audiences at courts, has made its imprint clearly: it is the expression of a self-negation before the nations of the earth, those masters of falsehood and fist, whose ideals have become lodged in the hearts of the ethical stragglers among our people during this bitter period.

The eagerness for the Zionist cure is a sign both of inner doubt and of inner pain which had not expressed themselves so openly before. The reaction to the Balfour Declaration revealed already a long-standing self-depreciation before the territorial nations and the desire to become like unto them, a humiliating state of spirit which had hesitated to bare itself previously.

But suddenly a sign appeared. The powerful of the planet went forth to fight, destroying by fire a thousand forests and farms in their flaming conquests, covering the earth with corpses. And when the final word had been declared by cannons, the victors met to divide the planet into tiny kingdoms which would pay heed to them. At this point our ethically wayward hastened to plead before them: give us, too, a tiny piece of land, whose name shall be "the Jewish State." Our worthiness has already been proved by the "Jewish Legion" which we recruited and sent with you to shed blood in "liberating Palestine" from Turkey. Thus did the self-designated Jewish delegation go to Paris to enter the Club and collect a share of the spoils of the bloodiest war in human history.

3.

"Save us and give us the land of Israel," shouted the Jewish politicians at the Versailles Congress, waiting about for a share of the spoils. Putting aside all moral questions about the Versailles "redemption," and granting even that our "statesmen" were successful, the outcome was not worthy of Jewish celebration, representing, as it does, an alien and perverse accomplishment.

Furthermore, during these ten years of Balfourist redemption, the situation of the Jews has worsened in the world. All the new League-established or aspiring sovereign states find it useful to persecute the Jews as they pursue their nationalist aims, and for the grace of a similar state to which we can escape, we are to be grateful to Balfour and his cronies!

5.

But apart from this physical catastrophe of our people, to which the trumpeters of the Balfour declaration have contributed by drowning the anguished cries of persecuted Jews with shouts of rejoicing at their nationalist "redemption," they have contributed to a moral catastrophe as well, both for Jews and for the world.

The World War should have been truly assessed for what it was: an unmixed defeat for humanity. Any decent man should have scorned its outcome, never excusing its brutality and blood-letting by any purported future results—for nothing can compensate for millions of young lives lost, millions of parents deeply bereaved, and millions of joyless, suffering disabled. And what of the utter pollution of the spiritual atmosphere, which turned men into beasts of prey and ambush! And what of later hardships inflicted on people, when parliaments decided to revise retroactively economic systems, and made no provision for the livelihoods of those directly affected by such radical changes! Not until after the World War did such cruelties occur, but now arrogant leaders can easily reason: if one could send millions to the slaughter for war, surely we can toss some into the ash heap to starve if that be necessary. Thus men have become wolves to one another, life has deteriorated seriously, and Jews, always the target, are more maligned than ever.

But our political Zionists have taken it upon themselves to praise and glorify this period and orient people positively to the World War, for never do they cease from their hymns in praise of this age of a new heaven and a new earth created by the war—so that when, in days to come, these adventurers are themselves prompted to create their own version of the new heaven and the new earth, they can with ease start the new conflagration from which they, too, may be crowned with praise as were their predecessors.

Our Balfour lovers never cease from singing the praise of the spirit of "liberty" and "justice" which has awakened in the world as the result of nations girding themselves with swords and going forth to "free lands," or of the "righteousness" which has been awakened in the hearts of nations to correct the "historic burden" of Israel by returning it to its "birthplace."

So cynical are the Zionists in calling darkness light, that they are not even embarrassed to abuse the testimony of the prophets. Thus the exalted visions of the end of days have been appropriated and applied by the nationalists to this present disgraceful and vile period—when the abstractions of "nations" and "sovereign states" are "liberated" and actual human beings are murdered!—when "national symbols" are invented while man, the living symbol of the King of Kings, the Holy One, Blessed be He, is erased! For our political careerists, however, all this is quite acceptable.

6.

Not only in theory and words have our Balfourists shown solidarity with the rulers of the earth, but in practice as well. They founded the "Jewish Legion" to fight with "Nikolai Nikolovitz"—otherwise a persecutor of Jews—to "liberate" Palestine from Turkey.

Nor was this help insignificant. Physically, of course, the help of a few hundred Jewish soldiers was inconsequential compared with the millions of men fighting in the Allied cause. The ethical help, however, was substantial indeed, consisting as it did in the destruction of ethical feeling and the removal from men's hearts of any remains of religious reverence, prerequisites for enabling men to wage war and attack others whom they had not previously so much as seen or known. Such was the very considerable moral contribution of the "Jewish Legion" to "Nikolai Nikolovitz."

The "Jewish Legion" was especially "beautiful" since, until the outbreak of hostilities, the Zionists were loud in proclaiming their love for Turkey and in praising the conditions under which Jews there lived, in contrast to the conditions in Europe. Dr. Herzl himself designated the sultan "a dear friend of the Jews," but when political fortunes changed and powerful nations attacked Turkey, the Zionists, too, joined her attackers. Thus to the besmirching of Jewish honor the Zionists contributed in two respects: by shedding blood, the ravaging of the wolf; and by deceitful espionage, the wiliness of the fox. For after England had conquered, one often read in Zionist literature how the Jews in Palestine had spied cleverly on behalf of the British. In this fashion did the Balfourists (who declare themselves the bringers of the Messiah to Israel!) add to the stream of corruption which was needed to anoint the wheels of the World War.

7.[91]

Small and humble is Jacob, and his ability to influence humanity for good is indeed limited. On the other hand, his ability to corrupt and pollute the moral atmosphere of the earth, should he pervert his way, is greater than anyone else's. For it unfortunately follows logically: if this frail and tender

---

[91] The following sections are full translations of Tamares.

people, whose existence has always been secured by moral force, at last acknowledges the sword, how shall one answer those nations who have always lived by the sword? If the people scattered and plucked by the ravages of war beyond any other—which has felt more keenly than any other the pain and suffering, the shame and violence of war—now goes forth in national garb to "liberate lands," what can one any longer say to others?

For Jews have suffered each time they saw, even from afar, the glittering helmets and flashing spears of a troop of soldiers approaching, and know well the terror which sends innocents running from shelter to shelter. If, despite this, there is not implanted within the heart of the Jewish people an absolute revulsion to such tactics, but she too now produces young men who, of their own volition, don uniforms and helmets of legionnaires and rush to join those who would "liberate lands" by the sword—what shall we then expect of those happy, misguided youths of other nations who, from earliest childhood, have been taught such games as: "Play the madman, shoot, kill, and then reply, 'I was only playing.'"

But it is not only because of Israel's extraordinary suffering at the blade of the sword that Jacob, should he, too, now begin to lust after sword and ammunition, has this special capacity to befoul the ethical atmosphere more than any other nation; it is also because of his distinction as "the chosen people."

How terrible is that corruption which would result from any evil example set by "Jacob, selected by God, Israel, His special treasure," were he, also, at last to adopt the faith of Esau. It may have been that, because of his lack of material might, the arrogant nations were previously unable to recognize the moral value of Jacob's ethical comportment and refused to follow his example. One may be sure, however, that when Jacob behaves deviously or dishonorably, the example will be duly noted along with his distinction, and suddenly he will become a valued authority who serves to sanction their own misdeeds.

"The wisdom of the poor man is despised," but the corruption of the wise, even if he be poor, will be noticed by thousands of curious and gloating eyes, and set as a lamp unto their feet.

The Junker philosopher, Nietzche, may have scorned the Jewish ethic of justice, and dubbed it "slave morality," but the "Jewish Legion" of Jabotinsky, however questionable its recruits, was welcomed with open arms and great rejoicing, just as missionaries rejoice when they catch in their nets a Jew who strays from our midst.

It is not a new phenomenon. Our sages, interpreting the verse from Isaiah (10:10) which speaks of "those whose carved images were more than those of Jerusalem or Samaria," remark the early idolaters, neighbors of Israel, loved most of all those idols from Jerusalem and Samaria. Why? Coming from the Jews, they made the greater impression.

This characteristic is also implied in the provision found in the Laws of Idolatry: "The effects of idolatry committed by heathen can be nullified, but those committed by Jews can never be nullified." For indeed, when falsehood proceeds from the dwelling place of truth, its effects are overpowering.

How great the pain and how tragic the loss! Perhaps there was one people on earth, the Jewish people, which truly cherished the vision of Isaiah: "Nation shall not lift up sword against nation." But came the Balfour enthusiasts and this, too, was defiled as they mocked, far more than others, the sacred teachings of our tradition. For the other nations, whose hands had never let go of the sword, not even for a moment, were well-confirmed in strife and fighting, and this momentum of the generations naturally propels them into wars. But those Jews who would suddenly delight in the beauty of the "loin of the warrior," girded with sword, must go forth with high hand to revile the prophet Isaiah!

8.

The end result of all the songs and dances, shouts and praises in honor of the right obtained from Balfour for the promised "redemption" of Israel is, by now, sadly known. Our Balfourists sounded a rousing ta-ra-rum here on every sidewalk whenever a caravan of immigrants "went up" to the "homeland," thus calling the Jewish community to respectful attention of their accomplishments at the courts of kings in building a Jewish State; and they sounded an equally rousing ta-ra-rum there whenever a group of immigrants would enter the land.

Travelers to Israel never entered as simple immigrants, merely desirous of a peaceful place in which to work and create a life for themselves, a place which would satisfy their romantic desire to hear echoes of the Biblical age still resounding on the mountains of Judah and which would, in due course, nourish their spirits with that revivifying air of the land of Israel.

A modest arrival of this sort would not have frightened and aroused the Arabs, and so it would have been possible gradually to establish there, in the land of our forefathers, a Hebrew settlement to the satisfaction of Jews everywhere, even though this yishuv did not dream dreams of "statehood" and "sovereignty," nor presume to dominate Jews everywhere as "teacher of all Jews in the Diaspora." It would have been possible to establish a simple Jewish settlement in the land of Israel like Jewish settlements everywhere on this earth, that the land of our forefathers not be less than lands elsewhere. Thus Jews in the land of Israel would have joined Jews everywhere in waiting for the true coming of the Messiah, that ideal moral redemption which is anticipated in Scripture and Rabbinic Teachings.

But our Balfourists, whose every limb and sinew desired a nationalist career, could not be content with this. The same hullabaloo with which they bade farewell to the immigrants as they left their residences here, proclaimed their entry into the land of Israel. Thus they entered amidst noise and shouting, with that ostentatious pride of "occupiers" who have conquered a land and come into it to impose their dominion on the original inhabitants.

Armed with a piece of paper, the official permit obtained from Balfour, and with that pride which comes from having seen the face of the king, the Zionist leaders began to proclaim loudly and openly that they had come to establish a "Jewish State" and to become lords of the land. They further began to urge Jews to hasten from the four corners of the earth to the land of Israel, not because Jews personally needed to emigrate, but in order to achieve a Jewish "majority" and thereby become the "dominant people," outnumbering the original Arab inhabitants of the land, who would then become a "tolerated" minority.

At that time the small number of immigrants—following the custom of those engaged in "nationalist rebirth"—had already spread themselves throughout the land, as if in their father's vineyard. Everywhere there resounded the incessant singing of "Hatikvah," (for all the nationalist appurtenances were prepared in advance), and everywhere were to be seen waving the blue and white banners as the hora was danced without pause.

Relying on the strength of Balfour and drunk with pride at being near him, the Zionists hid their eyes from the fact that the actual place was not a newly-discovered, unsettled island located at the far ends of the earth, but was a place already inhabited by a people which was sure to feel the "nationalist" and "sovereign–political" aims as a needle in its living flesh.

Thus the result resembles the tale told by Rabba bar bar Hanna (Baba Batra 73b). A group of seafarers saw a slope which from afar resembled an island, and so they approached, left their boats, and spent several days resting on it. During this interval they wandered about, spread themselves out, and soon felt like absolute owners of the place. Finally they lit a fire with which to bake bread and roast meat, and at last discovered that, although it had appeared to their eyes as a lump of inert clay, this was not an island but rather a living whale. As soon as the fire was felt by the fish, he turned on his back, quaked, raged, and tossed them all into the sea. Had their boats not been near to rescue them, they might have drowned in the sea. The application is painfully evident.

9.

But even after this latest tragedy our errant leaders, the Balfour sectarians, have had no misgivings about their strategy nor have they so much as begun to search their deeds. Instead, they first of all attack England for not having kept her promises to help them establish a "national home," and organize noisy demonstrations against her.

The first demonstration by the Zionists in New York emphasized the merits of the "Jewish Legion" with such slogans as these: "For naught we went arm in arm with General Allenby!" "For naught we shed our blood with the English to liberate Palestine!" This approach to the English meant to say: the demand for help in putting the Arabs in stocks and establishing a "Jewish State" is not a request for charity; rather is it the collecting of a debt incurred when Jews stood as brothers to the English in driving Turkey from Palestine. For whoever helps conquer a country by sword and bow surely has claim to all within it, from inanimate to animate being, as the spoil.

Hence there has been no confession of guilt, not even this admission: we are responsible for the terrible catastrophe which has just befallen the Jews in the land of Israel, and we recognize it as a form of chastisement because of the folly and wickedness of forming "Jewish Legions" to take the sword and go out to "liberate lands."

It was we who incited our people to do this; it was we who taught Israel to go in the ways of the nations and commit even the most heinous of sins, the shedding of blood.

No! Instead, the blue-and-white flag wavers have begun to shout because their pay for this very fine work has been withheld! They are, indeed, fulfilling the words of Isaiah (1:5): "Where will you still be smitten that you continue in your defection?"

The government of England was not at all moved by the demonstrations and demands, perhaps rightly. For if a landlord hire a group of ne'er-do-wells to beat up a poor neighbor of the landlord, is such a wicked arrangement to be honored, especially when the original suggestion came not from the landlord but from the ne'er-do-wells themselves? For in the case of Jabotinsky's legion, it was the legionnaires who entreated the British to hire them for this fine work; and is the debt now to be collected in court?

When the Balfourists saw that the demonstrations against the British had no effect, they then turned to the League of Nations, appealing to the "sense of justice" of these nations which had promised at San Remo to help "correct the historic burden which the Jewish people has carried for two thousand years."

That these League members strangle Jews every ten years in their own lands seems, to the Balfourists, no reflection on their inner "sense of justice," for after all, the Jews there are "aliens" in lands not their own, and we all know that aliens are for slaughter. But that the League of Nations should be negligent in giving aid to the Jews to establish themselves as a "Jewish State" in their "historic land," over some "uncultured" people which stole into the land and has lived there a mere 1,500 years (but a day and a half in the eyes of those who boast an historical perspective in which a thousand years are but a day!); that the League of Nations not keep its word, uttered at the propitious moment after the orgy of World Slaughter, authorizing the Jews to go forth and subdue that "uncultured" people now living there and so establish a "national home"—this the Balfourists find to be a grievous sin without parallel, for which the nations shall never be forgiven!

In the demonstrations against England, then, they cited the "Jewish Legion" and exalted our young Jewish warriors. But when they turned to the League of Nations to appeal to "justice," the Balfourists seized the ethical staff and pointed with pride to the young men who are "breakers of stones and drainers of swamps" in Palestine. Before the League they argued: how can you ignore such a quiet, humble, and peaceable people as these, a people which did not come to the land with sword or bow but with hammer and plow, to work there quietly? How can you fail to help such a people establish there a "Jewish Dominion?"

10.

Let me state loudly and clearly that the honor due these young men who are toiling to break stones and drain swamps in the land of Israel is beyond question. I, too, rejoice in them and admire them without reserve. I love the youth of Israel, those fine young people who are not interested in personal gain or diplomas from gymnasia, but who see clearly the glory of menial labor and who appreciate fully the satisfaction and exaltation of the toil of one's hands. For them I have the greatest respect, and henceforth I speak only of their masters and manipulators in Russell Street, who misuse the bodily toil of our young halutzim for their own political purposes, and who for the previous ten years, in fact, have scorned or ignored such young people and their work.

When the Weizmann circle wanted to establish before the world its right to found a "Jewish State" in the land of Israel, it first spoke at length of "historical rights" of the Jews to Palestine, and invoked the youth of the "Jewish Legion," who had been seduced by the Weizmann group to don the sword and go forth to kill and be killed, in order to "liberate Palestine" from Turkey.

Then, when the chorus of their praise for the idol of "homeland" had drawn a whole band of self—sacrificing and devoted young people to Israel to break stones and drain swamps on behalf of a "Jewish State," the Weizmannites began to cite their accomplishments, too, in vocal claims to further their own political careers. They then began to trumpet the accomplishments and "creations of the halutzim in the land of Israel achieved by virtue of their diligent toil and their love of work."

(How miserably these dedicated young people lived, with hardly enough for bread and water! And even this meager support the Weizmannites imposed upon poor Jews throughout the Diaspora, never ceasing to collect "for the poor workers in Eretz Yisrael," not to speak of the tolls for the support of the "government in exile" and its esteemed workers!)

Not for a moment did the Weizmann group stop to consider the reproach which its claims cast upon the Jewish people, nor did it seem to mind that all the mud which the halutzim drained from the swamps in the Valley of Jezreel was cast upon the entire Jewish people in the Diaspora by the lords of Russell Street! For by constantly proclaiming to the nations of the earth this wonder, that young Jews were toiling in the land or Israel, they spoke as if these were the descendants or wandering parents whose only occupations had been horse-stealing or card-playing, as if all Jews in the Diaspora wanted only to eat, not to work, and that therefore the sufferings which afflict them daily are deserved!

It is surely a special distinction which the Jews will thus find in the eyes or the nations: Millions of Jewish parasites among the nations (according to the testimony of the Zionist leaders themselves), and a handful of stone-breakers in the land of Israel, whose every blow of the hammer is heard around the world, and whose praise passes all boundaries—as though no other people in the world had ever managed to build a road elsewhere!

At the beginning, then, the Weizmann circle used the halutzim merely as one more claim in addition to their basic one of the "Jewish Legion" which took spear in hand and went forth with Nikolai Nikolovitz to drive out Turkey and "liberate" Palestine. Now, however, after the frightful events which have so recently befallen us in Israel—inflicted by bands of Arab killers who take pride in their role as nationalist "liberators of the homeland"—now one hears only the basic motif of "breakers or stone" from the Weizmann crowd as it pleads before the League of Nations. That is to say, a people which has produced such diligent young workers, whose esteem for work extends even to "the religion of work," surely deserves your help in founding a "Jewish State" and "national home" in Palestine, without any regard to the protests of the Arab people who were there at the time. For in all the thousand years it has dwelt in Palestine, this uncultured people has failed to build a single railway or electric station. So ill, in fact, was this savage people, that despite all these centuries breathing the air of Israel which makes men wise, it had not even invented the steam engine or electricity before these were dreamt of in Europe!

And the Weizmann group need not fear that the League of Nations will respond to its claims on behalf of the halutzim in these terms: If your young men love work so much and esteem labor so highly, why do they strive so hard for "sovereignty" and a "Jewish State?"

These aims cast some shadow on the work which you so loudly praise, and raise the suspicion that your young men work not for the sake of work but rather in order to "build a homeland." Instead, let your young men, respecters of work, remain in the land of Israel as a minority, simply as a people without dominion, and then their breaking or stones will, indeed, be pure and without ulterior motives.

However, as we remarked above, the Weizmann circle need hardly fear such a retort, for already that group has cast such aspersions on all Jews of the Diaspora—portraying them as lazy shnorrers—that should anyone reply as suggested, they would simply respond: Look at how Jews live in alien lands; do they show any inclination to labor? Without the bribe or the establishment of a "Jewish State," it is impossible to motivate this people to labor, sunk as it has been in sloth and idleness from generation to generation.

11.[92]

Political Zionism, as developed thus far, clearly imperils the character of Judaism, which has survived so many centuries free from the defilements of "nationalism" and "homeland-ism."

Additionally, the establishment of the desired political state with a Jewish majority would affect adversely Jews elsewhere, both physically and spiritually. Physically, this proclaimed preferable place for Jews gives implicit sanction to persecutors elsewhere who would like to oust "alien" Jews from other lands, for they can now say: Jews, what complaints have you against us? Why do you insist on residing here where, by your own Zionist admission, you are mere temporary aliens? Go on to your own country, Palestine, where you are now the dominant majority; and en route, be sure to thank us for our kindness in recognizing your "historic rights" to the land of Israel!

As for the spiritual damage to Jews elsewhere, by exaggerating the delights and the incomparable dignity which Jews supposedly enjoy in the "fatherland," Jews elsewhere will come to despair of the quality of their lives as Jews.

The Zionists, of course, insist that everywhere in the world Jews will point with pride to Israel and the people there will come to subject themselves to the "fatherland," and will finally accept it as the source of a spiritual revolution. They will, it is asserted, make their ears as funnels to catch every sound emanating

---

[92] The remainder of this essay is presented in summarized excerpts.

from the mouths of their big brothers in Israel, where flags of blue and white flutter as in a dream, and recruits are conscripted by gendarmes whose caps gleam with the emblem of the star of David.

Yet I find these consolations offered the millions of Jews outside of Israel—namely, knowing that there, in the "homeland," a handful of Jews live a "life of honor" and "are equal to all men"—are even emptier than the promise of the Feast of Leviathan which others offer to currently suffering Jews. For the latter at least promises a personal recompense in the future for the sufferings of the present, while the prophets of the idol called "homeland" offer merely generic consolations: that lowly Jews in the Diaspora shall enjoy vicariously the lives of the proud Jews in Tel Aviv who dance the hora, and be satisfied that they are members of the same family. And even this only on condition that the Jews of the Diaspora place themselves under the influence of the fortunate ones in Israel.

Do you hear? We had always imagined that as a Diaspora people, purified and cleansed of the pride of the sword, we should be able to share a goodly teaching with others. But now come the Balfourists and reveal to us the secret that we are lowly creatures who have no salvation except to listen to what proceeds from the mouths of our distinguished brothers in the "homeland," to make of their teachings a crown for our heads, and whose words shall be our light.

However, if it is simply by virtue of dwelling in a "homeland" or a "fatherland" that our Balfourists have become superior men, sanctified already in the wombs of their mothers to be teachers and guides, providers of fare for the souls of all the Diaspora, then consider: Distinguished teachers such as these already abound for Jews in the Diaspora! For in every single land where Jews dwell, there are many who try with all their might to stuff us with their own cultures, the culture of "by your sword shall you live." The Jews of the Diaspora have no need whatsoever to bring from afar such false bread as this!

12.

Not for nothing did the blue-and-white contingent dub itself "the kingdom on the way" (ha-m'lu-cha ba-de-rech). But more accurate still would be "in the way of the kingdom" (ba-de-rech ha-m'lu-cha). For the way of rulers is exactly that which they imitate, not the way of men of Torah. For the latter, the life of man is precious above all else. Respecting the individual, the motto of our Sages, may their memory be a blessing, was: "nothing takes precedence over saving a human life." As for the people as a whole, the people takes precedence over the land; the land was to be sacrificed for the people: "that his land atone for him."

Even in the case of the noted destruction of the Temple, the Sages expressed their satisfaction that the Holy One, Blessed be He, poured out His wrath on the land and not the people.

Quite the opposite is the way of the nationalists, the men of dominion. They would sacrifice their people for their land. Did not Wilhelm proclaim that he was prepared to see all 50 million of his people slain rather than yield one inch of German soil? It is in these paths that our nationalist leaders are prepared to go.

13-17.

Jewish nationalists view with equanimity the disappearance of Judaism in the Diaspora. They are not anxious for it to disappear rapidly, for they need it to build the "homeland," but their essential attitude accepts this disappearance.

Meanwhile, there is a strange capitulation of Diaspora Jews to the Balfourists. Periodicals show almost exclusive reliance upon material from Israel, or that having to do with Zionist politics. Jewish educators know only to teach the map of Israel, Zionist songs, significant Zionist anniversaries, love of "fatherland," and Sephardic pronunciation.

It would appear to be widely accepted that the true task of Diaspora Jews, including the intellectuals, is simply to do piecework at home for the chief culture factory in Israel.

20.

Noticing that people will turn out at midnight for Balfourist demonstrations, our writers and teachers assume that by subordinating their work to the Balfourist mood, they too will benefit from this association. But they are wrong. First of all, by their Zionism they alienate both left and right wings in Judaism. Secondly, even that center section which follows the Zionists eagerly has no interest in Hebrew in the Diaspora, for it intends to become "masters" in its "homeland." It is a serious error for Jewish intellectuals to attach themselves as tail to the horse of political Zionism.

21.

The "renaissance of Hebrew language and culture" cannot take place unless the recently accepted subordinate role of handmaiden to political Zionism be rejected, and the movement reassert its Independence and return to its proper tasks on behalf of world Judaism.

Jewish culture must be the whole, and Zionism but one part of it; then the two may flourish. Jewish culture will then fulfill its ethical mission of enabling our people throughout the world to serve as a living challenge to the idols and abominations of this world. Thus Jewish culture will help bring about the realization of the prophecy of Isaiah: "Though darkness cover the face of the earth, and dark clouds the nations, the Lord will shine upon you." Zionism, meanwhile, will echo the aspirations of Rabbi Jehudah Halevi.

Jewish culture will serve to correct the souls of our people, confirming the

Jewish people in its exalted task and vital mission in this world. And Zionism will serve as a resource for the individual Jewish soul. Thus one who has the possibility to travel to the land of Israel and establish himself there in some work or business may do so, and at the end of the day feast his eyes on the sights, hiking among the mountains of Judah, contributing to Zion the blessing of "peace from the prisoner of hope, whose tears flow as the dew of Hermon, and who desired to shed them on her mountains."

But on this scheme the one who travels to the land of Israel must go for his own sake, not for the purported sake of the Jewish people. Let him there build for himself a house, plant for himself a vineyard, take for himself a wife, sire unto himself children and grandchildren. But let him not build a "national home" for the Jewish people nor a "spiritual center" for Judaism!

He who enters the land of Israel with trumpets and shouting, who proclaims that he "goes up" for our sake, the community of the Diaspora, that he goes to the "homeland" and the "national refuge"—such a one is, plainly put, a "troubler of Israel." For whoever builds a "national refuge" acts mistakenly, conceding thereby the Sodomite measure by which the dwellers of this planet are declared to be either "owners" or "intruders," with the former having the privilege of disposing of the latter as they see fit. Furthermore, such a one narrows the universal image of Judaism, demeans the image of Diaspora Jews, and casts upon them shadows of despair.

As for building a "spiritual center" for Judaism, such advocates reveal a failure to grasp the nature of Judaism.[93] For Judaism at root is not some religious concentration which can be localized or situated in a single territory, with a "throne" for the sacred, anointed leader who draws the heavenly stream earthward through the doors of the heavens which are opened directly opposite that "sacred place," he being intermediary between mortal men and God. Neither is Judaism a matter of "nationality" in the sense of modern nationalism, fit to be woven into the famous three-fold mesh of "homeland, army, and heroic songs." No, Judaism is Torah, ethics, and exaltation of spirit.

If Judaism is truly Torah, then it cannot be reduced to the confines of any particular territory. For as scripture said of Torah: "Its measure is greater than the earth..." (Job 11:9).

Neither is Torah the monopoly of particular men or particular places. Our Sages said of Torah (Yoma), and it is repeated by Maimonides (Laws of the Study of Torah): "The crown of Torah is prepared for all Israel." And in Avot

---

[93] The reader will notice that Tamare's attempt, in Chapter 7 of *The Community of Nations and the Wars of Nations* (p. 205) to give some acceptable meaning to the notion of a territorial "spiritual center," is here abandoned.

our Sages said: "Prepare yourself to learn Torah, for it is not a biological inheritance." If Torah is not inherited from the womb, all the less is it the automatic inheritance of any "country."

If Judaism is ethics and exaltation of spirit, then its task is not simply to perfect peoples, societies, or other such abstractions, neglecting on their behalf the particular human being. Rather is its task the perfection of the individual person, living and actual.

Hence the true locus and center of Judaism is within the heart, within the heart of every Jew whose heart is of flesh, not of stone. Wherever on all this earth such a Jew is found, there is the place of Judaism.

Logic cannot accept the fixing of a particular piece of ground as "the spiritual center" of Judaism.

This is the basis for the decision stated clearly above. For the Jew who travels to the land of Israel for self-improvement, without pretending thereby to improve Judaism as such, well and good. This brings personal satisfaction to Jews everywhere that co-religionists are living there in the land of such fond associations and precious memories. But one who "goes up" with patriotic shouts of improving Diaspora life by a national ingathering in the birth-land, such a one, to speak plainly, is a troubler of Israel, diminishing the image of Israel in the world and casting shame and discouragement upon those dwelling in the Diaspora.

The propaganda for a "national ingathering" implicitly sanctions the Sodomite division of the world into nationals and aliens, here casting Jews in the Diaspora as aliens, lost. The vicarious rewards of "nationalist life" in Israel are small compensation for this belittlement. Not one in a thousand will actually live there, and all are subject to the incessant, empty sounds of imitation of European nationalism with the slogan of a state on the way to formation. All are herded toward the dark mountains of false counsels and tainted goals.

Toward this end, the lords of the "kingdom on the way" occupy rooms in the ranking hotels of London, Paris, and other capitals of Europe, their "love of Zion!" exhausted by this: loudly reciting the Sacred Name "Zion!" "Zion!," thus to become the guardians and administrators of Jewish life in the Diaspora, ensnaring the innocent, unsuspecting Jews. But even the simple Jews, if they go to Israel thinking that they will thus improve our Diaspora life by a "National Home," lose our sympathy. By such slogans they assist those who transgress and would take charge of our Diaspora lives.

This is as we asserted above. If "Zionism" is recognized as only one part of Judaism and "Jewish Culture," the improvement of world Judaism is "the whole," well and good. If however, Zionism is seen as "the whole" and "Jewish language and culture" as merely a portion of Zionism, then both are invalidated. Zionism becomes a recruiting technique "to shed the last drop of blood for the Homeland"[94] while Jewish culture becomes part drunken war hymns and part "bible criticism."

22.

"The movement for Revival of Hebrew Language and Culture!" This may be a formula for the flourishing of Trumpeldor-oriented youth movements but is the reverse for Torah-oriented youth. Within the tents of Torah there is greater hope for the success of Hebrew language movement than in any other. The coupling of Hebrew language with the study of Torah is a more fitting and natural pairing than with the young lions of the Trumpeldor covenant.

Indeed the latter are more dependent upon Hebrew language, "the beautiful language" and "the national language," in order to conceal the emptiness of their wrapping themselves in military nationalist garb. This is in contrast to the tents of Torah, which have a purifying and uplifting content not dependent upon costuming in a national language, anointing war, or speaking Holy language, for Torah speaks in all tongues. Since Torah speaks all tongues, it does not require for its completion the Hebrew language as such, even though such revival of the Hebrew language is quite suitable to those tents. Without the study of Torah, "Hebrew culture" is a barren wasteland, lacking all content. This emptiness is in danger of being filled by the pretender of "Fatherland," which marks the end of our purpose (or mission as a Diaspora people). Nonetheless, the revival of Hebrew language and culture is desirable within the tents of Torah. This revival certainly deserves the love and esteem accorded it as bone of our bone and flesh of our flesh. Holy Scripture, after all, was transmitted to dwellers on this earth through the Hebrew language. The abundance of love that Talmud directed toward the Hebrew language is testified to by the term "the Holy language," and parents have the responsibility to teach their children the sacred language (J. Talmud Sukkot end Chapter 3). And it is the parental responsibility, when the child is able to speak, to initiate him/her into the Hebrew language, the language of Torah, the key to our accumulated spiritual treasures. The coupling of the revival of the Hebrew language with the zealous young activist is called by our sages "marrying one's daughter to an ignorant man: it is as if he cast her before a lion which tramples and consumes her" (Talmud Pesachim 49b). The Zionist lions need the Hebrew language for

---

[94] An allusion to Joseph Trumpeldor, 1880-1920, a soldier in the Russian army, noted for his bravery. His Zionism was expressed in the hymn, "Two banks to the Jordan River, this one ours, this one also." His patriotism he expressed as he lay dying from wounds suffered in defense of a settlement: "Never mind, it is good to die for our country."

domination and direction, as they have seen among other nationalisms with their patriotic songs and hymns of might. The love of our Trumpledorists is, as it were, like the love of the adulterer for adulterous language, simply to satisfy their own passions. It once having served this seductive purpose, they send it to Azazel (Hell). They themselves establish the language of covenant with "homeland," "army," the hymn "Hatikvah" recited ten times daily together with other nationalist songs and sentiments celebrating might and power. The ceremony "unfurling the flag," that blue-white object of veneration, is practiced all the day long and perfected to professionalism.

23.

When the revival of Hebrew language and culture wants to abandon the society of Balfour enthusiasts that all the day long heaps abuse and disdain, and to seek an attitude that respects and puts all its trust in the world to come of the Jewish Commonwealth, with dancing the Hora in the streets of Tel Aviv, it must not lapse into a mourning society attitude of overemphasis on ritual piety, Hasidic self-deprivation, and other such values. Let the movement associate itself with the furtherance of that exaltation of spirit at Sinai and the Judaism of purposeful existence in the world at large. The study of Torah must give to the people of Israel its exalted purpose, the enrichment of the inner soul that derives from the study of Torah in a manner unsurpassed. Amidst all the wisdom of the world and all the inspired teachers, no jewel is more precious for fending off zoological animality, "the corruption of the primordial serpent." Nothing compares with this well of purity; for this cleansing of the spirit: "Our table is greater than their table, our crown surpasses theirs." Before kings I stand not ashamed, for the mastery of the sacred language in its original sources, together with its classic commentaries, is for us a glory in the world at large, a garb of distinction for a distinctive life of a people apart. They may not know or recognize our inwardness, nor have they reached the point of understanding our inspired Torah purpose, hence they judge only by our external garments.

The summary of the matter: "The Hebrew language and culture" that must be learned must be the Zionism of "Rabbi Judah Halevi" and not the Fatherlandish Zionism of Trumpledor.

Bibliography of Aaron Samuel Tamares

Judaism and Liberty / *Hayahadut v'haherut*
Perspectives on Judaism and its striving for freedom and justice and an analysis of political Zionism from those perspectives
    by One of the Passionately Concerned Rabbis
    Odessa, 1905

The Ethics of Torah and Judaism / *Musar hatorah v'hayahadut*
    A collection of sermons
    by Aaron Samuel Tamares
    Rabbi in Mielyczyce
    One of the Passionately Concerned Rabbis
    Vilna, 1912

Pure Faith and Popular Religion / *Haemunah hat'hora vhadat hahamonit*
    by One of the Passionately Concerned Rabbis
    Odessa, 1913

The Community of Israel and the Wars of the Nations / *Knesset yisrael umilchamot hagoyim*
    by Aaron Samuel Tamares
    ("One of the Passionately Concerned Rabbis")
    In Mielyczyce
    Warsaw, 1920

Yad Aharon / *The Hand of Aaron*
    Fresh insights into Torah
    by Aaron Samuel Tamares
    Pietrokov, 1923
    (reprinted 2008)

Three Improper Pairings / *Shlosha Zivugim Bilti Hagunim*
    by One of the Passionately Concerned Rabbis
    Pietrokov, 1930

About Rabbi Everett Gendler

Everett Gendler was born in Chariton, Iowa, in 1928. When his family moved to Des Moines in 1939, he found that the nearby very liberal midwestern Conservative rabbi and synagogue provided "nourishment for my neshama" while the regional American Friends Service Committee (Quakers) "helped shape and support my conscience." He later studied at University of Chicago and Jewish Theological Seminary (rabbinic ordination 1957), with additional graduate work at Columbia University and Union Theological Seminary.

After serving congregations in Mexico, Brazil, and Princeton, N.J., he was rabbi to Temple Emanuel, Lowell, M.A., for 24 years. During 19 of those years he was also Jewish Chaplain and Instructor in Philosophy and Religious Studies at Phillips Academy, Andover, M.A.

Long active in organic food growing, environmental issues, liturgical renewal, and the struggle for racial and economic justice and world peace by nonviolent means, since "retirement" Rabbi Gendler and his wife, Mary, travel regularly to India, helping the Tibetan exile community develop a community-wide educational program in strategic nonviolent struggle.

Reflections on the weekly Torah portion from *Ben Yehuda Press*

An Angel Called Truth and Other Tales from the Torah by Rabbi Jeremy Gordon and Emma Parlons. Funny, engaging micro-tales for each of the portions of the Torah and one for each of the Jewish festivals as well. These tales are told from the perspective of young people who feature in the Biblical narrative, young people who feature in classic Rabbinic commentary on our Biblical narratives and young people just made up for this book.

Torah & Company: The weekly portion of Torah, accompanied by generous helpings of Mishnah and Gemara, served with discussion questions to spice up your Sabbath Table by Rabbi Judith Z. Abrams. Serve up a rich feast of spiritual discussion from an age-old recipe: One part Torah. Two parts classic Jewish texts. Add conversation. Stir... and enjoy! "A valuable guide for the Shabbat table of every Jew." —Rabbi Burton L. Visotzky, author *Reading the Book*

Torah Journeys: The Inner Path to the Promised Land by Rabbi Shefa Gold. Rabbi Gold shows us how to find blessing, challenge and the opportunity for spiritual transformation in each portion of Torah. An inspiring guide to exploring the landscape of Scripture... and recognizing that landscape as the story of your life. "Deep study and contemplation went into the writing of this work. Reading her Torah teachings one becomes attuned to the voice of the Shekhinah, the feminine aspect of God which brings needed healing to our wounded world." —Rabbi Zalman Schachter-Shalomi

American Torah Toons 2: Fifty-Four Illustrated Commentaries by Lawrence Bush. Deeply personal and provocative artworks responding to each weekly Torah portion. Each two-page spread includes a Torah passage, a paragraph of commentary from both traditional and modern Jewish sources, and a photo-collage that responds to the text with humor, ethical conscience, and both social and self awareness. "What a vexing, funny, offensive, insightful, infuriating, thought-provoking book." —Rabbi David Saperstein

The Comic Torah: Reimagining the Very Good Book. Stand-up comic Aaron Freeman and artist Sharon Rosenzweig reimagine the Torah with provocative humor and irreverent reverence in this hilarious, gorgeous, off-beat graphic version of the Bible's first five books! Each weekly portion gets a two-page spread. Like the original, the Comic Torah is not always suitable for children.

we who desire: poems and Torah riffs by Sue Swartz. From Genesis to Deuteronomy, from Bereshit to Zot Haberacha, from Eden to Gaza, from Eve to Emma Goldman, *we who desire* interweaves the mythic and the mundane as it follows the arc of the Torah with carefully chosen words, astute observations, and deep emotion. "Sue Swartz has used a brilliant, fortified, playful, serious, humanely furious moral imagination, and a poet's love of the music of language, to re-tell the saga of the Bible you thought you knew." —Alicia Ostriker, author, *For the Love of God: The Bible as an Open Book*

Eternal Questions by Rabbi Josh Feigelson. These essays on the weekly Torah portion guide readers on a journey that weaves together Torah, Talmud, Hasidic masters, and a diverse array of writers, poets, musicians, and thinkers. Each essay includes questions for reflection and suggestions for practices to help turn study into more mindful, intentional living. "This is the wisdom that we always need—but maybe particularly now, more than ever, during these turbulent times." —Rabbi Danya Ruttenberg, author, *On Repentance and Repair*

Jewish spirituality and thought from *Ben Yehuda Press*

The Essential Writings of Abraham Isaac Kook. Translated and edited by Rabbi Ben Zion Bokser. This volume of letters, aphorisms and excerpts from essays and other writings provide a wide-ranging perspective on the thought and writing of Rav Kook. With most selections running two or three pages, readers gain a gentle introduction to one of the great Jewish thinkers of the modern era.

Ahron's Heart: Essential Prayers, Teachings and Letters of Ahrele Roth, a Hasidic Reformer. Translated and edited by Rabbi Zalman Schachter-Shalomi and Rabbi Yair Hillel Goelman. For the first time, the writings of one of the 20th century's most important Hasidic thinkers are made available to a non-Hasidic English audience. Rabbi Ahron "Ahrele" Roth (1894-1944) has a great deal to say to sincere spiritual seekers far beyond his own community.

A Passionate Pacifist: Essential Writings of Aaron Samuel Tamares. Translated and edited by Rabbi Everett Gendler. Rabbi Aaron Samuel Tamares (1869-1931) addresses the timeless issues of ethics, morality, communal morale, and Judaism in relation to the world at large in these essays and sermons, written in Hebrew between 1904 and 1931. "For those who seek a Torah of compassion and pacifism, a Judaism not tied to 19th century political nationalism, and a vision of Jewish spirituality outside of political thinking this book will be essential." —Rabbi Dr. Alan Brill, author, *Thinking God: The Mysticism of Rabbi Zadok of Lublin*

Return to the Place: The Magic, Meditation, and Mystery of Sefer Yetzirah by Rabbi Jill Hammer. A translation of and commentary to an ancient Jewish mystical text that transforms it into a contemporary guide for meditative practice. "A tour de force—at once scholarly, whimsical, deeply poetic, and eminently accessible." —Rabbi Tirzah Firestone, author of *The Receiving: Reclaiming Jewish Women's Wisdom*

Enlightenment by Trial and Error: Ten Years on the Slippery Slopes of Jewish Mysticism, Postmodern Buddhist Meditation, and Heretical Flexidox Spirituality by Rabbi Jay Michaelson. A unique record of the 21st century spiritual search, from the perspective of someone who made plenty of mistakes along the way.

The Tao of Solomon: Finding Joy and Contentment in the Wisdom of Ecclesiastes by Rabbi Rami Shapiro. Rabbi Rami Shapiro unravels the golden philosophical threads of wisdom in the book of Ecclesiastes, reweaving the vibrant book of the Bible into a 21st century tapestry. Shapiro honors the roots of the ancient writing, explores the timeless truth that we are merely a drop in the endless river of time, and reveals a path to finding personal and spiritual fulfillment even as we embrace our impermanent place in the universe.

Embracing Auschwitz: Forging a Vibrant, Life-Affirming Judaism that Takes the Holocaust Seriously by Rabbi Joshua Hammerman. The Judaism of Sinai and the Judaism of Auschwitz are merging, resulting in new visions of Judaism that are only beginning to take shape. "Should be read by every Jew who cares about Judaism." —Rabbi Dr. Irving "Yitz" Greenberg

Recent books from *Ben Yehuda Press*

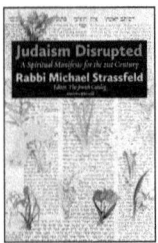

Judaism Disrupted: A Spiritual Manifesto for the 21st Century by Rabbi Michael Strassfeld. "I can't remember the last time I felt pulled to underline a book constantly as I was reading it, but *Judaism Disrupted* is exactly that intellectual, spiritual and personal adventure. You will find yourself nodding, wrestling, and hoping to hold on to so many of its ideas and challenges. Rabbi Strassfeld reframes a Torah that demands breakage, reimagination, and ownership." —Abigail Pogrebin, author, *My Jewish Year: 18 Holidays, One Wondering Jew*

The Way of Torah and the Path of Dharma: Intersections between Judaism and the Religions of India by Rabbi Daniel Polish. "A whirlwind religious tourist visit to the diversity of Indian religions: Sikh, Jain, Buddhist, and Hindu, led by an experienced congregational rabbi with much experience in interfaith and in teaching world religions." —Rabbi Alan Brill, author of *Rabbi on the Ganges: A Jewish Hindu-Encounter*

Liberating Your Passover Seder: An Anthology Beyond The Freedom Seder. Edited by Rabbi Arthur O. Waskow and Rabbi Phyllis O. Berman. This volume tells the history of the Freedom Seder and retells the origin of subsequent new haggadahs, including those focusing on Jewish-Palestinian reconciliation, environmental concerns, feminist and LGBT struggles, and the Covid-19 pandemic of 2020.

Duets on Psalms: Drawing New Meaning from Ancient Words by Rabbis Elie Spitz & Jack Riemer. "Two of Judaism's most inspirational teachers, offer a lifetime of insights on the Bible's most inspired book." — Rabbi Joseph Telushkin, author of *Jewish Literacy*. "This illuminating work is a literary journey filled with faith, wisdom, hope, healing, meaning and inspiration." —Rabbi Naomi Levy, author of *Einstein and the Rabbi*

Weaving Prayer: An Analytical and Spiritual Commentary on the Jewish Prayer Book by Rabbi Jeffrey Hoffman. "This engaging and erudite volume transforms the prayer experience. Not only is it of considerable intellectual interest to learn the history of prayers—how, when, and why they were composed—but this new knowledge will significantly help a person pray with intention (*kavvanah*). I plan to keep this volume right next to my siddur." —Rabbi Judith Hauptman, author of *Rereading the Rabbis: A Woman's Voice*

Renew Our Hearts: A Siddur for Shabbat Day edited by Rabbi Rachel Barenblat. From the creator of *The Velveteen Rabbi's Haggadah*, a new siddur for the day of Shabbat. *Renew Our Hearts* balances tradition with innovation, featuring liturgy for morning (*Shacharit* and a renewing approach to *Musaf*), the afternoon (*Mincha*), and evening (*Ma'ariv* and *Havdalah*), along with curated works of poetry, art and new liturgies from across the breadth of Jewish spiritual life. Every word of Hebrew is paired with transliteration and with clear, pray-able English translation.

Forty Arguments for the Sake of Heaven: Why the Most Vital Controversies in Jewish Intellectual History Still Matter by Rabbi Shmuly Yanklowitz. Hillel vs. Shammai, Ayn Rand vs. Karl Marx, Tamar Ross vs. Judith Plaskow... but also Abraham vs. God, and God vs. the angels! Movements debate each other: Reform versus Orthodoxy, one- two- and zero-state solutions to the Israeli-Palestinian conflict, gun rights versus gun control in the United States. Rabbi Yanklowitz presents difficult and often heated disagreements with fairness and empathy, helping us consider our own truths in a pluralistic Jewish landscape.

Recent books from *Ben Yehuda Press*

Reaching for Comfort: What I Saw, What I Learned, and How I Blew it Training as a Pastoral Counselor by Sherri Mandell. In 2004, Sherri Mandell won the National Jewish Book award for *The Blessing of the Broken Heart*, which told of her grief and initial mourning after her 13-year-old son Koby was brutally murdered. Years later, with her pain still undiminished, Sherri trains to help others as a pioneering pastoral counselor in Israeli hospitals. "What a blessing to witness Mandell's and her patients' resilience!" —Rabbi Dayle Friedman, editor, *Jewish Pastoral Care: A Practical Guide from Traditional and Contemporary Sources*

Heroes with Chutzpah: 101 True Tales of Jewish Trailblazers, Changemakers & Rebels by Rabbi Deborah Bodin Cohen and Rabbi Kerry Olitzky. Readers ages 8 to 14 will meet Jewish changemakers from the recent past and present, who challenged the status quo in the arts, sciences, social justice, sports and politics, from David Ben-Gurion and Jonas Salk to Sarah Silverman and Douglas Emhoff. "Simply stunning. You would want this book on your coffee table, though the stories will take the express lane to your soul." —Rabbi Jeff Salkin

Just Jewish: How to Engage Millennials and Build a Vibrant Jewish Future by Rabbi Dan Horwitz. Drawing on his experience launching The Well, an inclusive Jewish community for young adults in Metro Detroit, Rabbi Horwitz shares proven techniques ready to be adopted by the Jewish world's myriad organizations, touching on everything from branding to fundraising to programmatic approaches to relationship development, and more. "This book will shape the conversation as to how we think about the Jewish future." —Rabbi Elliot Cosgrove, editor, *Jewish Theology in Our Time*.

Put Your Money Where Your Soul Is: Jewish Wisdom to Transform Your Investments for Good by Rabbi Jacob Siegel. "An intellectual delight. It offers a cornucopia of good ideas, institutions, and advisers. These can ease the transition for institutions and individuals from pure profit nature investing to deploying one's capital to repair the world, lift up the poor, and aid the needy and vulnerable. The sources alone—ranging from the Bible, Talmud, and codes to contemporary economics and sophisticated financial reporting—are worth the price of admission." —Rabbi Irving "Yitz" Greenberg

Why Israel (and its Future) Matters: Letters of a Liberal Rabbi to the Next Generation by Rabbi John Rosove. Presented in the form of a series of letters to his children, Rabbi Rosove makes the case for Israel — and for liberal American Jewish engagement with the Jewish state. "A must-read!" —Isaac Herzog, President of Israel. "This thoughtful and passionate book reminds us that commitment to Israel and to social justice are essential components of a healthy Jewish identity." —Yossi Klein Halevi, author, *Letters to My Palestinian Neighbor*

Other Covenants: Alternate Histories of the Jewish People by Rabbi Andrea D. Lobel & Mark Shainblum. In *Other Covenants*, you'll meet Israeli astronauts trying to save a doomed space shuttle, a Jewish community's faith challenged by the unstoppable return of their own undead, a Jewish science fiction writer in a world of Zeppelins and magic, an adult Anne Frank, an entire genre of Jewish martial arts movies, a Nazi dystopia where Judaism refuses to die, and many more. Nominated for two Sidewise Awards for Alternate History.

www.ingramcontent.com/pod-product-compliance
Lightning Source LLC
Chambersburg PA
CBHW050550160426
43199CB00015B/2608